GENDER MATT

A manual on addressing gender-ba_ _ _ _ _ _ _ _ _
affecting young people

Second edition – fully revised and updated

Written and edited by

ANCA-RUXANDRA PANDEA, DARIUSZ GRZEMNY, ELLIE KEEN

Final Editor

RUI GOMES

Authors and editors of the first edition

ANNETTE SCHNEIDER, DENNIS VAN DER VEUR,
GORAN BULDIOSKI, KAROLINA VRETHEM,
GAVAN TITLEY, GYÖRGYI TÓTH, YAEL OHANA

Council of Europe, 2019

Acknowledgements

We would like to express our gratitude to all those who contributed to this edition of the manual, in particular:

- CÉCILE GREBOVAL and her colleagues at the Gender Equality Division
- ALICE BARBIERI, Gender Equality Rapporteur of the Joint Council on Youth
- EMIE VALIQUETTE, ENRICO ELEFANTE, FABRIZIO PROVENZANO, KAAN SEN, VINCENT SCANLAN, trainees at the European Youth Centre, NATHALIE GUITER and JOANNE HUNTING for their useful advice and care.

We have made every possible effort to trace references of texts and activities to their authors and give them the necessary credits. We apologise for any omissions or inaccuracies and will be pleased to correct them.

GENDER MATTERS
A manual on addressing gender-based violence affecting young people
Second edition, 2019

All other correspondence concerning this document should be addressed to the Youth Department of the Council of Europe:

European Youth Centre Strasbourg
30, rue Pierre de Coubertin
F- 67075 Strasbourg Cedex – France
Email: *youth@coe.int*

Credits for photos:

- Cover and pages 14, 56, 174, 194: Alan Poulson, Filip Warulik, WAYHOME studio, Anatol Misnikou © Shutterstock.com
- Page 230: Ivelin Radkov © Shutterstock.com
- Page 180: Metoo - Mihai Surdu

Layout, design and illustrations: Pedro Meca

Printed in Hungary

ISBN: 978-92-871-8958-5

Poster created by the No Hate Ninjas (Portugal) for the No Hate Speech Movement youth campaign.

**Snežana
Samardžić-Marković**
Director General
of Democracy,
Council of Europe

PREFACE
Gender equality does matter

Gender-based violence is one of the most widespread forms of human rights abuse and a violation of human dignity anywhere. Gender-based violence is a problem in all member states of the Council of Europe and affects millions of women, men and children regardless of their social status, cultural or religious background, civil status, sexual orientation or gender identity. Gender-based violence undermines the core values of human rights on which the Council of Europe is based and to which its member states have subscribed.

As the Council of Europe Istanbul Convention affirms, there can be no real equality between women and men if women experience gender-based violence on a large scale and state agencies and institutions turn a blind eye. It is the responsibility of state authorities to take measures to prevent violence, protect the victims and prosecute the perpetrators.

Legal action, however essential, cannot be the only response if we want to reduce and eradicate such forms of violence. The values of human rights, non-violence and gender equality can be neither imposed nor simply advertised; they must be accepted and respected in real life. The key is education, information and awareness-raising. Only through combined efforts can we ensure that the patterns of oppression and humiliation are not repeated from generation to generation.

The Council of Europe youth sector has taken this matter seriously because young people are more vulnerable to forms of gender-based violence; they must also be the agents of the changes required to eradicate it. The Youth for Democracy programme consistently combats all forms of discrimination and promotes gender equality with an intersectional approach. A Gender Impact Study concluded that there is adequation between the aims of the programme and the promotion of gender equality. The programme is sensitive to the promotion of diversity and the inclusion of minorities and vulnerable individuals; it has gender equality among its priorities, and its work is in contrast with the current gender inequality patterns in the member states of the Council of Europe. The objectives of the programme are also effective responses to ongoing discriminatory, transphobic and homophobic narratives.

The work of the Council of Europe's youth sector relies on its youth multipliers. The role of young people and youth work is thus very important to reach out to the rest of society to prevent and combat gender-based violence. Gender Matters was first published to support this work. It builds on the educational approaches of *Compass*, the manual on human rights education with young people which enables millions of young people across Europe to learn about, through and for human rights.

Gender Matters is a manual on gender-based violence affecting young people. It is a useful introduction to gender and gender-based violence for people who work with young people, providing reflections on gender and gender-based violence, a background to key contemporary issues and, especially, methods and resources for education and training activities with young people.

We hope that youth workers and activists alike will find in this manual inspiration and resources to resist the backlashes to equality and dignity for all and overcome the narratives of supremacy, sexism, hate and violence. Gender equality matters. Gender-based violence has no future.

TABLE OF CONTENTS

Introduction to this edition

Introduction to this edition

Welcome to the second edition of Gender Matters, a manual on addressing gender-based violence affecting young people.

Gender Matters was first published in 2007, within the Human Rights Education Youth Programme of the Council of Europe. It followed and built on the publication of *Compass – a manual on human rights education with young people* and *Compasito – a manual on human rights education for children*. Both of these publications make reference to issues of gender, gender equality and gender-based violence.

Gender Matters is a manual on **gender-based violence** affecting young people. The manual constitutes a useful introduction to gender and gender-based violence for people who work with young people, by providing reflections on gender and gender-based violence, a background to key social, political and legal issues, and methods and resources for education and training activities with young people.

Gender Matters has been used as an educational resource in numerous educational activities run at the European Youth Centres in Strasbourg and Budapest. Translated into several languages, the manual has reached youth groups and youth organisations across Europe, supporting work against the gender-based violence which affects young people today.

Gender-based violence undermines the core values on which the Council of Europe is based, notably human rights, democracy and the rule of law. In the years following the first edition of Gender Matters, the Council of Europe introduced a number of legal instruments and policies related to gender equality and protection from gender-based violence, including:

- The Convention on Preventing and Combating Violence against Women and Domestic Violence (Istanbul Convention) – the most far-reaching international treaty designed to address violence against women. It breaks new ground by requesting states to criminalise the various forms of violence against women;
- The Convention on the Protection of Children against Sexual Exploitation and Sexual Abuse, also known as the Lanzarote Convention. The treaty demands that all types of sexual offences against children be criminalised;
- The Convention on Action against Trafficking in Human Beings, which entered into force in 2008 and strengthens the protection afforded to victims of trafficking;
- Recommendation CM/Rec(2010)5 of the Committee of Ministers to member states on measures to combat discrimination on grounds of sexual orientation or gender identity. This was the first instrument in the world to deal specifically with one of the most persistent and difficult forms of discrimination.

In the youth sector, a series of recommendations of the Committee of Ministers to member states have reinforced the importance of gender equality as an integral part of youth policies and programmes:

- The Charter on Education for Democratic Citizenship and Human Rights Education (2010) affirms *gender equality as an essential element of EDC/HRE*
- The *Enter!* Recommendation (2015) on Access of Young People from Disadvantaged Neighbourhoods to Social Rights stresses the need to develop *gender-sensitive approaches to the elaboration of youth policies in disadvantaged neighbourhoods, and provide support for the capacity building and equal participation of young women and young men, as well as to address bullying, sexual harassment, gender-based violence, and all other forms of violence prevalent in disadvantaged neighbourhoods;*
- The Recommendation on Young People's Access to Rights (2016), which asks member states to establish strategies to improve young people's access to rights that reflect *the principles of the universality and indivisibility of human rights, non-discrimination and equal opportunities and gender equality;*
- The Recommendation on Supporting Young Refugees in Transition to Adulthood (2019) which calls upon member states to provide to young refugees in transition to adulthood the support and protection they require and give due consideration to the needs of all young refugees at risk, *such as survivors of sexual and gender-based violence, trafficking in human beings or exploitation. States are also recommended to take due consideration to the specific needs and situations of young women and of young men* in the implementation of the Recommendation.

These new treaties and recommendations, as well as other developments such as the experience of the No Hate Speech Movement campaign regarding sexist, homo- and transphobic hate speech, made the need to revise and update Gender Matters particularly pressing. The growing awareness of gender inequality and gender-based violence as obstacles to the full participation and development of young people needs to be accompanied by up-to-date and accessible educational resources.

Gender Matters is an important resource in support of the Council of Europe youth sector strategy 2030 and the Youth for Democracy programme, notably regarding young people's access to rights, human rights education and combating all forms of discrimination with an intersectional approach.

This manual is also useful for pursuing the UN Sustainable Development Goals, particularly Goal 5 on Gender Equality, and the Council of Europe's Gender Equality Strategy.

What has changed

This second edition has been substantially rewritten, taking into account feedback from users, and changes in legislation and policy – particularly from the Council of Europe.

- **The structure has changed**
  The manual still includes four chapters, but these have been organised differently from the first edition. Users still find a theoretical chapter addressing the issues of gender, gender-based violence and human rights instruments (Chapter 1), and a set of activities (Chapter 2). Taking action against gender-based violence is now a chapter on its own. There is also a new chapter, 'Themes relating to gender and gender-based violence', where readers can find information on different topics which may be useful when exploring issues like feminism, intersectionality or sexuality. A glossary of terms relating to gender and gender-based violence has also been added.

- **Language has been simplified**
  Talking about gender can be very difficult and often includes complicated terms or theories, which may be hard to understand for young people – and the detail is not always necessary. To make the content clearer and the manual more readable for young people we have tried to use more user-friendly language, but without over-simplifying content.

- **The language is more inclusive**
  We have tried to use gender-sensitive language throughout the manual and avoid the trap of gender binary. However, this was not always possible, for example in parts of the manual where the content deals with different legal instruments which sometimes use less gender-sensitive language.

- **A new set of experiential activities**
  There are new activities in Chapter 2 which take into account new legal instruments and deal with topics absent from the first version, such as remembrance. Some of the activities have been adapted from *Compass* or *Bookmarks*.

What has not changed

The purpose, educational approach and methods proposed remain largely valid; if anything, they are probably improved in this edition.

Gender Matters provides information, ideas and resources to deepen youth and educational activities addressing issues related to gender and gender-based violence and places these issues within the framework of human rights education.

Gender Matters does not aim to be an exhaustive publication and will not provide readers with all possible theories or ideas related to gender or gender equality. Nor does it deal with all aspects of gender-based violence. Instead, it focuses on issues and concerns relating to gender-based violence which are likely to be relevant to young people's lives. These issues and concerns may differ depending on social and political context, and some of the material and activities may need to be adapted in order to respond to the concrete needs of young people in a given community, region or country.

While there is no particular starting point, and it is our intention that readers are able to choose the parts that are relevant for them, we strongly recommend you look through the whole manual to gain an overall picture of the contents, and read the parts of the conceptual chapters most closely related to the issues being addressed by your work with young people. Working with the topic of gender and gender-based violence can be challenging and requires sensitivity and specific competences to be able to deal with the ethical issues which may arise.

Gender Matters is for everybody who wants to explore the topics related to gender and gender-based violence through human rights education. It does not provide all the answers – and may instead create new questions! The manual should be used as a resource to guide young people in the world of human rights issues, helping them to become more aware of their own actions and the actions of others, and contributing to a better understanding of how to stay safe and secure and how to support those who have experienced violence in their lives.

CHAPTER 1
Gender identity, gender-based violence and human rights

Gender identity, gender-based violence and human rights

Gender equality is an essential aim for any society based on human rights, democracy and the rule of law. Gender equality concerns almost every aspect of social interaction and public policy, including youth policy and youth work. Every individual is directly and personally affected by issues relating to gender equality and gender-based violence.

However, discussing gender and gender-based violence can be difficult, as these discussions include concepts and terms which are not always clear, which may change over time, and which cut across different disciplines such as psychology, sociology, culture, medicine, law, education, activism or politics.

The baseline is that gender-based violence is a human rights violation and affects not only people who are directly targeted by it, but also the whole of society.

The Spotlight Initiative of the United Nations and the European Union provides the following data[1]:

35% of girls and women in the world have experienced physical or sexual abuse;

70% of all human-trafficking victims worldwide are girls or women;

more than **700** million women alive today were married before the age of 18;

200 million women and girls alive today have been victims of female genital mutilation.

In addition:

- 1612 transgender people were killed in 62 countries between 2008 and 2014[2];
- almost half of the respondents to an EU LGBT survey stated that they had experienced discrimination or harassment because of their sexual orientation[3].

These statistics show a little of the extent of gender-based violence, but it is important to note that most examples of the problem continue to go unreported. Acting against gender-based violence requires active involvement from state authorities, from institutions, NGOs and indeed from all members of society. Addressing the problem is a key task for youth work.

1. What is gender-based violence?

'Gender-based violence' and 'violence against women' are two terms that are often used interchangeably, as most violence against women is inflicted (by men) for gender-based reasons, and gender-based violence affects women disproportionately. The UN Declaration on the Elimination of Violence against Women defines violence against women as

> any act of gender-based violence that results in, or is likely to result in, physical, sexual or psychological harm or suffering to women, including threats of such acts, coercion or arbitrary deprivation of liberty, whether occurring in public or in private life[4].

In more recent legal documents, there are examples of the two terms being merged, and the term 'gender-based violence against women' is used. For example, in the Council of Europe's Convention on Preventing and Combating Violence Against Women and Domestic Violence (Istanbul Convention), Article 3 offers the following definition:

> gender-based violence against women shall mean violence that is directed against a woman because she is a woman or that affects women disproportionately[5].

Definitions such as these apply to instances where gender is the basis for violence carried out against a person. However, there is more to gender than being male or female: someone may be born with female sexual characteristics but identify as male, or as male and female at the same time, or sometimes as neither male nor female. LGBT+ people (lesbian, gay, bisexual, transgender and other people who do not fit the heterosexual norm or traditional gender binary categories) also suffer from violence which is based on their factual or perceived sexual orientation, and/or gender identity. For that reason, violence against such people falls within the scope of gender-based violence. Furthermore, men can also be targeted with gender-based violence: statistically, the number of such cases is much smaller, in comparison with women, but it should not be neglected.

Using the definition of 'gender-based violence against women' from the Explanatory report to the Istanbul Convention[6] as a starting point we can say that:

> **Gender-based violence refers to any type of harm that is perpetrated against a person or group of people because of their factual or perceived sex, gender, sexual orientation and/or gender identity.**

Gender-based violence is based on an imbalance of power and is carried out with the intention to humiliate and make a person or group of people feel inferior and/or subordinate. This type of violence is deeply rooted in the social and cultural structures, norms and values that govern society, and is often perpetuated by a culture of denial and silence. Gender-based violence can happen in both the private and public spheres and it affects women disproportionately.

Gender-based violence can be sexual, physical, verbal, psychological (emotional), or socio-economic and it can take many forms – from verbal violence and hate speech on the Internet, to rape or murder. It can be perpetrated by anyone: a current or former spouse/partner, a family member, a colleague from work, schoolmates, friends, an unknown person, or people who act on behalf of cultural, religious, state, or intra-state institutions. Gender-based violence, as with any type of violence, is an issue involving relations of power. It is based on a feeling of superiority, and an intention to assert that superiority in the family, at school, at work, in the community or in society as a whole.

Why is gender-based violence a problem?

- **Gender-based violence is a human rights violation**
  It is an unrelenting assault on human dignity, depriving people of their human rights. Freedom from violence is a fundamental human right, and gender-based violence undermines a person's sense of self-worth and self-esteem. It affects not only physical health but also mental health and may lead to self-harm, isolation, depression and suicidal attempts.

- **Gender-based violence threatens a person's physical and psychological integrity**
  Everyone has the right to feel safe and secure, and where this is not present, people's ability to function in the family, community and society is likely to be impaired, as self-realisation and development are affected. Gender-based violence is an obstacle to the realisation of every person's well-being and to their right to fulfilment and self-development.

- **Gender-based violence is discrimination**
  It is deeply rooted in harmful stereotypes and prejudices against women or other people who do not fit into a traditional gender binary or heteronormative society. For that reason, gender-based violence can have the effect of pushing women and others who are affected to the margins of society and making them feel inferior or helpless. In the case of men who do not act according to dominant masculine gender roles, gender-based violence has the function of

correction by example. The severity of the 'punishment' for men who do not act according to expectations concerning male gender roles (whether gay, bisexual or heterosexual) may be related to the perceived danger that their difference presents to normalised and dominant assumptions about gender. Their very lives might collide and appear to contradict the idea that there are natural forms of behaviour and social roles in general for men and women.

- **Gender-based violence is an obstacle to gender equality**
  Gender equality is central to safeguarding human rights, upholding democracy and preserving the rule of law. Gender-based violence contributes to cultivating a heteronormative society and perpetuates the power of men. Gender equality, on the other hand, entails equal rights for people of all genders, as well as equal visibility, and equal opportunities for empowerment, taking responsibility and participating in all spheres of public and private life. Gender equality also implies equal access to, and equal distribution of resources between women and men.

- **Gender-based violence is under-reported and there is often impunity for perpetrators**
  Common myths, such as that 'what happens at home should stay at home' or that 'it is nobody's business what happens in the family' are very powerful. This makes denouncing violence in the family difficult, and it may affect the provision of help and support services, thereby exposing the abused person to greater harm, with possibly fatal consequences. Furthermore, violence very often silences those who are affected by it. By failing to speak out against domestic violence we also mirror the techniques used by perpetrators. In some countries, most types and forms of gender-based violence are illegal and punishable by law, but there are countries which lag behind in this respect. The Istanbul Convention of the Council of Europe asks for criminalisation of different forms of gender-based violence.

- **Gender-based violence affects everyone**
  Children raised in families where a woman is abused are also victims of violence (sometimes not physically, but always psychologically). The children witness violence and may form the impression that such behaviour is justified or 'normal'; in other words, they assimilate violent norms. They are also brought up in a culture of violence that may negatively affect their self-development and ability to function in society. Gender-based violence affects family members, friends and colleagues.

- **Gender-based violence has a very heavy economic cost.**
  It requires the involvement of different services - medical, psychological, the police or justice system – and it results in the loss of resources or of employment by victims. It makes people underachieve at work and in education, and it negatively affects their productivity. Many people who suffer from gender-based violence cannot stay at home and need a place to stay, which sometimes

results in homelessness. Shelter services need to be provided for such people, and while there are services for abused women and their children in many places in Europe (although not in sufficient numbers), the inadequate number of shelters for LGBT+ people remains critical.

Poster created by the No Hate Ninjas (Portugal) for the No Hate Speech Movement youth campaign.

2. What causes gender-based violence?

Gender-based violence, and in particular violence against women, is one of the most pronounced expressions of the unequal power relations between women and men. The main cause of the violence is the perpetrator him or herself: it is very important to keep in mind that a person who has been affected by gender-based violence is never responsible for the perpetrator's actions.

There is no single factor that can explain gender-based violence in our societies, but rather a myriad of factors contribute to it, and the interplay of these factors lies at the root of the problem. Four types of factors can be identified: cultural, legal, economic and political.

Cultural factors

Patriarchal and sexist views legitimise violence to ensure the dominance and superiority of men. Other cultural factors include gender stereotypes and prejudice, normative expectations of femininity and masculinity, the socialisation of gender, an understanding of the family sphere as private and under male authority, and a general acceptance of violence as part of the public sphere (e.g. street sexual harassment of women), and/or as an acceptable means to solve conflict and assert oneself.

Religious and historical traditions have sanctioned the physical punishment of women under the notion of entitlement and ownership of women. The concept of ownership, in turn, legitimises control over women's sexuality, which, according to many legal codes, has been deemed essential to ensure patrilineal inheritance.

Sexuality is also tied to the concept of so-called "family honour" in many societies. Traditional norms in these societies allow the killing of women suspected of defiling the "honour" of the family by indulging in forbidden sex or marrying and divorcing without the consent of the family. Norms around sexuality also help to account for the high numbers of homeless LGBT+ young people, and for the prevalence of hate crimes against them, on the grounds that they are considered a "threat" to societal norms. The same norms around sexuality can help to account for the mass rape of women.

Legal factors

Being a victim of gender-based violence is perceived in many societies as shameful and weak, with many women still being considered guilty of attracting violence against themselves through their behaviour. This partly accounts for enduring low levels of reporting and investigation.

Until recently, the law in some countries still differentiated between the public and private spaces, which left women particularly vulnerable to domestic violence.

The Istanbul Convention ensures the right for everyone, particularly women, to live free from violence in both the public and the private spheres.

While most forms of gender-based violence are criminalised in most European countries, the practices of law enforcement in many cases favour the perpetrators, which helps to account for low levels of trust in public authorities and for the fact that most of these crimes go unreported.

The decriminalisation of homosexuality is still very recent in many societies. While progress has been achieved in many states by adopting equal marriage, this has sometimes led to a backlash, for example by strengthening opinions holding the traditional family to be the union between a man and a woman, or where countries have adopted laws that forbid "homosexual propaganda".

Economic factors

The lack of economic resources generally makes women, but also LGBT+ people particularly vulnerable to violence. It creates patterns of violence and poverty that become self-perpetuating, making it extremely difficult for the victims to extricate themselves. When unemployment and poverty affect men, this can also cause them to assert their masculinity through violent means.

Political factors

The under-representation of women and LGBT+ people in power and politics means that they have fewer opportunities to shape the discussion and to affect changes in policy, or to adopt measures to combat gender-based violence and support equality. The topic of gender-based violence is in some cases deemed not to be important, with domestic violence also being given insufficient resources and attention. Women's and LGBT+ movements have raised questions and increased public awareness around traditional gender norms, highlighting aspects of inequality. For some, this threat to the status quo has been used as a justification for violence.

3. Types of gender-based violence

Violence is often associated only with physical violence, neglecting other non-physical forms. Violence is a complex issue and categorising different 'types' of violence can never be exact. The Council of Europe Istanbul Convention mentions the following types of violence:

- psychological violence (Art. 33)
- stalking (Art. 34)
- physical violence (Art. 35)
- forced marriages (Art. 37)
- sexual violence, including rape (Art. 36)
- female genital mutilation (Art. 38)
- forced abortion and forced sterilisation (Art. 39)
- sexual harassment (Art. 40)
- aiding or abetting and attempt (Art. 41)
- unacceptable justifications for crimes, including crimes committed in the name of so-called "honour" (Art. 42).

Using these as a basis, in this publication, we shall distinguish five inter-related types of violence:

- Physical
- verbal (including hate speech)
- sexual
- psychological, and
- socio-economic.

There also two other categories of violence that can be found in this chapter: domestic violence and (sexual) harassment – both of which may be a combination of all five types of violence mentioned above. In reality, some or many forms of violence can be present at the same time, particularly in abusive relationships. All forms can occur both in the private sphere (in families and intimate relationships) and in the public sphere, committed by (unknown) individuals in public space, or by organisations, institutions, and states.

Physical violence

Physical violence includes beating, burning, kicking, punching, biting, maiming or killing, or the use of objects or weapons. Some classifications also include human trafficking and slavery in the category of physical violence because initial coercion is often experienced, and the people involved often end up becoming victims of further violence as a result of their enslavement. Physical violence is an act attempting to cause, or resulting in, pain and/or physical injury. As with all forms of violence, the main aim of the perpetrator is not only – or may not always be – to cause physical pain, but also to limit the other's self-determination. Physical violence sends a clear message to the victim from the perpetrator: "I can do things to you that you do not want to happen." Such violence demonstrates differences of social power, or may intend to promote particular demands, sometimes regularly, through coercion. Physical violence in intimate relationships, often referred to as domestic violence, continues to be a widespread phenomenon in every country.

Physical violence in the private sphere also affects young people. As mentioned above, witnessing the abuse of one parent by another leads to serious psychological harm in children. Often, children and young people who are present during an act of spousal abuse will also be injured, sometimes by accident and sometimes because they try to intervene. Young men sometimes commit criminal offences against the abusive parent (mostly fathers), in order to protect their mother and siblings, and children regularly become victims of an act of revenge by the abuser against the mother. In fact, for many mothers a prime motivation to stay in an abusive relationship is that the abuser threatens to harm or kill the children if she tries to leave.

Physical violence also appears in the intimate relationships of young people. The fact that they might not live together often adds to the difficulties in talking about it.

Gender-based violence in public is often related to assumptions and expectations concerning gender roles. Verbal abuse, name-calling, threats and attacks may take place, and it is common that LGBT+ people or those perceived to be gay, lesbian or 'different' may become victims of public violence. Violence against LGBT+ people can be organised (groups going to well-known meeting places of gay men to beat them up) or 'spontaneous' outbursts, for example, when a lesbian woman is attacked when she walks in the street holding hands with her partner. In this respect, public affection becomes a safety issue, and research shows that many LGBTs refrain from showing affection in public. This kind of street violence usually remains under-reported.

Verbal violence and hate speech

Many cultures have sayings or expressions to the effect that words are harmless, and there is a long tradition that teaches us to ignore verbal attacks. However, when these attacks become regular and systematic and purposefully target someone's sensitive spots[7], the object of the attacks is right to consider themselves victims of verbal abuse.

Verbal violence can include issues that are specific to a person, such as put-downs (in private or in front of others), ridiculing, the use of swear-words that are especially uncomfortable for the other, saying bad things about the other's loved ones, threatening with other forms of violence, either against the victim or against somebody dear to them. At other times, the verbal abuse may be relevant to the background of the victim, such as their religion, culture, language, (perceived) sexual orientation or traditions. Depending on the most emotionally sensitive areas of the victim, abusers often consciously target these issues in a way that is painful, humiliating and threatening to the victim.

Most of the verbal violence that women experience because of being women is sexualised, and counts as sexual violence. Verbal gender-based violence in the public sphere is also largely related to gender roles: it may include comments and jokes about women or may present women as sex objects (e.g. jokes about sexual availability, prostitution, rape). A great deal of bullying is related to the (perceived) sexuality of young people (especially boys). The regular negative use of words such as 'queer' or 'fag' is often traumatising for those perceived as gays and lesbians. This is very likely one of the reasons why many gays and lesbians only 'come out' after secondary school.

Verbal violence may be classified as hate speech. It can take many forms: words, videos, memes, or pictures that are posted on social networks, or it may carry a violent message threatening a person or a group of people because of certain characteristics. The European Commission on Racism and Intolerance defines hate speech as:

> (…) advocacy, promotion or incitement, in any form, of the denigration, hatred or vilification of a person or group of persons, as well as any harassment, insult, negative stereotyping, stigmatisation or threat in respect of such a person or group of persons and the justification of all the preceding types of expression, on the ground of "race"[8], colour, descent, national or ethnic origin, age, disability, language, religion or belief, sex, gender, gender identity, sexual orientation and other personal characteristics or status[9].

Gender-based hate speech mainly targets women (in this case, it is often called 'sexist hate speech') [10]and LGBT+ people, on the basis of sex, gender, sexual orientation or gender identity both in the private and public spheres. This includes the Internet, which is considered a public sphere. However, people may also be affected by this kind of gender-based violence in private e-mails or messages sent using online messaging software.

Gender-based hate speech can take many different forms – jokes, spreading rumours, threats, slander, incitement of violence or hate. It aims at humiliating, dehumanising and making a person or group of people scared. As with any type of violence, gender-based hate speech is usually very destructive for the person targeted: people who experience hate speech often feel helpless, and do not know what to do. They feel uneasy, frightened, and they lose self-confidence and sometimes even attempt suicide. Hate speech can sometimes lead to hate crimes – crimes that are motivated by prejudices targeting a person whose identity is different from the perpetrator's. Hate crimes can take various forms: physical violence, destroying property, arson or killing. The victims are deliberately chosen because of certain characteristics that they are perceived to possess.

Psychological violence

All forms of violence have a psychological aspect, since the main aim of being violent or abusive is to hurt the integrity and dignity of another person. Apart from this, there are certain forms of violence which take place using methods which cannot be placed in other categories, and which therefore can be said to achieve psychological violence in a 'pure' form. This includes isolation or confinement, withholding information, disinformation, and threatening behaviour.

In the private sphere, psychological violence includes threatening conduct which lacks physical violence or verbal elements, for example, actions that refer to former acts of violence, or purposeful ignorance and neglect of another person.

One common example of such violence in the public sphere includes the isolation of young women or men who do not act according to traditional gender roles. Isolation in the public sphere is most often used by peer groups, but responsible adults – such as teachers and sports coaches – can also be perpetrators. Most typically, isolation means exclusion from certain group activities. It can also include intimidation, in a similar fashion to psychological abuse in the private sphere.

Sexual violence

As more and more information has become available about the circumstances surrounding sexual violence, it has become clear that sexual violence, like other forms of violence, is an abuse of power. Sexual violence includes: engaging in non-consensual vaginal, anal or oral penetration with another person, by the use of any body part or object; engaging in other non-consensual acts of a sexual nature with a person; or causing someone else to engage in non-consensual acts of a sexual nature with a third person. Marital rape and attempted rape constitute sexual violence. Examples of forced sexual activities include being forced to watch somebody masturbate, forcing somebody to masturbate in front of others, forced unsafe sex, sexual harassment, and abuse related to reproduction (e.g. forced pregnancy, forced abortion, forced sterilisation, female genital mutilation).

Certain forms of sexual violence are related to a victim's personal limits, and are more typical of the private sphere. The perpetrator deliberately violates these limits: examples include date rape, forcing certain types of sexual activities, withdrawal of sexual attention as a form of punishment, or forcing other(s) to watch (and sometimes to imitate) pornography.

All forms of sexual violence can appear in both the private and the public spheres. There are, however, three particular forms of sexual violence in the public sphere which are worth noting: sexual harassment at the workplace, sexual violence as a weapon of war and torture, and sexual violence against (perceived) LGBT+ people as a means of 'punishment' for abandoning prescribed gender roles.

Socio-economic violence

Socio-economic deprivation can make a victim more vulnerable to other forms of violence and can even be the reason why other forms of violence are inflicted. Global economic data clearly show that one of the consequences of globalisation is the feminisation of poverty[11] (making women generally more economically vulnerable than men), however economic vulnerability is a phenomenon that also exists on the personal level. It has been recognised in a vast number of abusive relationships as a distinct phenomenon, which is why it deserves a category of its own. However, even when the relationship is reversed, and a woman has a higher economic status in a relationship, this does not necessarily eliminate the threat of violence: conflicts about status and emasculation may arise, particularly in already abusive relationships.

Typical forms of socio-economic violence include taking away the earnings of the victim, not allowing them to have a separate income (giving them 'housewife' status, or making them work in a family business without a salary), or making the victim unfit for work through targeted physical abuse.

Socio-economic violence in the public sphere is both a cause and an effect of dominant gender power relations in societies. It may include denial of access to education or (equally) paid work (mainly to women), denial of access to services, exclusion from certain jobs, denial of pleasure and the enjoyment of civil, cultural, social and political rights. In the case of LGBT+ people, they may even be subject to criminalisation.

Some public forms of socio-economic gender-based violence contribute to women becoming economically dependent on their partner (lower wages, very low or no child-care benefits, or benefits being tied to the income tax of the wage-earning male partner). Such a relation of dependency then offers someone with a tendency to be abusive in their relationships the chance to act without fear of losing their partner.

Domestic violence or violence in intimate relationships

Domestic violence, or intimate partnership violence, is the most common type of gender-based violence. It also requires special attention, because it is a relational type of violence, and the dynamics are therefore very different from violent incidents that occur among strangers.

The fact that domestic violence was long considered to be a private, domestic issue has significantly hampered recognition of the phenomenon as a human rights violation. The invisibility of the phenomenon was reinforced by an understanding of international human rights law as applicable only to relations between individual and the state (or states). However, it is now recognised that state responsibility under international law can arise not only from state action, but also from state inaction, where a state fails to protect citizens against violence or abuse (the "due diligence" principle).

According to the Istanbul Convention, domestic violence includes "acts of physical, sexual, psychological or economic violence that occur within the family or domestic unit or between former or current spouses or partners, whether or not the perpetrator shares or has shared the same residence with the victim". Although the vast majority of domestic violence is perpetrated against women by men, it actually occurs in same sex relationships just as frequently as in heterosexual relationships, and there are cases of women abusing their male partners. Domestic violence such as rape, battering, sexual or psychological abuse leads to severe physical and mental suffering, injuries, and often death. It is inflicted against the will of the victim, with the intention to humiliate, intimidate and exert control over her or him. Very often the victim is left without recourse to any remedies, because police and law enforcement mechanisms are often gender-insensitive, hostile or absent[12].

A question often asked in relation to domestic violence is 'why doesn't (s)he leave?' There is no simple answer to this question, because domestic violence is a complex phenomenon which often involves physical, psychological, emotional and economic forms of abuse. It may often lead to 'battered woman syndrome', where a woman in an abusive relationship starts feeling helpless, worthless, powerless, and accepting of the status quo. However, this syndrome does not explain why some women kill their violent partners and detracts attention from other reasons why women end up staying in a violent relationship. Such reasons may include financial dependence on the abuser, social constraints, and a lack of alternatives such as shelters for abuse victims. Domestic violence often involves isolation of the victim from family and friends, deprivation of personal possessions, manipulation of children, threats of reprisals against the individual, against children, or against other family members. Furthermore, common social pressures regarding the nature of a family – 'some kind of father is better than no father for your children' – often makes getting out of an abusive relationship not only difficult, but also extremely dangerous.

One further reason why people stay in abusive relationships can be understood through the so-called 'Cycle of Violence'[13]:

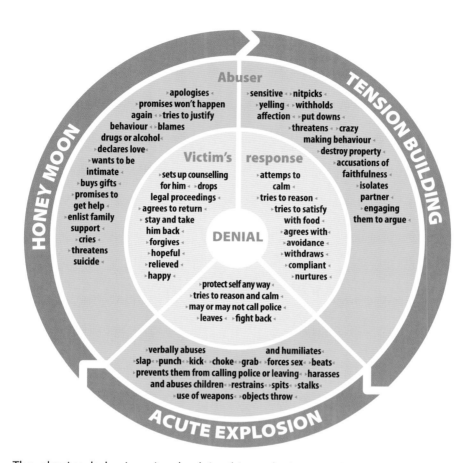

The abusive behaviour involved in this cycle is sometimes instinctive and reactive, and sometimes planned and deliberate. It aims to keep the abused person in the relationship through promises and denials. The basic cycle consists of an outburst of violence, which is followed by a so-called 'honeymoon period' characterised by a sudden positive change in the behaviour of the abuser. It is known as the honeymoon period because victims often describe this period as being very similar to the early part of the relationship. The abuser is typically very apologetic about his or her behaviour, makes promises to change, and may even offer presents. However, this period does not last long, as its only function is to eliminate the worries of the victim regarding the future of the relationship. The victim is typically engaged and involved at this stage, as nobody likes to remember negative experiences. The victim therefore welcomes the apparent changes and promises made.

Once the victim's worries have been silenced, the old power structure is re-asserted. The many typical characteristics of domestic violence will again breed the kind of tension that eventually erupts in a further act of violence on the part of the abuser. Early in a relationship, violent incidents may be as far apart as six months or even a year, making it difficult to recognise the cyclical nature. Early incidents are likely to be verbal incidents followed by minor acts of physical violence, also making it hard for the victim to recognise the cycle, or to realise that put-downs, breaking of cups, even shoves and slaps are likely to escalate and end in beatings or worse.

The cycle does not only escalate as far as the severity of violence is concerned, but the incidents typically become closer to each other. Eventually, the honeymoon phase can disappear completely, and in some abusive relationships it may not exist at all. Instead, it may be replaced, particularly in social groups where domestic violence and rigid gender roles are less accepted, by attempts to minimise or deny the violence altogether.

In contexts where gender roles are more rigid, the perpetrator has greater freedom to deny responsibility. The set of gender roles that we are taught to adhere to as women and men contain many contradictions or demands that cannot be fulfilled. At the same time, part of the hegemonic male gender role is to oversee women and children in fulfilling their roles, and if necessary, to discipline them. These two conditions combine to create common justifications for those who are abusive in relationships: they can easily find one thing or another to blame the woman for in cases of violence inflicted, and thereby to claim the right to inflict it.

In many countries, physical abuse and emotional abuse, often accompanied by acts of sexual violence, are seen as acts or crimes of 'passion', motivated by jealousy or the failure of the partner to fulfil expectations. Such a portrayal is particularly common in the media. However, this kind of vocabulary should be avoided when talking about forms of gender-based violence as it perpetuates ideas of impunity and implies responsibility on the part of the victim. The influence of alcohol is also often cited as a mitigating factor in cases of sexual abuse or exploitation, but this ignores the fact that abuse is perpetrated in a systematic way. As Ronda Copelon remarks, alcohol does cause violence, but "many men get drunk without beating their wives and…men often beat their wives without being drunk. To the extent that alcohol facilitates male violence, it is an important factor in the effort to reduce violence, but it is not the cause"[14].

Harassment and sexual harassment

Can I hug my colleague at work without asking, or is this sexual harassment?
Is it OK to comment on a woman's body?

When, in fact, does harassment start? It is helpful to note, from the start, that any form of harassment is usually humiliating and degrading and threatens the physical and mental integrity of a person. The Istanbul Convention of the Council of Europe defines sexual harassment as:

> any form of unwanted verbal, non-verbal or physical conduct of a sexual nature with the purpose or effect of violating the dignity of a person, in particular when creating an intimidating, hostile, degrading, humiliating or offensive environment.[15]

Harassment and sexual harassment are also defined in EU Directive 2002/73/EC[16]. Harassment is said to occur "where an unwanted conduct related to the sex of a person occurs with the purpose or effect of violating the dignity of a person, and of creating an intimidating, hostile, degrading, humiliating or offensive environment". Sexual harassment is "where any form of unwanted verbal, non-verbal or physical conduct of a sexual nature occurs, with the purpose or effect of violating the dignity of a person, in particular when creating an intimidating, hostile, degrading, humiliating or offensive environment". This EU Directive states that harassment is both a form of discrimination and that it is illegal.

Verbal examples of sexual harassment may include: making sexual comments about a person's body, making sexual comments or innuendos, asking about sexual fantasies, preferences, or history, asking personal questions about someone's social or sex life, making sexual comments about a person's clothing, anatomy, or looks, repeatedly trying to date a person who is not interested, telling lies or spreading rumours about a person's sex life or sexual preferences.

Examples of non-verbal harassment include: looking a person up and down ('elevator eyes'), following or stalking someone, using sexually suggestive visuals, making sexual gestures with the hands or through body movements, using facial expressions such as winking, throwing kisses, or licking lips.

Instances of physical harassment include: giving someone a massage around the neck or shoulders, touching another person's clothing, hair, or body, hugging, kissing, patting, touching or rubbing oneself sexually against another person.

The key concept in understanding harassment is that any overtures are unwelcome. A person may welcome and accept a sexist remark or a comment about their body, but this is likely to depend on the particular situation and circumstances. However, it is important to remember that even if someone accepts – or welcomes – the behaviour, it may still be degrading and humiliating. In addition, such acceptance may not be fully voluntary: it may be a result of often invisible pressure from the outside world.

4. Exploring gender and gender identity

Gender enters into all our social relations. When people interact, their view of themselves, including their identity and their rights and possibilities, comes up against the way they are perceived by other people, and the way that others behave towards them. However, it often appears that gender in its truest sense is absent from our social relations, because the way in which most people perceive gender tends to be internalised so deeply that it appears 'normal' and natural. Understanding how we live together means being able to question the things we take for granted in our everyday lives. This includes a key part of our identity: our gender.

This manual is a resource for working with others, but it is also a resource that underlines the need constantly to work with oneself. It could even be said that one is not really possible without the other. In some ways, the reasoning behind this can be expressed easily: each of us is a person with our own subjectivity and experience of living with others in society – so everyone is personally involved in discussions of gender. It is easy to test this out: most people have had experiences where someone's appearance does not immediately signal 'male' or 'female'. Perhaps fewer people then go on to ask themselves what this indicates about gender, or about how they perceive gender stereotypes. In fact, on a daily basis, it is common for people to organise their perceptions according to gendered assumptions that have never been questioned.

The concept of 'gender awareness' reminds us that we all need to be aware of issues such as the following:

- We are likely to see ourselves within such categories as male/female or man/woman, but these categories do not in fact do justice to the complexity of gender and sexual identities;
- We consciously and unconsciously express our gendered selves in numerous ways, including in our relations with others;
- We interpret and evaluate other people's gender and this affects the ways that we interact with them;
- We use images, associations, assumptions and normative standards to interpret the gender(s) and sexualities of others, and are often unaware of the way this happens or how these influences originate;
- Gender is of key importance in defining the power, privilege and possibilities that some people have and some people do not have in a given society. It affects progress towards equality and freedom from discrimination.

Gender awareness is necessary as an end goal for everyone, but deliberate work on this issue is particularly important for youth workers and young people who want to address issues of gender and violence with their peers. Gender awareness is necessary because no one is ever completely able to 'step outside' of the social and cultural processes that partly shape our identities, values and perceptions, but we can still develop ways of reflecting and ways of interrogating ourselves, and this is very important for group work and group interaction. Gender awareness should also be seen as a process, because our ways of thinking about ourselves and others as gendered, sexual beings shift over time and in different contexts.

Sex and gender

Different terms are regularly used in theories of sexuality and gender, for example sex, gender, gender identity, gender expressions, gender roles, sexual orientation. It is important to be clear about the meanings of such terms.

Gender is an area that cuts across thinking about society, law, politics and culture, and it is frequently discussed in relation to other aspects of identity and social position, such as class, ethnicity, age and physical ability. Gender is also an important concept within a range of social and political debates and may influence these debates differently according to cultural context.

'Gender' is a 'heavy' word: politicians and public figures often use it with negative connotations, for example in referring to 'gender police', or to ideologies that 'threaten our kids'. These are examples of how gender can be misunderstood and politicised.

There are some languages which do not have a word for 'gender'. In such cases, the word 'sex' is normally used, and in order to distinguish between sex and gender, different terms may be employed, for example 'biological sex' may be used to refer to 'sex', and 'cultural and social sex' may be used to refer to 'gender'. However, even when the terms exist in the language, 'sex' and 'gender' are often used interchangeably.

Definitions of sex and gender

A number of definitions have been put forward by different organisations. They provide a useful starting point for discussion.

The World Health Organisation summarises the difference between sex and gender in the following way:

Sex refers to "*the different biological and physiological characteristics of males and females, such as reproductive organs, chromosomes, hormones, etc.*"

Gender "*refers to the socially constructed characteristics of women and men – such as norms, roles and relationships of and between groups of women and men. It varies from society to society and can be changed. The concept of gender includes five important elements: relational, hierarchical, historical, contextual and institutional. While most people are born either male or female, they are taught appropriate norms and behaviours – including how they should interact with others of the same or opposite sex within households, communities and work places. When individuals or groups do not "fit" established gender norms they often face stigma, discriminatory practices or social exclusion – all of which adversely affect health[17]."*

The Council of Europe Convention on preventing and combating violence against women and domestic violence is the first international human rights document that contains a definition of gender. In Article 3, gender is defined as "socially constructed roles, behaviours, activities and attributes that a given society considers appropriate for women and men."[18]

The European Institute for Gender Equality, an autonomous body of the European Union, provides very extensive definitions of sex and gender:

"Sex refers to the biological and physiological characteristics that define humans as female or male. These sets of biological characteristics are not mutually exclusive, as there are individuals who possess both, but these characteristics tend to differentiate humans as females or males."

"Gender refers to the social attributes and opportunities associated with being female and male and to the relationships between women and men and girls and boys, as well as to the relations between women and those between men. These attributes, opportunities and relationships are socially constructed and are learned through socialisation processes. They are context- and time-specific, and changeable. Gender determines what is expected, allowed and valued in a woman or a man in a given context. In most societies, there are differences and inequalities between women and men in responsibilities assigned, activities undertaken, access to and control over resources, as well as decision-making opportunities. Gender is part of the broader sociocultural context. Other important criteria for sociocultural analysis include class, race, poverty level, ethnic group and age."[19]

Other definitions have been proposed[20], but the general differences between the terms can be summarised as follows:

SEX

- 'Sex' refers to biological differences between males and females (e.g. gonads, sexual organs, chromosomes, hormones).
- Sex is usually assigned at birth (there are examples when it is assigned later, when sex characteristics do not clearly indicate the sex of the baby, for example in the case of 'intersex' people).
- Sex can be changed: in the case of transsexual people, who are born with the sex characteristics of one sex and gender identity of the other, sex reassignment surgeries are performed. This includes a change of sex organs and the administration of hormones.

GENDER

- Gender is a social, psychological and cultural construct and it is developed in the process of socialisation. Different societies and cultures may therefore have different understandings of what is 'masculine' or 'feminine'. Societies create norms and expectations related to gender, and these are learned in the course of people's lives – including in the family, at school, through the media. All of these influences impose certain roles and patterns of behaviour on everyone within society. Gender norms – often limited to notions of masculinity and femininity – change over time, but are usually based on a heteronormative order which stipulates that there are two sexes (genders) and they are attracted to each other. People who do not appear to fall under this binary notion of gender often suffer from exclusion, discrimination and violence.

- Gender is both an analytical category – a way of thinking about how identities are constructed – and a political idea which addresses the distribution of power in society.

- Gender norms are learned and internalised by all members of society.

- Gender norms vary across different cultures and over time.

- Traditional gender norms are hierarchical: they presuppose an unequal power structure related to gender that disadvantages mostly women.

- Gender is not necessarily defined by biological sex: a person's gender may or may not correspond to their biological sex. Gender is more about identity and how we feel about ourselves. People may self-identify as male, female, transgender, other or none (indeterminate/unspecified). People that do not identify as male or female are often grouped under the umbrella terms 'non-binary' or 'genderqueer', but the range of gender identifications is in reality unlimited.

- Gender is deeply personal to every individual: some people recognise their gender identity early in childhood, and some only later on.

- Gender intersects with other categories, such as class, skin colour, ethnicity, religion or disability. (You can read more about intersectionality in Chapter 4).

- Gender is something we express (gender expression), sometimes intentionally, and sometimes without thinking. We communicate our gender in a number of ways, for example by the way we dress, the way we move, our hair style, and the way we interact with others[21].

Gender expression can vary for an individual from day to day or in different situations, but most people can identify a range on the scale where they feel the most comfortable. Some people are comfortable with a wider range of gender expression than others.

Gender may appear to be a complicated idea, but once the biological determinism common in everyday thinking about differences between women and men is challenged, it becomes easier to understand gender.

Aspects of sex will not vary substantially between different human societies and over time, while aspects of gender may vary greatly.

Examples of sex characteristics:

- Women can menstruate while men cannot.
- Men have testicles while women do not.
- Women have developed breasts that are usually capable of lactating (producing milk) while men have not.
- Men generally have bigger bones than women.

Examples of gender characteristics:

- In most countries, women earn significantly less than men.
- In some countries, the tobacco industry targets women by "feminising" cigarettes packaging for certain brands (small "purse" packs that resemble cosmetics and evoke slimness, the use of "feminine" colours, such as pink).
- In most countries of the world, women do more housework than men.
- In some countries, the law allows people to marry a partner of the same sex; in other countries this is not allowed.

Facilitating discussion on gender issues

Before examining gender and socialisation, it is important to bear in mind some considerations about approaching gender and gender issues in a local context, including how this relates to working with young people.

- Gender is a sensitive issue. Understandings and feelings about gender and gender issues can often be deeply personal, and approaching these issues can trigger memories and feelings about past or current experiences. When we deal with issues concerning identity, it is not always possible to know 'who is in the room'. Before engaging in discussions such as these with your youth group, you need to think carefully about how to conduct them with sensitivity and responsibility.
- Gender is a political issue. Discussions around gender often become heated and are likely to raise political issues where there are strong disagreements, often based on different ideological, religious or other firmly held beliefs. Facilitating such discussions is challenging, and involves being acutely aware of our own attitudes and beliefs and understanding how to support others to discuss these issues in a meaningful way.
- Key terms are generally not well understood. Despite the definitions and differentiations offered above, you will hear the terms 'gender' and 'sex' used interchangeably in society. For example, some questionnaires or forms may ask for your 'gender' and simply provide the categories 'male' and 'female' for you to choose from, neglecting other options.
- Gender is everyone's concern. Awareness of gender issues has primarily

been brought about as a result of the work of the women's movement and of feminist politics, which includes work on gender equality, challenging the status and roles of women and men in society, and addressing the creation of gendered stereotypes. For this reason, there is a tendency to associate gender with women and women's issues alone. However, it is important to note that everyone has a gender identity, and discussing gender is not only about discussing women's issues.

• Gender relations are relations of power. A proper gender analysis cannot examine the construction of male and female identities in relation to each other without considering how these relations are a function of power, and how they serve to reproduce differences in access to power and resources – and other inequalities. In general, these relationships tend to privilege men and subordinate women. It is also important to recognise that "…current norms of gender marginalise many men and that cultural constructions of gender exclude and alienate those who do not fit neatly into the categories of male or female".[22]

Gender and socialisation

Humans learn the norms of society through the experience of living within it and interacting socially. However, we are not necessarily always aware of how or what we are experiencing and learning. In other words, people may be highly attuned to signs of gender in the environment, while not necessarily being able to reflect on how these signs have become gendered.

Our everyday knowledge includes a sense of values, norms, roles and ways of evaluating behaviour, and this kind of knowledge is constantly expanding and constantly being fine-tuned: "although deeply immersed in our daily routines, informed by practical knowledge oriented to the social settings in which we interact, we often do not pause to think about the meaning of what we have gone through; even less frequently do we pause to compare our private experiences with the fate of others…".[23] Reflecting on how we learn about gender involves a challenge: it invites us to take a critical distance from ourselves and our daily modes of seeing and interacting, and to pause and think about the meaning of gender, and of how we have been able to acquire such a vast and seemingly 'natural' knowledge of gender roles, values and identities.

We have all been born into socio-cultural arrangements and meanings that pre-date us. 'Socialisation' is the term that is often given to how we learn, from early childhood, to fit into and negotiate the normative expectations which allow us to be able to behave and fit into society. This applies, among other things, to the sets of masculine and feminine codes, roles and behaviours. Being born as a 'he' or 'she' does not merely mean acquiring a biological sex category, but marks the 'him' or 'her' out as the inheritors of characteristics that women and men ought to have, together with preconceptions about how they should behave, play, be played with, dress, react and express emotions. As Jane Pilcher and Imelda Whelehan explain:

> The concept of socialisation features in explanations of gender difference, where emphasis is given to the process of how individuals learn to become masculine or feminine in their identities, appearance, values and behaviour. The primary stage of socialisation occurs during infancy and childhood, via interaction between adults (especially parents) and children. Socialisation is, though, a life-long process. As individuals grow up and older, they continually encounter new situations and experiences and so learn new aspects of femininity and masculinity throughout their lives.[24]

However, knowing that something called 'socialisation' takes place is different from analysing how it takes place, and this can be a challenging topic for discussion, particularly given the many different contexts in which a resource such as this manual may be read. A key concern for anthropologists who study gender is that the ways in which women and men relate to each other and interact, and the social senses in which the sexes themselves are conceptualised vary enormously from place to place. With this in mind, we can talk about socialisation in two ways. It is (a) a general concept relating to processes that shape and orient us over time through our interaction with others, resulting in the acquisition of a gendered identity, and (b) a concept that has a more specific history in sociology.

Generally, theories of socialisation suggest that we learn about prevalent gender roles, differences and values through interaction with important agents. Such agents include the family, teachers, peer groups, and mediated images and information. However, this general idea becomes more complicated when we look at the divergence of views concerning the processes by which socialisation takes place. Key questions include:

- How much importance should different agents of socialisation be given in our considerations?
- To what extent, and in which ways, are people able actively to negotiate these influences and fashion their own concepts of gender identity?

Theories of role-learning, which were most influential in the 1970s and which have become widely accepted, argue that children learn and internalise correct gender roles and behaviours through interaction with adults, especially their parents. In everyday situations, it is argued, parents often sanction and set boundaries of appropriate gendered behaviour for children, such as which games and toys to play with. They also implicitly offer themselves as gendered role models through their own behaviour. Children learn to travel as girls or boys by using maps that reflect the important directions, laid down by key adult influencers. Thus, across theories of socialisation that emphasise role-acquisition, recurring ideas include the ways in which boundaries for behaviour – the rigidity of which depend on the context – are reinforced by logics of positive and negative reaction, resulting in the internalisation of norms for feminine and masculine roles and behaviours.

Agency (personal involvement) in gender construction

Although we are unable to do full justice to role-learning theories here, it is useful to note some of the limits to this kind of approach. Role-learning theories may be useful for suggesting how 'dominant' or 'hegemonic' gender roles are formed, but they do not give a satisfactory account of how some men and women come to oppose sexism and heterosexism (sexism directed at people on the basis of sexual orientation). Neither do such theories explain how, in many ways, gender roles have become more complex and confused. Why, for example, do some people seem to accept and live within certain roles, and others reject or subvert them?

For example, a stereotypical gender role constructs a man as a father working outside the home, and associates the male historically with the role of soldier. However, in some European countries it is becoming increasingly common to see fathers who have both been in the army for national service and taken parental leave to be the primary carer of a child. Similarly, while schools have been identified as associated with stereotyped femininities and masculinities, in many contexts this identification does not stand up to analysis, given the changes in the ways in which educational materials and curricula now reflect an increased sensitivity to gender. However, a lot of work still needs to be done in this area.

Perhaps most importantly, over-emphasising socialisation as a force that guarantees conformity is as limiting as denying the influence of society on the individual. After all, the educational logic of resources such as this one is based on a belief that our understandings of gender can change, and that people can and do adapt gender norms in their own lives. For that reason, many contemporary theories of gender emphasise the power that people have to reflect on, shape and construct their own gender identities. Young people in particular, in their use of style, popular culture and networking have, in many contexts, increased their autonomy with respect to how they represent themselves and live in their bodies. Such considerations have led to a tendency to opt for a balance between accounts of socialisation and the autonomy of the individual.

Gender equality and gender mainstreaming

The notion of gender equality[25] is often used to refer to equality between women and men. It describes a state of affairs in which women and men enjoy equal rights and opportunities, where the behaviour, aspirations, wishes and needs of women and men are equally valued and favoured. An equal distribution and access to resources is also implied.

However, gender equality can also refer to broader notions of equality in relation to gender identity (social expectations and norms attached to the masculine and the feminine) and sexual orientation.

The Council of Europe has adopted a number of standards relating to gender equality, for example addressing violence against women, balanced participation in political and public decision-making, gender equality in media, education, health and sport.[26] These standards interpret gender equality as equality between women and men. Issues relating to gender identity and sexual orientation are dealt with separately by the Council of Europe.[27]

For the Council of Europe, gender equality means:

> an equal visibility, empowerment and participation of both sexes in all spheres of public and private life. Gender equality is the opposite of gender inequality, not of gender difference, and aims to promote the full participation of women and men in society. It means accepting and valuing equally the differences between women and men and the diverse roles they play in society. Gender equality includes the right to be different. This means taking into account the existing differences among women and men, which are related to class, political opinion, religion, ethnicity, race or sexual orientation. Gender equality means discussing how it is possible to go further, to change the structures in society which contribute to maintaining the unequal power relationships between women and men, and to reach a better balance in the various female and male values and priorities.[28]

Although a great deal has been achieved internationally to guarantee gender equality, many women are still confronted with discrimination and violence. Globally, women in the labour market still earn 24% less than men on average,[29] and in Council of Europe member states, women account for only about 25% of members of parliaments and 13% of mayors.[30] One of the UN's Sustainable Development Goals (Goal 5) is "Achieving gender equality and empowering all women and girls". [31]

A number of different models and theories have been put forward to explain how men have predominantly placed themselves, and been placed, in social hierarchy over women. The idea of 'patriarchy' is often used as a shorthand for male dominance, and it has also itself been the subject of more detailed theories. In general, patriarchy describes the way in which gender roles and possibilities have tended to subordinate women to men. Patriarchy involves the acceptance of fundamental ideas about the nature and value of women, their potential, and their roles – including the heterosexual norms of wife and mother. Such ideas tend to be based on appeals to biological reasoning, for example, on suggestions that women are more "naturally" suited to be carers. Some discussions of patriarchy argue that it is dependent on divisions in labour that have tended to dominate in industrial capitalist societies. In other words, the predominance of men at work in the public sphere, and of women's work in the private sphere 'making a home' has deeply influenced the durability of traditional gender roles. However, it is important to recognise that this is a partial story, as it fails to take account of women's role in the work force of industrial societies, and does not acknowledge the many changes that have taken place in work-gender roles in societies where heavy industry has been replaced by the service and information industries.

One important contribution of feminist theory and the women's movement has been to include the private sphere within political and economic discourse. This has led to heightened awareness about the invisible contribution of women to the economy and to general well-being, and to the adoption of policies advocating the equal distribution of unpaid care work between women and men as an essential step towards gender equality in the public sphere and in paid employment.

Heteronormative societies impose a very distinct way of understanding the role of men and women. As Mary Holmes puts it: "Social rules about 'normal' gender and sexuality demand that you must be clear about who are boys and who are girls, so that boys and girls can grow up, fall in love with each other, and have more little boys and girls."[32] Such assumptions and norms lead to direct or indirect discrimination of LGBT+ people in the public sphere, limiting their access to – or even denying them access to different services. LGBT+ people also experience systemic discrimination and violence. In many countries, they cannot legally enter into a civil union or get married; and in some countries, they can be sentenced to death simply because of their sexual orientation or gender identity. You can find more information on gender-based violence affecting LGBT+ people in Chapter 4, in the section on LGBT+.

Gender mainstreaming

The concept of gender mainstreaming arose because it was recognised that a new approach to policymaking was needed – one which took into account the concerns and needs of both women and men. Gender mainstreaming means integrating a gender equality perspective into policies, programmes and projects, at every level. Women and men have different needs and circumstances, and unequal access to power, resources, and the justice system, including human rights institutions. The men and women's circumstances also differ according to country, region, age, ethnic or social origin, and other factors. The aim of gender mainstreaming is to take into account these differences when designing, implementing and evaluating policies, programmes and projects, so that the benefits accrue equally to women and men, and do not increase inequality but enhance gender equality. Gender mainstreaming aims to solve gender inequalities, even when they are hidden. It is a tool for achieving gender equality.

Gender mainstreaming is one of the objectives of the Council of Europe Gender Equality Strategy, and different parts of the organisation have been actively working to implement this Strategy, including in the areas of sports, media, audiovisual, health, and more. Gender mainstreaming is also an objective of the European Union, as provided by Article 8 of the Treaty on the functioning of the EU.[33]

Gender mainstreaming does not take the place of specific policies aimed at redressing gender inequalities. It should go hand in hand with specific policies for the advancement of women, including positive actions designed to reach gender equality. Gender mainstreaming is a transformative tool to reach this goal.

5. Gender-based violence and human rights

Gender-based violence is a human rights concern. People who experience gender violence may suffer from different human rights violations – for example the right to life, freedom from torture and degrading treatment, freedom from discrimination and the right to safety and security. All these rights can be found in international and regional human rights documents, in particular by the United Nations and by the Council of Europe.

United Nations

The right to life, gender equality, prohibition of discrimination on the grounds of sex, protection of physical integrity, the right to health - to mention a few of the human rights impacted by gender-based violence - are safeguarded in the Universal Declaration of Human Rights and the International Covenants on Civil and Political Rights and on Social, Economic and Cultural Rights.

In order to step the combat against violence and discrimination against women, the United Nations adopted specific instruments and measures.

Convention on the Elimination of All Forms of Discrimination Against Women' (CEDAW)

One of the most important international human rights documents dealing with women's rights is the United Nations Convention on the Elimination of All Forms of Discrimination Against Women (CEDAW). This Convention prohibits discrimination on the basis of sex. It defines discrimination against women as:

> Any distinction, exclusion or restriction made on the basis of sex which has the effect or purpose of impairing or nullifying the recognition, enjoyment or exercise by women, irrespective of their marital status, on a basis of equality of men and women, of human rights and fundamental freedoms in the political, social, cultural, civil or any other field.[34]

States that are parties to this Convention are obliged to adopt all necessary measures to ensure that women enjoy equality with men. This means that State Parties should adopt necessary legislation to combat discrimination and advance women's rights. It should be noted, however, that the aim of equality for women does not mean that they can be denied special protection where this is needed – for example, in relation to maternity.

CEDAW reviews states' compliance with the Convention. State Parties have to submit periodic reports on any measures undertaken to implement the

Convention, and the CEDAW Committee monitors states' compliance. However, the implementation mechanism is regarded as weak, and relies primarily on the force of moral persuasion. Implementation is further weakened by the many reservations and exceptions to the original document which have been negotiated by states.

Unlike other women's issues – such as suffrage (the right to vote), equality, or discrimination – violence against women has only recently been recognised as deserving of special attention by international human rights law. CEDAW dates back to 1979, and came into force in 1981. It makes no mention of violence, rape, abuse or battery.[35] However, in 1992, General Recommendation 19 was issued by the CEDAW Committee, recommending that violence against women should also be reported on by the States Parties. An individual complaint mechanism was added to CEDAW, whereby individuals, after exhausting domestic remedies, were able to file a complaint against the State in relation to provisions of the Convention.

In 1993, in Vienna, the United Nations General Assembly adopted the 'Declaration on the Elimination of Violence Against Women'. This Declaration was significant in that it made violence against women an international issue, not subject to claims about cultural relativism. The Declaration therefore included a variety of issues such as female genital mutilation, rape and torture, domestic battery and female sexual slavery, all of which had previously been regarded, in some quarters at least, as acceptable or beyond the realm of the law. The inclusion of such practices within the realm of international law was an important statement from the UN, and it placed individual rights to physical integrity above claims of cultural rights. It also recognised that national or cultural support for such practices ignores the wishes of women themselves, as well as the many voices, even in supposedly homogenous cultures, which are opposed to such practices.

Another aspect of the Declaration is that it recognises the need to re-draw the apparently 'natural' boundaries between public and private – a challenge long advocated by feminist groups. The UN Declaration prohibits not only state violence against women, but also private violence, including '…battering, sexual abuse of female children in the household, dowry-related violence, marital rape, female genital mutilation and other traditional practices harmful to women, non-spousal violence or violence related to exploitation'.[36] The Declaration also prohibits violence against women based on cultural practices.

Although it is not a binding document, the Declaration made an important contribution towards breaking a wall of silence, and recognising violence against women as an international human rights violation.

Independent Expert on Sexual Orientation and Gender Identity

In 2016, the UN Secretary General appointed an Independent Expert on Sexual Orientation and Gender Identity, with a mandate "to assess the implementation of existing international human rights instruments with regard to ways to overcome violence and discrimination against persons on the basis of their sexual orientation or gender identity, and to identify and address the root causes of violence and discrimination".[37]

COUNCIL OF EUROPE

As a human rights issue, gender equality and gender-based violence are addressed firstly by human rights instruments such as the European Convention on Human Rights and the European Social Charter. The growing awareness of the extent and persistence of the problem has led to the creation of specific instruments addressing gender-based violence in its various forms.

The European Convention on Human Rights

The European Convention on Human Rights and Fundamental Freedoms (ECHR), includes a number of articles relevant to gender-based violence:

> **Article 8** of the ECHR protects the right to private and family life, and gives people of marriageable age the right to marry.
>
> **Article 14** forbids discrimination on any grounds in relation to any of the other rights in the Convention. This includes discrimination on the grounds of sex or gender.
>
> **Article 5** of Protocol 7 to the Convention states that spouses should have equal rights in marriage.
>
> **Protocol 12** to the Convention extends the prohibition of discrimination in Article 14 to cases not engaged by other rights in the Convention.

The European Convention has a strong and well-known enforcement mechanism, the European Court of Human Rights (ECtHR), which is able to address complaints from individuals against their state, as well as state vs. state complaints.

The European Social Charter

The European Social Charter (ESC) was adopted in 1961 and revised in 1996 and complements the European Convention on Human Rights. The ESC addresses economic and social rights, and guarantees the enjoyment of rights in the areas of housing, health, education, employment, legal and social protection and the movement of persons. All rights in the Social Charter must be implemented without discrimination on any grounds, and this includes on grounds of sex or gender. The revised form of the Charter provides for equality between women and men in education, work and family life, for positive measures to ensure equal opportunities, and the right to equal remuneration.

The Lanzarote Convention

The Council of Europe Convention on the Protection of Children against Sexual Exploitation and Sexual Abuse (Lanzarote Convention)[38] entered into force on 1 July 2010. It has been signed by all 47 member states of the Council of Europe (but not ratified by all).

The Lanzarote Convention is a comprehensive international legal instrument for the protection of children against sexual exploitation and sexual abuse. The Convention covers sexual abuse within a child's family and in the "circle of trust" as well as acts carried out for commercial or profit-making purposes. It also tackles all possible kinds of sexual offences against children (including sexual abuse of a child, exploitation of children through prostitution, grooming and corruption of children through exposure to sexual content and activities and offences related to child abuse material). According to the Convention, governments in Europe and beyond should develop legislation to criminalise all forms of sexual exploitation and abuse against children, and should take concrete measures designed to prioritise the best interests of children, in four areas:

- **Prevention**: children should be made aware of the risks of sexual exploitation and sexual abuse and should be empowered to protect themselves; persons working in contact with children should be screened and trained; intervention programmes or measures for sexual offenders (whether convicted or potential) should be regularly monitored.
- **Protection**: reporting any suspicion of sexual exploitation or sexual abuse should be strongly encouraged; telephone and Internet helplines should be set up; programmes to support victims and their families should be established; therapeutic assistance and emergency psychological care should be provided; child-friendly judicial proceedings for protecting the victim's safety, privacy, identity and image should be put in place (e.g. the number of interviews with child victims has to be limited, the interview has to be carried out in a reassuring place, with professionals trained for the purpose).
- **Prosecution**: the Convention requires states to criminalise all sexual offences against children (including sexual abuse within the family or circle of trust, exploitation of children through prostitution, pornography, participation in pornographic performances, corruption of children, solicitation of children for sexual purposes). The Convention requests that countries extend their statute of limitation on sexual offences against children, so that proceedings may be initiated after the victim has reached the age of majority. It also establishes common criteria to ensure that an effective and proportionate punitive system is put in place in all countries, and foresees the possibility

of prosecuting a citizen for a crime even when committed abroad ("extraterritoriality principle"). For example, prosecution can be brought against sexual offenders when they return to their home country.

- **Promotion of national and international co-operation**: Co-operation helps countries to identify and analyse problems, find and apply common solutions, share data and expertise, combat impunity and improve prevention and protection measures. The Lanzarote Convention is open to accession from non-European as well as European countries, in order to facilitate international co-operation in fighting the problem of sexual offences against children.

The implementation of the Convention is monitored by the Committee of the Parties to the Convention (the Lanzarote Committee), which assess the protection of children against sexual violence at national level on the basis of information provided by national authorities and by other sources. The Lanzarote Committee also acts as a platform to discuss and give visibility to challenges arising and examples of good practice.

Istanbul Convention

The Council of Europe Convention on preventing and combating violence against women and domestic violence (Istanbul Convention) was adopted by the Committee of Ministers and opened for signature in Istanbul on 11 May 2011. The Convention entered into force on 1 August 2014, and recognises gender-based violence against women as a violation of human rights and a form of discrimination.

It focuses on several areas, obliging States Parties to the Convention to take a number of measures to act against violence against women and domestic violence, including:

- **Prevention**: States should regularly run awareness-raising campaigns, train professionals in close contact with victims, include within teaching materials issues such as gender equality and non-violent conflict resolution in interpersonal relationships, set up treatment programmes for perpetrators of domestic violence and for sex offenders, work closely with NGOs, and involve the media and the private sector in eradicating gender stereotypes and promoting mutual respect.
- **Protection**: This includes granting the police the power to remove a perpetrator of domestic violence from their home, ensuring people's access to adequate information on available services in a language they understand, setting up easily accessible shelters in sufficient numbers and in an adequate geographical distribution, making available state-wide 24/7 telephone helplines free-of–charge, and setting up easily accessible rape crisis or sexual violence referral centres.
- **Prosecution**: The Convention defines and criminalises the various forms of violence against women, including domestic violence. States that have

signed and ratified the treaty must introduce a number of new offences where these do not already exist, for example, psychological and physical violence, sexual violence and rape, stalking, female genital mutilation, forced marriage, forced abortion and forced sterilisation. In addition, States Parties will need to ensure that culture, tradition or so-called "honour" are not regarded as a justification for any of the above-listed courses of conduct. States parties will have to take a range of measures to ensure the effective investigation of any allegation of violence against women, including cases of domestic violence. This means that law enforcement agencies will have to respond to calls for help, collect evidence, and assess the risk of further violence to adequately protect those at risk. In addition, judicial proceedings should be run in a manner that respects the rights of victims at all stages of the proceedings and that avoids secondary victimisation.

- **Development of integrated policies**: It is difficult for one institution alone to act against violence. For that reason, the Convention asks States Parties to implement comprehensive and co-ordinated policies involving government agencies, NGOs, and national, regional and local parliaments and authorities. The aim is for policies to prevent and combat violence against women, including domestic violence, to be carried out at all levels of government and by all relevant agencies and institutions.

The Convention sends a clear message to the whole of society, that violence is never the right way to solve difficulties and cannot lead to a state of peace – either in private or public life. It reinforces the importance of understanding that violence against women is not acceptable and will not be tolerated. While the focus of the Convention is on all forms of violence against women, including domestic violence, it also recognises that there are other victims of domestic violence, such as boys and men. This may include gay men, transgender men or men that do not conform to what society considers to be appropriate behaviour. The Convention devotes an entire chapter to women migrants and asylum-seekers facing gender-based violence. It also recognises the work of NGOs, and seeks to ensure greater political and financial support for their work.

The Convention establishes a monitoring mechanism, consisting of two bodies:

- GREVIO (Group of Experts on Action Against Violence Against Women and Domestic Violence), which is a body of independent and impartial experts known for their expertise in the fields of human rights, gender equality, violence against women, or assistance to and protection of victims; or having demonstrated relevant professional experience in any of these fields. GREVIO draws up and publishes reports on legislative and other measures taken by countries that have ratified the Convention, designed to give effect to its provisions (evaluation procedure). In specific circumstances, the group may initiate inquiries (inquiry procedure).
- The Committee of Parties is composed of representatives of the Parties to the Convention. The Committee may adopt recommendations on measures to be taken to implement conclusions contained in GREVIO's reports. The

Committee also supervises the implementation of its own recommendations, examines the findings of any inquiry conducted by GREVIO members, and considers any necessary measures pursuant to these findings.

The Istanbul Convention is in many ways an innovative document:

- It is the first international document that contains a definition of gender.
- It calls for the involvement of all relevant state agencies and services, so that violence against women and domestic violence are tackled in a co-ordinated way. This means that agencies and NGOs are encouraged not to act alone, but to work out protocols for co-operation.
- It criminalises offences, such as female genital mutilation, forced marriage, stalking, forced abortion and forced sterilisation. This means that states will be obliged, for the first time, to legislate against these serious offences.
- It recognises violence against women as a violation of human rights and a form of discrimination. States are held responsible if they do not respond adequately to such violence.
- It obliges states which have signed and ratified the Convention to invite their parliaments to participate in the monitoring process.

Recommendation on the Protection of Women Against Violence

Recommendation Rec(2002)5 of the Committee of Ministers of the Council of Europe on the Protection of Women Against Violence sets out a series of measures to end all forms of violence against women.[39] These measures include legislative and policy measures to prevent and investigate violence against women, to assist victims, work with perpetrators, increase awareness, education and training, and collect relevant data. Implementation of this Recommendation is regularly monitored and member states are provided with information on progress achieved and any existing gaps.

Convention on Action Against Trafficking

The Council of Europe Convention on Action against Trafficking in Human Beings[40] was adopted by the Committee of Ministers of the Council of Europe on 3 May 2005 and entered into force on 1 February 2008. The Convention builds on existing international instruments, but goes beyond the standards previously established, and strengthens protections afforded to victims.

The Convention has a broad scope and covers all forms of trafficking, national and transnational, whether or not it is linked to organised crime. It also takes in all victims of trafficking (women, men and children). The forms of exploitation covered by the Convention include sexual exploitation, forced labour or services, slavery and similar practices, servitude and the removal of organs.

The main innovations of the Convention are the human rights perspective it brings, and the focus on victim protection. The Preamble defines trafficking in human beings as a violation of human rights and an offence to the dignity and integrity of the human being. The body of the Convention then outlines a series of rights for victims of trafficking, in particular the right to be identified as a victim, to be protected and assisted, to be given a recovery and reflection period of at least 30 days, to be granted a renewable residence permit, and to receive compensation for any damages suffered.

Another important innovation introduced by the Convention is the monitoring system set up to supervise the implementation of the obligations contained within it. This monitoring system consists of two pillars: the Group of Experts on Action against Trafficking in Human Beings (GRETA) and the Committee of the Parties.

The Convention is not restricted to Council of Europe member states: non-member states also have the possibility of becoming Party to the Convention, as does the European Union.

Recommendation on sexual orientation and gender identity

On 31 March 2010, the Council of Europe Committee of Ministers adopted Recommendation CM/Rec(2010)5 on measures to combat discrimination on grounds of sexual orientation or gender identity.[41] This Recommendation is the first instrument in the world to deal specifically with discrimination against LGBT+ people. It begins by setting out principles relevant to this group, deriving from existing European and international instruments, with particular emphasis on the European Convention on Human Rights and case law from the European Court of Human Rights. The review process for implementation of the Recommendation is carried out periodically by the Steering Committee for Human Rights (CDDH) in the Council of Europe. This helps to provide an overall picture of the state of discrimination against LGBT+ people in Europe and enables the Council of Europe to establish priority areas for its work. More information about this Recommendation can be found in Chapter 4, in the section on LGBT+.

Recommendation on Preventing and Combating Sexism

In March 2019, the Council of Europe Committee of Ministers adopted a Recommendation on Preventing and Combating Sexism. This text contains the first ever internationally agreed definition of sexism.

It also proposes a set of concrete measures to combat this wide-spread phenomenon including through legislation and policies and through awareness-raising. The recommendation proposes specific tools and measures to prevent and combat sexism and sexist behaviour in the areas of language and communications, Internet and social media, media and advertising. The recommendation proposes specific attention to sexism in justice and education institutions, in culture and sport, as well as in the private sector.

Action at national level remains essential

Despite the significant progress achieved with the instruments mentioned above, recognition and existing legal measures are not sufficient. Effective mechanisms and processes for violence prevention and gender mainstreaming need to be put in place. In addition to the international human rights mechanisms, important policies or bodies at national level need to include:

- National committees for gender advancement with a clear plan of action;
- Equality ombudsman;
- Effective legislation to ensure legal and substantive equality;
- Affirmative action, such as quotas for women in education and employment;
- Women's NGOs, LGBT+ organisations and women's or LGBT+ studies in universities. These may play an important role in advocacy or lobbying efforts.

6. Youth work and youth policy responses to gender and gender-based violence

The youth sector of the Council of Europe plays an important role in establishing and promoting standards to address the challenges faced by young people. The Youth Department guides member states in the development of their national youth policies, using recommendations from the Committee of Ministers, as well as other texts. All guidelines are firmly based on the Council of Europe's values, and aim to ensure a minimum level of standards in youth policy throughout Europe.

Issues related to gender, gender equality and gender-based violence have always been a part of the Council of Europe youth sector's strategy and activities. In 2008, at the 8th Conference of Ministers responsible for Youth, a strategic document on youth policy – known as Agenda 2020 – was approved by the Youth Ministers. This strategic document set the implementation of gender equality and the prevention of all forms of gender-based violence as one of the priorities for the youth sector.[42]

Attention has been given to this priority at the level of the Council of Europe as a whole, and also at national level, where it has been taken into account by member states in their youth policy development and implementation. The principle of gender equality is applied in the educational programme of activities which strives to include people of different genders and which addresses the topics of gender, gender equality and gender-based violence. In 2017, the Joint Council on Youth, which is jointly responsible for decision making in the Youth Department,[43] adopted the "Guidelines on integrating and mainstreaming gender equality into the intercultural youth activities of the Council of Europe and its partners".[44] These Guidelines were intended to support organisers and educational teams in intercultural youth activities of the Council of Europe and its partners in ensuring gender equality in all phases of an activity or project.

The work on gender, gender equality and gender-based violence has been particularly visible in human rights education programmes run by the Council of Europe youth sector. The experiences of the training courses, study sessions and educational resources developed in the European Youth Centres, such as the *Compass* manual, contributed greatly to the development of the Council of Europe Charter on Education for Democratic Citizenship and Human Rights Education. This document establishes gender equality as one of the aims of human rights education and education for democratic citizenship.

The No Hate Speech Movement youth campaign implemented by the Council of Europe between 2013 and 2018 mobilised hundreds of thousands of young people to act against hate speech online, including sexist and homophobic hate speech.

In 2009, the Council of Europe's youth sector initiated the *Enter!* project, to develop youth policy responses to exclusion, discrimination and violence affecting young people – particularly in disadvantaged neighbourhoods. Based on the activities of the project, the Committee of Ministers of the Council of Europe adopted Recommendation CM/Rec(2015)3 on the access of young people from disadvantaged neighbourhoods to social rights. The Recommendation calls on member states to develop gender-sensitive approaches to the development of youth policies in disadvantaged neighbourhoods, and provides support for capacity building and for the equal participation of young women and young men aiming to improve gender equality among young people living in disadvantaged neighbourhoods.

Gender-related issues cut across all areas of the Youth Department's work, including in dealing with challenges faced by marginalised groups, such as refugees or Roma people. The Youth for Democracy programme, within which these activities are implemented, prioritises combating all forms of discrimination and exclusion and addressing intersectionality (including gender equality, sexual orientation LGBTQI, gender identity and disability).

In 2018, the Committee of Ministers of the Council of Europe adopted a Recommendation on Youth Work (CM/Rec(2017)4).[45] This Recommendation encourages member states to develop and strengthen youth work policies and practice. It also includes proposals for the youth sector of the Council of Europe to support member states in this task, maximising the positive contribution that youth work can make to Europe's future through co-operation, peer learning and collaboration. Youth work is defined in the document as:

> a wide variety of activities of a social, cultural, educational, environmental and/or political nature by, with and for young people, in groups or individually. Youth work is delivered by paid and volunteer youth workers and is based on non-formal and informal learning processes focused on young people and on voluntary participation. Youth work is quintessentially a social practice, working with young people and the societies in which they live, facilitating young people's active participation and inclusion in their communities and in decision making.

The Recommendation on Youth Work draws special attention to the fact that youth work needs legal and political support, sustainable funding and structures, improved co-ordination both across sectors, and between local and national levels, as well as a competency-based framework for the education and training of youth workers. Such demands are particularly important when working with issues of gender, gender-equality and gender-based violence: work on these issues can be particularly challenging in contexts where there is a hostile environment or where strong gender stereotypes prevail.

Endnotes

1 Source: *http://www.un.org/en/spotlight-initiative/resources.shtml*.

2 Discrimination and violence against individuals based on their sexual orientation and gender identity. Report of the Office of the United Nations High Commissioner for Human Rights, 2015.

3 EU LGBT survey: European Union lesbian, gay, bisexual and transgender survey. Results at a glance, Luxembourg: Publications Office of the European Union, 2013, p. 16: *http://fra.europa.eu/en/publication/2013/eu-lgbt-survey-european-union-lesbian-gay-bisexual-and-transgender-survey-result*.

4 UN Declaration on the Elimination of Violence against Women, Article 1, *http://www.un.org/documents/ga/res/48/a48r104.htm*.

5 Council of Europe Convention on preventing and combating violence against women and domestic violence (Istanbul Convention), Article 3, *https://rm.coe.int/168008482e*.

6 The Explanatory Report to the Council of Europe Convention on preventing and combating violence against women and domestic violence, *https://rm.coe.int/16800d383a*.

7 'Sensitive spots' can be anything that one is especially emotional about. It can be an important person, one's religion or ethnic identity. It can be also something that one is ashamed of (whether it is justified or not, whether it is the product of internalised oppression or personal conviction).

8 Since all human beings belong to the same species, ECRI rejects theories based on the existence of different races. However, in this Recommendation ECRI uses this term "race" in order to ensure that those persons who are generally and erroneously perceived as belonging to another race are not excluded from the protection provided for by the Recommendation.

9 ECRI General Policy Recommendation No. 15 on combatting hate speech, adopted on 8 December 2015, Council of Europe: *https://www.coe.int/t/dghl/monitoring/ecri/activities/GPR/EN/Recommendation_N15/REC-15-2016-015-ENG.pdf*.

10 You can read more about sexist hate speech at: *https://rm.coe.int/CoERMPublicCommonSearchServices/DisplayDCTMContent?documentId=0900001680651592* (Factsheet on Sexist Hate Speech) and *https://rm.coe.int/CoERMPublicCommonSearchServices/DisplayDCTMContent?documentId=09000016806cac1f* (Report of the Seminar on Sexist Hate Speech 10 – 12 February 2016).

11 UN Women, The Feminisation of Poverty Fact Sheet No 1: *http://www.un.org/womenwatch/daw/followup/session/presskit/fs1.htm*.

12 Copelon, R., (1994). 'Understanding Domestic Violence as Torture' in Cook, R. (Ed.). Human Rights of Women. National and International Perspectives. Philadelphia: University of Pennsylvania Press. (p.116- 152).

13 Based on: *https://www.whiteribbon.org.au/understand-domestic-violence/what-is-domestic-violence/cycle-of-violence*

14 Copelon: p.128-129.

15 Council of Europe Convention on preventing and combating violence against women and domestic violence, Article 40 *https://www.coe.int/en/web/conventions/full-list/-/conventions/rms/090000168008482e*.

16 DIRECTIVE 2002/73/EC OF THE EUROPEAN PARLIAMENT AND OF THE COUNCIL of 23 September 2002 amending Council Directive 76/207/EEC on the implementation of the principle of equal treatment for men and women as regards access to employment, vocational training and promotion, and working conditions: *http://eur-lex.europa.eu/LexUriServ/LexUriServ.do?uri=OJ:L:2002:269:0015:0020:EN:PDF*.

17 Source: *http://www.who.int/gender-equity-rights/knowledge/glossary/en/*.

18 The Council of Europe Convention on preventing and combating violence against women and domestic violence: *https://rm.coe.int/168008482e*.

19 Source: *http://eige.europa.eu/rdc/thesaurus/terms/1361*.

20 You can find more definitions in the Gender Equality Glossary, Council of Europe 2016: *https://edoc.coe.int/en/gender-equality/6947-gender-equality-glossary.html*.

21 Source: *http://www.gendersanity.com/diagram.html*.

22 Alsop, R., Fitzsimons, A. & Lennon, K. (2002). Theorising Gender, Oxford: Polity, p. 5.

23 Ibid, p.7

24 Pilcher, J. & Whelehan, I. (2004). 50 Key Concepts in Gender Studies. London: Sage, p. 7.

25 More information: *https://www.coe.int/en/web/genderequality*.

26 More information : *https://www.coe.int/en/web/genderequality/standards-and-mechanisms*.

27 More information: *http://www.coe.int/en/web/sogi*.

28 Council of Europe Gender Equality Glossary, March 2016. For the full definition please refer to Chapter V.

29 Source: *http://www.un.org/sustainabledevelopment/wp-content/uploads/2016/08/5_Why-it-Matters_GenderEquality_2p.pdf*.

30 Balanced participation of women and men in decision-making - Analytical Report - 2016 data, Council of Europe, 2017: *https://rm.coe.int/analytical-report-data-2016-/1680751a3e*.

31 Read more: *http://www.un.org/sustainabledevelopment/gender-equality/*.

32 Mary Holmes, What is Gender? Sociological Approaches, SAGE Publications, 2007, p. 21.

33 For more information about the gender mainstreaming work of the Council of Europe, please visit: *https://www.coe.int/gender-mainstreaming*.

34 Convention on the Elimination of All Forms of Discrimination Against Women' (CEDAW), Article 1: *http://www.un.org/womenwatch/daw/cedaw/text/econvention.htm*.

35 Keck, M.E., & Sikkink K. (1998). Activists Beyond Borders. Advocacy Networks in International Politics. Ithaca and London: Cornell University Press, p.168.

36 United Nations Declaration on the Elimination of Violence against Women (DEVAW), General Assembly Resolution 48/104, 20 December 1993 Article 2 (a): *http://www.un.org/documents/ga/res/48/a48r104.htm*.

37 *http://www.ohchr.org/EN/Issues/SexualOrientationGender/Pages/Index.aspx*.

38 The Council of Europe Convention on the Protection of Children against Sexual Exploitation and Sexual Abuse (Lanzarote Convention): *https://rm.coe.int/168046e1e1*.

39 *https://www.coe.int/en/web/genderequality/recommendation-rec-2002-5-and-other-tools-of-the-council-of-europe-concerning-violence-against-women*

40 *https://www.coe.int/en/web/conventions/full-list/-/conventions/rms/090000168008371d*

41 *https://search.coe.int/cm/Pages/result_details.aspx?ObjectID=09000016805cf40a*

42 "The future of the Council of Europe youth policy: AGENDA 2020", 8th Council of Europe Conference of Ministers responsible for Youth, Kyiv, Ukraine, 10-11 October 2008: *https://rm.coe.int/1680702429*.

43 Read more about co-management in the Youth Department of the Council of Europe here: *https://www.coe.int/en/web/youth/co-management*.

44 Gender equality in the intercultural youth activities of the Council of Europe and its partners, Guidelines adopted by the Joint Council on Youth at its 36th meeting – March 2017: *https://rm.coe.int/guidelines-for-gender-equality-in-international-youth-activities/16807840f2*.

45 *https://pjp-eu.coe.int/documents/1017981/10886476/CM+REC.pdf/ba2e3081-680e-2200-f6cc-1acb89c6fd22*.

CHAPTER 2

Activities to address gender and gender-based violence with young people

Activities to address gender and gender–based violence with young people

Educational approaches and guidance for facilitators

This manual has been developed to be used primarily with youth groups in non-formal education settings, although it can also be easily adapted and used in formal education settings. The principles of non-formal education apply throughout, especially in the running and facilitation of activities proposed in this chapter.

All the activities proposed draw on the experience of human rights education. The manual adopts a human rights approach to gender-based violence and uses human rights education as a basis for young people to learn about, and act against, gender-based violence.

This section provides essential information and practical tips on human rights education and non-formal education and outlines their general application to this manual. This should support facilitators in choosing the activities most adequate to their group, and should enable them to facilitate with confidence. Specific advice is also proposed about working on gender issues with young people.

Human rights education – more than an educational approach

Gender-based violence is a human rights violation. It can be prevented and addressed using a human rights framework, which human rights education (HRE) can help to explain.

Before starting to work with these activities, it is important to understand the educational approach within which the manual and activities have been developed. The underlying approach to human rights education is based on the approach outlined in *Compass – a manual for human rights education with young people*[1].

Human rights education is about education for change - both at a personal level and at the level of society. It is about developing young people's competence to be active and responsible citizens who participate in their communities. The educational process should therefore develop knowledge, skills, values and attitudes that are appropriate for positive action on behalf of human rights. In the case of this manual, such positive action concerns chiefly the area of gender-related human rights - for example whenever gender-based violence is concerned.

Compass defines human rights education as:

> ...educational programmes and activities that focus on promoting equality in human dignity, in conjunction with other programmes such as those promoting intercultural learning, participation and empowerment of minorities[2].

A more detailed definition of HRE can be found in the Council of Europe Charter on Education for Democratic Citizenship and Human Rights Education:

> ... education, training, awareness raising, information, practices and activities which aim, by equipping learners with knowledge, skills and understanding and developing their attitudes and behaviour, to empower learners to contribute to the building and defence of a universal culture of human rights in society, with a view to the promotion and protection of human rights and fundamental freedoms[3].

There are other definitions of human rights education. All such definitions incorporate three important dimensions:

- **Learning *about*** human rights – for example, knowledge and understanding of human rights, of what they are, and of how they are safeguarded or protected;
- **Learning *through*** human rights: this dimension recognises that the educational context and the way human rights learning is organised and imparted must be consistent with human rights values (e.g. participation, freedom of thought and expression, etc.). In human rights education, the process of learning is as important as the educational content;
- **Learning *for* human rights**: young people need to develop the skills, attitudes and values to be able to apply human rights values in their lives and to take action, alone or with others, to promote and defend human rights.

How can these three dimensions be translated into educational practice with young people? In the process of human rights education, it is recommended to respect the following principles:

- **start from what people already know**, from their opinions and experiences. From this base, enable them to search for and discover together new ideas and experiences, and contextualise these in universal human rights;
- **encourage the active participation** of young people in shaping the discussions and the educational content. Support them to learn from each other;
- encourage young people to translate their learning into **simple but meaningful actions and personal attitudes** that demonstrate their rejection of injustice, inequality, and the violation of human rights.

Knowledge, skills, attitudes and values supporting human rights education

In order for young people to work in the defence of human rights and towards a deeper understanding of human rights issues, they need a knowledge and understanding of certain issues, and certain key skills. They also need to develop and practice appropriate attitudes and values.

In terms of **knowledge**, young people need to develop an understanding of the main concepts and the historical development of human rights, as well as the standards demanded by the main instruments and mechanisms for human rights protection. This means knowing about one's own rights and the way they interact with other people's, as well as knowing how to defend human rights.

In terms of **skills**, young people need to be able to communicate and advocate for human rights in public and private, to be able to assess cases from a human rights standpoint, and to reflect on what constitutes an abuse of human rights. Other important skills include dealing with conflict and learning to transform it in a constructive manner, and participating actively and constructively in the community.

Finally, in terms of **attitudes and values**, young people need to develop motivation and a commitment to the protection of human dignity; empathy and solidarity for others; and a sense of justice and responsibility for their own actions and those of others.

In relation to gender equality and gender-based violence, it is important that young people feel confident and able to address and combat gender inequalities and gender stereotypes, including their own role in perpetuating or combating them, within a human rights framework. Knowledge of human rights instruments specifically concerned with gender equality is also important.[4]

It is essential that young people have a deeper understanding about how human rights relating to gender equality are based on people's needs, and why they have to be protected. Young people with no direct experience of gender-based violence may think that the issue is of no concern to them, but from a human rights perspective, such a position is not acceptable. People everywhere have a responsibility to protect the human rights of others, including rights related to gender.

People have different ways of understanding important values, and therefore perceive rights and responsibilities differently. This means that human rights issues, including those which are gender related, are often controversial. Human rights education provides a framework to address and deal with these differences in understanding values and which manifest themselves as conflicts of opinion. Human rights education with young people is also aboutequipping young people with the ability to appreciate different points of view about a question, even if they are not necessarily in agreementand helping them to develop skills to reach mutually agreeable solutions.

This manual and its activities are based on an understanding that conflicts of opinion can be used constructively for the learning process, provided that the facilitator feels confident in addressing possible conflicts, and confident about managing diverging opinions in a group. The purpose is not so much that everyone needs to agree with a given result, but rather that the participants are also able to learn from the process of discussion (e.g. by listening to each other, expressing themselves, seeking information, respecting differences of opinion, etc.).

Experiential learning – a basis for human rights education

Skills and values such as good communication, critical thinking, advocacy, tolerance and respect, cannot really be 'taught': they have to be learned through experience. For this reason, all the activities in this manual address sensitive issues around gender and gender-based violence, while promoting co-operation, participation, and learning through experience. The activities encourage young people to think, feel and act, and to engage their heads, hearts and hands in the defence of gender related human rights.

For this reason, the activities proposed in this manual have been developed in accordance with the David Kolbe's cycle of experiential learning cycle.

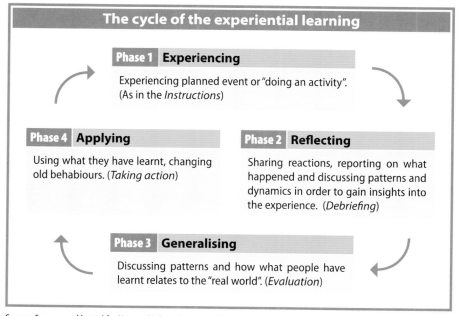

The cycle of the experiential learning

Phase 1 Experiencing
Experiencing planned event or "doing an activity". (As in the *Instructions*)

Phase 4 Applying
Using what they have learnt, changing old behabiours. (*Taking action*)

Phase 2 Reflecting
Sharing reactions, reporting on what happened and discussing patterns and dynamics in order to gain insights into the experience. (*Debriefing*)

Phase 3 Generalising
Discussing patterns and how what people have learnt relates to the "real world". (*Evaluation*)

Source: Compass – Manual for Human Rights Education with young people, Council of Europe, October 2012

This cycle suggests that it is not sufficient simply to run an activity (Phase 1 of the learning cycle). It is essential to follow any activity with a debriefing and evaluation, which enables people to reflect on what has happened and why (Phase 2); to evaluate their experience and extract learning points (Phase 3); and finally to decide what to do next (Phase 4). In this way, the cycle returns to Phase 1, and a new cycle of the learning process begins.

In a school setting, activities such as those included in this manual can help to break down artificial barriers between subjects, and can also provide ways of extending links between a school subject and areas of interest, in order to promote a more holistic approach to an issue. In a non-formal educational setting, the activities can awaken interest in issues and, because they promote learning in a non-didactic way, they are often intrinsically more attractive to young people.

Using the activities

Choosing activities

This manual contains educational activities to address gender-based violence with young people.

As facilitator of the learning process, you should choose activities that are at the "right" level for you and your group and that will fit into the time you have. Read carefully any activity you are planning to do, at least twice, and try to imagine how your group may react, and some of the things they may say. Make sure that you have all the materials you will need, and check that there will be enough space, especially if participants will be breaking up for small-group work.

The instructions for each activity should be understood only as guidelines: each facilitator should use the material to suit the needs and context of their group, including issues needing to be addressed, and taking into account their own experience and ability as facilitator. It is not possible to write activities that will fit exactly into every possible European – or international – context. Facilitators are therefore expected to adapt the activities, while preserving the key aims and dynamics.

Key to the presentation of the activities

Each activity is presented in a standard format.

Level of complexity

By complexity, we indicate both the complexity of the method, and the critical thinking, analytical and communication skills participants need to possess in order to be able to benefit from the activity. Most of the activities that require basic skills employ simple methods, take little preparation, and often do not take much time. On the other hand, those activities that require good communication and thinking skills are often divided into different stages, require more preparation, and take longer. They usually also require greater competence, including emotional competence, from the facilitator.

Levels 1 to 4 indicate the general level of intellectual and emotional competency required for participation, and the amount of preparation involved. The level also refers to the degree of difficulty for participants and for the facilitator. In general, these variables tend to go together: level 1 activities need very little preparation and demand little emotional competence from both participants and facilitator, while activities at level 4 need much more.

	Overview	This gives brief information about the type of activity and the issues addressed, including any specific thematic focus.
	Group size	This indicates the ideal number of people (including minimum and maximum) needed to run the activity.
	Time	This is the estimated time in minutes needed to complete the whole activity, including any discussion before or after the activity.
	Objectives	These outline the learning that the activity hopes to achieve for participants, in terms of knowledge, skills, attitudes and values.
	Materials	This is a list of equipment needed to run the activity.
	Preparation	This is a list of things the facilitator needs to do or prepare before starting the activity.
	Instructions	This is a list of instructions for how to run the activity.
	Debriefing and evaluation	This section includes suggested questions to help the facilitator to conduct the debriefing and to evaluate the activity (Phases 2 - 4 of the experiential learning cycle).
	Tips for facilitators	These include guidance notes, things to be aware of - especially for debriefing the activity - information on alternative ways of running the activity, additional background information relevant to the activity, and indications of where further information can be found.
	Suggestions for follow-up	These include ideas for what to do next and links to other activities that can be used to address similar issues or themes.
	Ideas for action	Suggestions, relating to the issues and themes addressed, for further steps or courses of action for young people to take.
	Handouts	These include role cards, action pages, background reading material, discussion cards or other materials that should be given to participants during the activity.

Advice on facilitation of activities

In this manual, we use the word 'facilitator' for the person who prepares, presents and coordinates the activities for participants. A facilitator is someone who helps people to discover how much knowledge they already possess, encourages them to extend their learning, and helps them to explore their own potential. Facilitation means creating an environment in which people learn, experiment, explore and grow. It differs from the process where one person - the 'expert' - imparts knowledge and skills to others. This terminology helps to emphasise that educational work on the themes of gender and gender-based violence requires a democratic and participative approach. We assume that you are facilitating groups of young people, for example in a classroom, in a youth club, on a training course, at a youth camp or at a seminar.

What follows are some general facilitation tips for work with groups of young people, and specific advice for working with the sensitive issues addressed by Gender Matters. Different approaches to facilitation exist, but all approaches require sensitivity to participants' context and to their special situations and needs. All activities in this manual can be adapted to specific circumstances with little effort. However, the facilitation of activities addressing gender issues, and in particular the issue of gender-based violence, requires particular sensitivity. It also demands careful attention to ethical questions and questions of responsibility.

- This manual does not require that facilitators have prior experience, however, it does recognise that working with the issues of gender and gender-based violence may be challenging. An interactive and participatory approach is essential, together with a sensitive approach to the issues, particularly where discussion is likely to lead to disclosures by participants on highly personal matters.

- Working on gender issues, as with other topics in human rights education, requires particular competences. Youth educators/trainers/activists always need to begin by working themselves, and reflecting on the attitudes, beliefs, knowledge and behaviour that they bring to youth work in general, and to work on gender in particular.

- Users of this manual do not have to read it in its entirety to be able to use it: this will depend on their own self-knowledge, the needs of the group, and the extent to which the facilitator feels competent in the area. However, use of this resource should always be preceded by a process of reflection on the issues.

- The manual asks those who use it to be 'translators' from one context to another. The information provided needs to be supplemented with information from, for example, national institutions, NGOs, legal and judicial systems, and local contexts. It is important also that users of the manual reflect on whether particular perspectives fit their own experience and youth work context; and that they adapt or substitute examples, ideas and explanations, where appropriate.

- Finally, working on gender, sex, gender-based violence and related issues should be an essential part of all youth work because it is something that concerns all young people. The questions and concepts that are addressed through this work are all relevant to young people's lives, and they relate directly to the world young people live in.

Specific ethical and practical considerations

Ethical considerations belong in any educational activity that brings people together, and these ethical considerations are particularly important when issues of identity and power are present, as in the case of many activities dealing with gender or gender-based violence. There are certain important issues to be taken into consideration when working on the issue of gender and gender-based violence with groups of young people, and these are particularly relevant when making decisions about which activities to choose.

- **Gender is a politically sensitive issue**
  Gender related issues can be highly politically charged. For example, equal rights for LGBT+ people or the rights of young women to determine their reproductive destinies have caused significant and often acrimonious debates in the public and political sphere between people of different political persuasions, as well as between people from different social, religious or cultural backgrounds. On a more personal level, people of authority surrounding young people - e.g. parents, teachers and professional youth workers - may have objections to certain issues being discussed or raised in the context of youth work or in leisure time activities, for example questions about sexuality. Facilitators need to be aware of such potential concerns before beginning to work on the issues with young people, and when choosing activities from this manual. It is also important to make sure that your organisation will support you, and that its policies and approaches do not conflict with the work that you are aiming to carry out.

- **Cultural difference matters**
  The cultural backgrounds of the members of the group you are working with may be a relevant factor in choosing your approach and the activities you will use. For some people and communities, specific gender related issues (such as sex, relationships and sexuality) should not be spoken about in public, or in mixed sex settings. Many young people may therefore find it difficult to engage in open discussion about such issues directly, especially if members of the other sex, or people that they do not know well, are present. Furthermore, the existence of domestic violence and sexual abuse is often denied in traditional (as well as in modern-secular) communities. The socialisation of a given participant in this relation will influence whether they will be willing to discuss or will be resistant to engaging with the activities you propose. However, the importance of cultural background can also be overestimated.

Not all young people who come from "traditional communities" will have difficulties in engaging with these issues. For example, a person's social background can often be more relevant than their religion to how they deal with sexuality. However, the fact that the young people you work with may come from very diverse cultural and social backgrounds, each of which may have a specific way of dealing with these issues, means that you need to consider the intercultural nature of your group, both in the development of your educational programmes and in the choice of the activities you propose.

- **The context of your work**
  It will be useful for you to consider your own reasons for undertaking to work on gender related issues in the context of (general) youth work. Ask yourself such questions as:

  - What is the relevance of such issues, and why the need to address them in this context?
  - Why do the young people you are working with want to or need to address such issues?
  - What are your educational objectives in undertaking the exploration of such issues?

Before you begin, you should think about such questions. Your responses will help you to select the kind of activity that is better suited for your purposes.

It is also important to consider how you will group your young people, considering your educational objectives at any given time. For example, when wishing to engage the members of your group on the question of female sexuality, you may consider beginning with work in single-sex groups to avoid participants feeling forced into discussing something they do not feel comfortable about with members of the other sex.

Finally, while you may consciously decide to engage in youth work with one or other target group, for reasons relating to the specificity of the context you are working in, you also must consider that you can never fully know 'who is in the room'. For example, even if working with an all-female group, you may not be aware of the sexual preferences of all members.

For this reason, you must also take into account that within single-sex and mixed groups there always exists a modicum of diversity that may complicate the dynamics, or enrich them. You should also bear in mind that the oppressed and marginalised are not immune to prejudice, any more than are members of the privileged classes or the majority. The most important thing is to remember that everyone needs to feel comfortable and respected, if they are to engage fully.

- **Disclosure may take place**

  Noting that one can never fully know "who is in the room", it is important to remember you cannot know whether or not there are participants who have experienced sexual or relationship abuse, or another form of gender-based violence. Although it is important to create a safe space for participants to discuss sensitive issues related to gender and gender-based violence, you should always be prepared for the possibility that creating such a safe space, and the dynamics of the activity, may lead young people to disclose painful personal experiences of gender-based violence. When this happens, it can be difficult for everyone concerned – for the participant disclosing, for other participants, and for the facilitator.

  It is difficult for a facilitator to prepare in advance for such a disclosure in the group. The disclosing participant may become very emotional, as may other participants listening to their story. In such an event, you should aim to observe the following points:

  - Do not interrupt or try to stop the participant.
  - Listen to the participant, for as long as they are willing to speak
  - Avoid pressing anyone else to go further or deeper in sharing experiences
  - You may want to call for a break and invite everyone to refresh themselves, in order to defuse the atmosphere
  - Pay special attention to the participant in question, and make sure that they are not left alone, if they do not want to be. You or another person that they trust might accompany them to another room to enable them to calm down and collect their strength. They may need a short time away from the group, or on their own.
  - It may be necessary, either immediately or at a later point, to come back to the disclosure in the whole group and speak about the fact that it took place.
  - Whatever you and your team decide to do, the decision should be made in consultation with the participant who made the disclosure. This also concerns how the disclosure is to be dealt within the group.

  Facilitators should not attempt to enter into a psychological support role or try to offer "therapy" to participants. There may be a need for such support, but this is neither the responsibility nor the role of a facilitator in an educational setting. You may, however, offer to provide details about support that is available.

  Finally, disclosure in the context of youth work is not only a matter of dealing with a complicated group dynamic or an emotionally charged situation. When a participant discloses something that they have experienced, the act of which constituted a crime (rape, sexual abuse, grievous bodily harm), then you may be obliged to inform the relevant authorities (police, social services, etc.), especially if the person who disclosed such information is a child (a person under the age of 18). In case such a situation arises you should be properly informed about your legal obligations. At the very least, and despite the importance of respecting confidentiality, you will need to tell your superior (e.g. the president of your organisation, a senior youth worker or your line manager or employer). You will need to decide together if further action is necessary. Of course you must keep the participant concerned fully informed and try to ensure that your action does not put them at any further risk.

Endnotes

1 The Spotlight Initiative to eliminate violence against women and girls - *https://www.un.org/en/spotlight-initiative*

2 COMPASS – Manual for human rights education with young people, Council of Europe, October 2012, p.17

3 Committee of Ministers Recommendation CM/Rec(2010)7 on the Council of Europe Charter on Education for Democratic Citizenship and Human Rights Education

4 See the Compilation of good practices for more about how to address gender stereotypes in education, including how to promote an education free from gender stereotypes and how to identify ways to implement the measures which are included in the Committee of Ministers' Recommendation on gender mainstreaming in education, Council of Europe 2015: *https://rm.coe.int/CoERMPublicCommonSearchServices/DisplayDCTMContent?documentId=0900001680590fe0*

Overview of the activities

Page	Time (min)	Title	Overview	Level	Number of participants
76	90	**About Maria**	This activity deals with the issue of forced sterilization of women with disabilities in recent history. Using a real story, participants explore, how gender-based violence can affect people. They then reflect on what the history of violence can teach us about preventing and acting against it today.	3	6-30
82	120	**Digital Media Bash**	This activity uses research techniques to address the presence and use of violence in the digital media.	1	10-30
86	120	**Gender Confusion**	This activity combines an analytical exploration of concepts (terms) used in work around gender equality and how they are understood / used by young people or presented in the media and by the educational authorities. It allows participants to reflect on the role of language in gender-based violence.	3	10-30
90	60-90	**Gender-in-a-box**	This activity raises awareness about gender and addresses problems associated with rigidly defined gender roles. It is based on the analysis of images of men and women in media.	3	6-30
94	60-90	**Good, Better, Best**	This activity looks at how gender stereotypes affect the lives of young people, and at the value society places on "feminine" and "masculine" qualities. Participants use sets of cards to discuss which qualities are more commonly regarded as masculine or feminine.	2	8-20

Page	Time (min)	Title	Overview	Level	Number of participants
99	90	**Greater Expectations?**	This activity uses brainstorming to help participants understand the different expectations towards and demands on girls/ young women and boys/young men in contemporary society. It allows participants to explore concepts of gender equality further.	1	15-30
102	60	**The Impact of Gender-Based Violence**	The participants look at various examples of gender-based violence and discuss the consequences for the individuals concerned and for society as a whole.	2	8-30
109	60	**Kati's Story**	This short simulation activity helps to build empathy towards victims of interpersonal or relationship violence and demonstrates that leaving a violent relationship generally takes place in stages. Participants listen to a story and use blankets to symbolise different stages of entering and leaving an abusive relationship.	4	10-20
116	60	**The Knight in Shining Armor**	This short role play introduces the difficulties of recognising abuse and looks at early warning signs to identify potential abusers. It provides a good basis for discussion on how society romanticises relationships which may involve violence and oppression.	3	10-20
120	190	**N vs Sweden**	This simulation activity looks at issues surrounding women seeking asylum, using a case brought to the European Court of Human Rights.	4	Any

Page	Time (min)	Title	Overview	Level	Number of participants
129	120	**No Violence Here**	This is a simulation activity, in which participants devise a policy on preventing and acting against gender-based violence in their school	4	10-30
140	45 Part 1 120 Part 2	**Our Daily Sexism**	In this activity, participants need to decide how they would respond to different examples of sexist hate speech online. They then develop an online action that they could implement to act against examples of gender-based violence.	2	6-20
147	60	**Safety in My Life**	This activity uses brainstorming to reflect about what people do to avoid violence and to identify common threats to safety according to sex. It highlights gender differences in relation to violence and addresses the absence of appropriate information for young people on the nature of interpersonal violence.	2	8-20
151	60-75	**Sex Sells?**	This activity addresses several issues concerning public perceptions of gender, sex and sexuality. Participants analyse how different genders are depicted in advertisements in newspapers and magazines using a special tool for analysis.	2	10-30
156	40-60	**Spaces and Places**	This activity looks at the safety of LGBT+ young people in different everyday settings. Participants position themselves along the length of a wall, according to how safe or unsafe they think it is for LGBT+ people to be "out" in particular settings.	2	10-30

Page	Time (min)	Title	Overview	Level	Number of participants
160	120	**Stella**	This activity uses ranking methods to expose the differences in participants' moral values, and to open discussion on questions of gender inequality and socialisation into gender-based stereotyping.	2	5-30
164	60	**Too Hard to Respond**	This activity uses brainstorming and role-playing to address ways of responding to unwanted sexual advances, sexual bullying and harassment.	3	6-30
168	60	**What to Do?**	This activity explores opinions in the group on common dilemmas relating to sex, sexuality, relationships and violence.	2	6-30

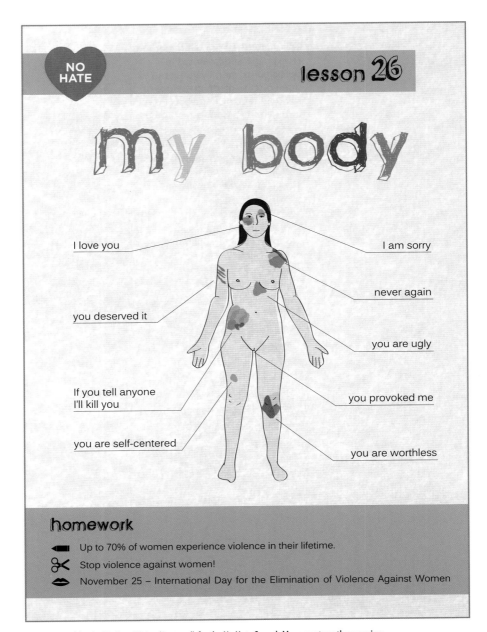

Poster created by the No Hate Ninjas (Portugal) for the No Hate Speech Movement youth campaign.

18 Educational activities to address gender-based violence with young people

> "The past is always tense, the future perfect."
> *Zadie Smith*

About Maria

Level 3

6 to 30

90 minutes

Complexity:	Level 3
Group size:	6 to 30
Time:	90 minutes
Overview:	This activity deals with the issue of forced sterilisation of women with disabilities in recent history. Using a real story, participants explore, how gender-based violence can affect people. They then reflect on what the history of violence can teach us about preventing and acting against it today.
Objectives:	To learn about and reflect on cases of gender-based violence and discrimination and consider their effect on people with disabilities today
	To understand which human rights are violated in different cases of gender-based violence
	To reflect on personal roles and consider the type of actions which could help to prevent gender-based violence today.
Materials:	Copies of "The story of Maria and her country" (one copy per group)
	Copies of the task for each group
Preparation:	You may want to review some of the terms relevant to this activity, such as forced sterilisation or eugenics.

Instructions

1) Start with a simple activity "Up and down". Tell participants that you will read out a series of different statements. If they agree with them, they should stand up, and if they do not agree, they should sit or crouch down. Different degrees of standing or crouching are possible: participants can stand with their arms raised if they agree completely with the statement; or they can sit on a chair, if they partly agree.

2) Read out the following statements, one by one, allowing people to adopt a position after each statement. This part of the activity should be done in silence.

   Statements:

   • Women should have the right to have babies
   • Women should have the right to decide if they want to have babies or not
   • Forcing women to have babies should be illegal
   • Forcing women not to have babies should be illegal
   • States that have performed surgery to make women infertile without their consent should pay reparations

3) Run a short debriefing after this part of the activity. You could ask the following questions:

   • How did you feel during the activity? Was it difficult to adopt a position?
   • How difficult / easy was it to answer the questions? Which ones were the most difficult and why?
   • Did you have any doubts when answering the questions? What were they?
   • Have you ever heard of cases when women have been forced to have an operation which makes them infertile? Can you give details – for example, who was involved, and which reasons were given? (you may want to explain to participants the meaning of the term "forced sterilisation")

4) Now ask participants to make smaller groups of 4-6 people. Give groups copies of the handout "The story of Maria and her country" and ask participants to read it. After they have read it, they should answer the questions below the text and write their answers to the last two questions (How do you think that forced sterilisation affected the rest of Maria's life? How do such acts affect the understanding of human rights?). Allow about 30 minutes for this part of the activity.

5) Once the groups are ready, ask them to present their answers to the last question. Allow some time for discussion of this question. You could also ask them to share their answers to the other questions. Tell participants that the case is about Sweden, and the story is based on the real-life experience of Maria Nordin, a Swedish citizen.

6) Finish the activity with a debriefing and evaluation, focusing on the types and extent of gender-based violence and discrimination experienced by people with disabilities today. Discuss how it affects them and relate the issues to human rights.

Debriefing and evaluation

Start with a general overview of the activity and ask the following questions:

- How did you feel during the exercise? Was it difficult or easy to connect with Maria's story?
- Did you expect the story to be about Sweden? If you guessed, which facts in the story gave this away? Were you surprised?
- Have you ever heard of eugenics? What is it? Can you think of other eugenic ideas or practices from history which classified certain people as inferior, and in doing so, appeared to justify violence against them – even killing them?
- Why do we need to remember gender-based violence and other crimes against people with disabilities which happened in Sweden and other countries in the recent past? What can we learn from such a look at history?
- What can governments of countries that allowed such violent practices do today to compensate the victims?
- People with disabilities face a great deal of discrimination today. Can you think of examples?
- Do you know about other violent practices that threaten bodily and mental integrity, which are performed on people today without their consent?
- Which human rights are violated when such practices are carried out?
- What can young people like you do to prevent or fight gender-based discrimination?

Tips for the facilitator

This activity deals with the forced sterilisation of people with disabilities in Sweden. However, it is important to remember that it is not only this country that has a history of such cruel treatment against – mainly - women from minority groups. Similar examples can be found in many countries of the world, for example Germany, Czech Republic (Czechoslovakia), Russia, Switzerland, China, United States and Australia. You could also refer to the forced sterilisation of Romani women which happened in Czechoslovakia, and later in the Czech Republic and Slovakia. The report of the European Roma Rights Centre, "Coercive and cruel", published in 2016, describes examples of such sterilisation from 1996 to 2016 and analyses the effects of such acts on the people concerned, on communities and on society as a whole.

The forced sterilisation of women constitutes an example of very cruel gender-based violence and a serious human rights violation. It violates such rights as the right to life, the prohibition of inhuman and degrading treatment, the right to safety, the right to privacy, and freedom from discrimination. The European Court of Human Rights has dealt with several cases concerning forced sterilisation, e.g. V.C against Slovakia (on the forced sterilisation of Romani woman) or A. P.,

E. Garçon and S. Nicot against France (on the forced sterilisation of transgender people). In both cases, the Court found forced sterilisation to be a human rights violation. Yet, in 2017 there were still 22 countries in Europe that demanded sterilisation for transgender people before they transition to another sex.

During the activity, participants may ask you whether sterilisation (including unforced) is allowed in your country, or anywhere in the world. You may want to check this fact before running the activity. There are many countries which do not permit sterilisation unless it has been recommended by a doctor for medical purposes. Sterilisation is usually permanent, but in some cases it can be reversed, although such a procedure is very risky and does not often end successfully.

You may want to read the first chapter of the manual, where you can find different examples of violence, before you run the activity. This may help with debriefing the activity.

Suggestions for follow-up

If the group is interested in exploring other historical examples of violence, you could suggest the activity "Dosta" from *Compass – the Manual for human rights education with young people*, in which participants plan and carry out an action project to raise awareness about Roma victims of the Holocaust.

You could also propose that participants look at the section on Intersectionality and multiple discrimination (in Chapter 4) to learn how gender intersects with other characteristics, such as skin colour, class, disability, ethnic origin or age.

Ideas for action

You could explore with participants whether forced sterilisation has ever been carried out in your country. Organise a visit to a local organisation which deals with challenges that people with disabilities face in your community and ask them what they do against gender-based violence.

The story is based on Sam Rowlands, Jean-Jacques Amy, Sterilisation of those with intellectual disability: evolution from non-consensual interventions to strict safeguards, Centre of Postgraduate Medical Research & Education, Bournemouth University and Learning Disabilities – Toward Inclusion, Helen L. Atherton and Debbie J. Crickmore (Ed.), Churchill Livingstone, Elsevier Ltd., 2011.

The story of Maria and her country
(based on a real story)

Maria lived in a country which she loved, but just as with every other country in the world, it had some sad historical chapters. In 1909, her country established *The Society for Racial Hygiene*, with the aim of influencing public policy and public opinion by spreading knowledge about eugenic methods, and their results. The Society distributed pamphlets about the importance of "racial hygiene" and presented the sterilisation of women considered 'unfit' as one way of maintaining a higher genetic pool within the country. The Society was later replaced by a government department called The State Institute for Racial Biology, which operated until the late 1950s.

In 1934, Maria's country adopted a law which allowed for the forced sterilisation of people with intellectual disabilities. Later, this law was extended to other groups of people who were considered 'unfit' for society.

When Maria was 17, she was identified as having a very low level of intelligence and was diagnosed by the school doctor as 'feeble-minded' (this is the term that was used to refer to people with intellectual disabilities). The doctor also said that because of this fact, Maria would be unable to raise children. She was later called to sign some papers. She was not sure what she was signing, and it turned out later on that by signing these papers she had agreed to be sterilised. In 1943, the doctors performed an operation on her and removed her ovaries, which made her infertile. It emerged later that the reason she was classified as 'feeble-minded' was because she was short-sighted (and had no glasses). This had made her unable to read the blackboard.

In 1997, in a newspaper interview, Maria (who was by then 72) said: "I'll never forget when I was called into the headmistress office… I was aware of it well before. I hid in the basement bathroom, crying all by myself. I thought of killing myself, and I have been thinking of it ever since. But I never wanted to give them [the government] the satisfaction of getting rid of me. I tried to let my hatred go, to melt it away. But it isn't possible for me'.

Maria demanded compensation from her government in 1996, but her claim was initially rejected. However, after prominent newspaper headlines about her story, an *ex-gratia* payment was made to her.

The law allowing forced sterilisation was operational until 1975, and it is estimated that some 60,000 people were sterilised, mainly women. How many of these sterilisations were on the grounds of intellectual disability is unknown. A similar law applied to transsexual people, who had to undergo sterilisation before a sex change. This law was abolished in 2013.

TASK FOR THE GROUP

After reading the story of Maria and her country, discuss the questions below in your group. Prepare a short report to present to the rest of the group, based on your answers to the last two questions. You will have about 2-3 minutes for your presentation.

Questions:

- What did you think about the story? Did it shock or surprise you? Why, or why not?
- Which country do you think Maria was from? Give a reason for your guess.
- Can you imagine Maria's feelings when she understood that she would be sterilised?
- How do you think that forced sterilisation affected the rest of Maria's life?
- How do such acts affect the understanding of human rights?

"You are what you share"
Charles Leadbeater

Digital Media Bash

Level 1

10 to 30

120 minutes

Complexity: Level 1

Group size: 10 to 30

Time: 120 minutes

Overview: This activity uses research techniques to address the presence and use of violence in the digital media.

Objectives:
- To share and discuss the use of violence in the digital media
- To learn how to recognise hate speech and act against it
- To develop gender awareness among participants

Materials:
- Computers, tablets or smartphones with access to the Internet (one for each group)
- Flipchart
- Copies of the handout (one for each group)

Preparation: Prepare links to a series of web pages for participants. These should include links to mainstream media sites and/or alternative media and social media. For social media, you could ask participants to open their social media pages. Look for web sites presenting different opinions, for example from different political perspectives. If you have less time available for the activity, select some articles and give participants links to these. Do not provide links to extremist web sites.

Instructions

1) Inform participants that they are going to analyse digital media using a pair of "gender / violence glasses". You may need to explain the concept of gender and gender-based violence.

2) Start the activity with a simple brainstorm, asking participants about examples of how violence and gender-based violence are presented online. Write down the answers on the flipchart. You could ask the group if they have ever heard of hate speech. If they have not, or if they are unclear about it, provide them with the definition in the glossary.

3) Split participants into smaller groups of 4-5 people and tell them that each group will be given a different web site and will analyse it using the "Research and analysis tool". Participants should look at different content on the web sites they have been given – for example, articles, pictures, photos, videos, memes, advertisements, comments, etc. This part of the activity may take some time, but you could limit it to 45 min. Provide the group with links to the web sites to be analysed. Tell the group that they can use their own social media profiles e.g. on Facebook, Twitter, Instagram, etc.

4) Ask the entire group in plenary to compare their findings and draw conclusions on the use of violence and its impact for young people of different genders.

5) After the presentations, go to the debriefing and evaluation

Debriefing and evaluation

Start with a few general questions on how participants felt about the activity, and then move to explore how online gender-based violence can be challenged and addressed. Use some of the following guiding questions:

- Have you ever looked at the issue of violence through gender glasses before? If not, what did you learn by taking this new perspective? Did anything surprise you?
- Is the material found and displayed representative of issues in your community?
- Did you find any gender stereotypes in the web sites? If yes, what were they?
- Were there more examples of violence committed by men? If yes, why do you think this is?
- Were there any "invisible" groups (e.g. LGBT+)? If yes, which? Why do you think they were not represented?
- Did you find examples of hate speech related to gender?
- Why do people use gender-related hate speech?
- Which human rights may be violated when people use hate speech online?
- Should hate speech be prohibited on digital media? Explain your answer
- How can the media be influenced to change the way it presents violence, stereo- typed images of perpetrators of violence, and different genders?

Tips for facilitators

This activity can take some time and requires preparation from the facilitator. It is important to prepare links to the web sites participants will analyse beforehand, and you should make sure to select web sites that differ in content and present opinions from different points of view, including different political viewpoints. Encourage participants to look at the comments under articles, as this is where most examples of hate speech can be found.

Suggestions for follow–up

If participants are interested in exploring the topic further and seeing how site administrators react to examples of violence, try the activity 'Reading the rules' from *Bookmarks*. In this activity, participants explore the terms of use or community guidelines of websites and take steps to report inappropriate content. Participants also discuss the positive and negative aspects of reporting.

For an in-depth exploration of bias and stereotyping in the media, you could run the activity 'Front Page', adapted to the issue of gender. This activity can be found in *Compass*.

Alternatively, you could suggest that participants review student text books and analyse these using "gender glasses".

Ideas for action

Encourage participants to contact local media outlets and ask them about their policy on reporting gender-based violence. Participants could challenge them to use "gender glasses" in their approach to reporting violence. You could organise a discussion in your group with media professionals and students about the responsibility of media professionals for the content and approach of their reporting.

Research and analysis tool

Review carefully the web site provided by the facilitator. Analyse the contents, looking at articles, pictures, videos, ads, photos, memes, comments, etc. You should analyse the content using gender/violence glasses, looking at how gender and violence is portrayed or reported. Discuss this within your group and answer the following questions, recording the answers on flipchart paper:

- What is the name of the web site?
- Comment on how the following are presented:
  - images of femininity:
  - images of masculinity:
  - images of people who are neither portrayed as stereotypically feminine, nor as stereotypically masculine (if any):
  - images of LGBT people (if any)
- Count how many times you see examples of violence, including violent expressions
- Count how many times men are described or portrayed as 'perpetrators', and how many times as 'victims' of violence
- Count how many times women are described or portrayed as 'perpetrators', and how many times as 'victims' of violence
- Are expressions of violence initiated by men and women treated or reported differently?
- Are there any examples of hate speech on the web site? Make a note of some of these. Do the examples refer to gender or to other characteristics?
- Is there any violence portrayed that you would identify as gender-based violence? Write down some examples
- Did you find any examples of encouragement or incitement to hate?
- Any other comments.

Gender Confusion

Level 3

10 to 30

120 minutes

Complexity: Level 3

Group size: 10 to 30

Time: 120 minutes

Overview: This activity combines an analytical exploration of concepts (terms) used in work around gender equality and how they are understood / used by young people or presented in the media and by the educational authorities. It allows participants to reflect on the role of language in gender-based violence.

Objectives:
- To understand the meaning of concepts such as sex, gender and sexual orientation
- To reflect on how different notions related to gender are presented in participants' environment and what impact it has on people and society at large
- To illustrate the dynamic and complex nature of gender identities

Materials:
- Pens and paper
- Appropriate visual aids and presentation equipment for the input
- Copies of the grid for group work

Preparation:
- Prepare a short input / presentation on terminology used in work around gender equality - covering at least terms such as sex, gender, transgender, sexual orientation, gender-based violence, gender-based discrimination. Definitions and explanations of these terms can be found in Chapter 1 of this manual and in the glossary at the end of the manual. The presentation can be made using flip-charts or as an electronic presentation.
- Copy handouts - one per each group

Instructions

1) Tell the participants that in this activity they will have time to reflect on how different terms related to gender and gender equality are understood by young people and other people or institutions in the society.

2) Divide participants into smaller groups: the number of groups should correspond to the number of terms you decide to explore together with the participants. Each group receives one term (e.g. gender) and the grid for group work, which you can find in the end of this activity. Tell the groups that they should first start with writing down their own understanding of the term, and then follow each box in the grid: how it is understood by other young people, how it is presented in the media and by educational authorities. Participants should base their reflection on what they know, what they heard or noticed in their own environment. Tell them that is it not a problem if they do not know some of the answers. Allow some 30 minutes for this part of the activity.

3) Once the groups finished their task, ask them to present their findings. You can allow some short time for questions after each presentation. The questions, however should only be asked if something is unclear. Do not open a discussion here.

4) At the end of the process give a brief presentation of the terminology used in the activity – use Chapter 1 and the Glossary of terms in this manual. Once it is done, continue with the debriefing and evaluation.

Debriefing and evaluation

Ask participants to sit in a circle, and ask them the following questions:

- How did you feel in this activity? How did you find the discussion in small groups? Were there any differences of opinion, or misunderstandings?
- Did your understanding of the term differ in comparison with the one presented in the end of the activity by the facilitator? What were these differences?
- Why do you think people have such different interpretations of terms relating to gender?
- Does the understanding of the terms by other young people and the way they are presented in the media and by educational authorities carry a positive or negative message? Why is it so? What impact does it have on the society?
- Do you agree that "gender" is political? Why yes / no?
- Can the use of language contribute to gender-based violence?
- How do gender related concepts, and the way they are used, contribute to discrimination? How can we avoid this?
- Is there any space for people in your community to discuss issues relating to gender and gender-based violence? To what extent are young people able to be involved in such debates? How could young people become more involved?

- Which human rights are violated in cases of gender-based violence? What can young people do to promote and protect human rights?

Tips for facilitators

Be aware that participants will have different approaches to, and knowledge of the topic. They may be confused about the meaning of terms, and there may be linguistic differences, particularly relating to transgender issues. Some participants in the group may have a better understanding of the concepts than others: it is important to reassure everyone that all opinions will be respected, and no-one should feel inhibited by other members of the group.

Try to explain and clarify, without giving participants the impression that you are telling them "the truth". Be aware that in some languages the English word "gender" may not have a direct equivalent.

Suggestions for follow-up

If you would like to explore the concept of gender further, try the activity "Expectations and demands", which uses brainstorming to help participants understand the different expectations towards, and demands upon, girls/ young women and boys/young men in contemporary society.

If the group has not already explored the human rights framework, and you would like to place gender issues in the wider context of human rights, you could try the activity "Act it out!" from *Compass – manual for human rights education with young people*.

Once participants have a basic understanding of the terms, it may be useful to explore stereotypes and prejudices related to gender and sexuality. Try running the activity "Let's talk about sex!" from *Compass*. This activity uses the "fish-bowl" technique to explore attitudes to sexuality, including homophobia.

Ideas for action

Consider inviting a guest speaker from a local LGBT+ or gender organisation to come and talk to the group about gender issues and the work they are doing. Participants could prepare questions before the meeting.

Participants could prepare a lesson plan and deliver a mini workshop to their peers (in the youth club or at school) explaining different terms related to gender.

Grid for group work

You will receive one term used when talking about gender and gender equality. Write in each box how, in your opinion, this term is understood and presented by different people, including you. You will have some 30 minutes to do the task.

Gender Confusion

Term:

1. How do you understand it?

2. How is it generally understood by your peers / other young people?

3. How it is presented / promoted in the media?

4. How is it officially presented / promoted by the educational authorities around you?

"Gender roles are so deeply conditioned in us that we will often follow them even when they chafe against our true desires, our needs, our happiness.

Chimamanda Ngozi Adichie

Gender-in-a-box

Level 3

6 to 30

60 to 90 minutes

Complexity:	Level 3
Group size:	6 to 30
Time:	60 to 90 minutes
Overview:	This activity raises awareness about gender and addresses problems associated with rigidly defined gender roles. It is based on the analysis of images of men and women in media.
Objectives:	• To understand the socially-constructed nature of gender roles and the mechanisms and agents of gender socialisation
	• To explore and reflect on personal experiences of gender socialisation
	• To discuss the connections between gender socialisation and gender-based violence
Materials:	• Magazines and advertising clippings, which show people in different life situations or electronic devices with Internet access
	• Flipchart with paper, scissors, glue sticks, marker pens (red, blue, green and black)
Preparation:	• Prepare several flipchart posters. Each poster should have one of the following headings: MEN, WOMEN , preferably each in a different colour
	• If you decide to use web sites, instead of magazines, prepare some links to web sites with ads that show men and women in different life situations

Instructions

1) Divide participants into smaller groups of three. Hand out magazines or clippings and ask the small groups to look through them and discuss the messages about "men" and "women" conveyed by the magazines. Instead of magazines, you can show some websites with ads that show people of different genders in different life situations.

2) While participants are talking, hang up the two flipcharts that you prepared before the activity.

3) After about 15 minutes, ask participants to come back into the circle and feed back on the qualities of 'men' and 'women', as presented through the magazines or web sites. Make notes of qualities they list on the two flipcharts. Try to use key words or short phrases.

4) Once the lists are complete, ask the group to cut out a few images from the magazines, if you use them, to illustrate some of the ideas. Stick them next to the keywords listed on the flipcharts. Give them five minutes for this task. Bring the group together and look again at the posters:

   · Ask participants to look at the lists and identify possible contradictions among characteristics listed under MEN and under WOMEN (e.g. under WOMEN: not hairy; long hair) Connect any such contradictions using a marker.
   · Ask participants to look for qualities that seem to be independent of "will" – for example, physical qualities, such as height, are largely a matter of genetics and can be influenced only to a certain degree. Put a box around these qualities.
   · Ask the group to find matching opposites in the men's and women's lists, and then circle and connect them using a marker of a different colour, e.g. submissive – dominant.

5) Proceed to the debriefing and evaluation to explore further the process of gender socialisation, and to make connections with gender-based violence.

Debriefing and evaluation

Explain to the group that despite arguments about certain words, different groups of people usually manage to agree on lists of characteristics normally attributed to men and women in a very short period of time. Explain that the reason for this is that we all learn about what women and men "should be" from common sources. The term used to describe these common perceptions is "gender roles". Gender roles tend to be presented to us as binary 'boxes' into which women and men are expected to fit.

Use the following questions to debrief the activity:

- How did you feel during the activity? Did you find out anything surprising?
- Where do we learn gender roles from?
- Are the roles or characteristics that you have listed the same for men and women all over the world? If they are not, what are some of the differences?
- How does society punish people who do not conform to society's expectations about their gender? How are people who do conform rewarded?
- "A rigid definition of gender roles contributes significantly to gender-based violence" - Do you agree with this statement? Why, or why not?
- Can you think of people who do not fit into the gender roles ascribed by society? Have you ever heard of non-binary people? How does gender-based violence affect them? How does such violence affect society as a whole?
- What can we do to challenge stereotypes about fixed and non-changeable gender roles? How can gender-based violence against people who do not fit into "gender norms" be prevented? How can we all act against it?

Tips for facilitators

The strength of this activity is that it brings the issue of gender roles and gender socialisation closer to participants. These issues are often dealt with only in theoretical discussions. If you have enough time, you can start this activity with an illustration of a real-life experience that participants are likely to have encountered. If you have come together for a one-off activity, you could create the experience in the form of a role-play (e.g. a boy and girl playing in a kindergarten or playground, and an adult instructing them to act like a boy and a girl), or using a video showing boys and girls or women and men in typical or atypical gender roles - for example, someone interviewing for a job atypical for their gender. If the group meets regularly, try to use a recent or typical experience, for example, that boys are usually called on to take out the trash or move the chairs, while girls might do the washing up or make the teas and coffees.

The first part of this activity could also be conducted in sub-groups. Each group would be given a selection of magazines or clippings (or web sites) and their own flipchart papers with MEN and WOMEN as headings. Introduce the activity by asking the group to give a few examples about messages that young people receive about how 'men' and 'women' are supposed to be, based on the video / role-play / experience they have in common. Take a few answers, then explain that the group will now work in two smaller groups, one on men, the other on women. If you have a bigger group, you can decide to create several groups that will work on gender roles ascribed to men and some that will work on women's gender roles. Each group should look through the magazines and clippings (or web sites) and use them as illustrations wherever possible. Tell participants that they should not limit themselves to what they have found in the magazines or web sites, but should also think of their own childhood, school years or adolescence, and add messages which they have received about gender roles to the list. The groups should work in separate locations, if possible. The facilitator should monitor the process.

Suggestions for follow-up

If you think it would be useful to continue the discussion and explore the concept of identity, try the activity "Who are I?" from *Compass*. You could also explore further how gender differences are related to the issue of violence, for example using the activity "Safety in my life".

Ideas for action

Gender socialisation can be seen in almost every aspect of life. The kind of examples that can be found in advertising or youth magazines can also be seen in many other areas of life. To supplement the discussion on 'Where do we learn gender roles from?', the group could examine different influences on gender socialisation, such as primary school text books, or the policies and activities in the youth group or other organisations.

The group could look into campaigns – including on the Internet - which address issues of gender socialisation and gender stereotyping, and could try to contribute to these campaigns by taking part in activities or creating publications or materials. If there are no appropriate campaigns already existing, they could think about starting their own campaign, or producing resources for other members of their school or youth group.

Adapted from Creighton, A. and Kivel, P. (1990). Helping Teens Stop Violence. A practical guide for educators, counsellors and parents. Hunter House, Alameda.

Once you label me you negate me
Søren Kierkegaard

Good, Better, Best

Level 2

8 to 20

60 to 90
minutes

Complexity: Level 2

Group size: 8 to 20

Time: 60 to 90 minutes

Overview: This activity looks at how gender stereotypes affect the lives of young people, and at the value society places on "feminine" and "masculine" qualities. Participants use sets of cards to discuss which qualities are more commonly regarded as masculine or feminine.

Objectives:
- To learn how people become socialised to regard certain qualities as feminine and others as masculine
- To understand why society considers certain qualities to be "positive" or "desirable", while other characteristics are considered to be "negative" or "undesirable"
- To discover how the widely adopted binary approach affects non-binary people

Materials:
- Two sets of cards with adjectives (see preparation and handouts)
- Instructions for each group
- 2 envelopes and sheets of A3 paper

Preparation:
- Make 2 copies of the set of cards at the end of this activity. Cut out the cards and shuffle them (keeping each set separate). Put one set of cards (20 cards) into each envelope.
- Prepare one sheet of A3 paper for group A: divide it into two columns, one labelled 'Feminine' and the other 'Masculine'.
- Prepare another sheet of paper divided into two columns for group B. The labels should read 'Positive / Desirable' and 'Negative / Undesirable'.

Instructions

1) Explain that this activity is about exploring how gender stereotypes work in society. Form two groups with equal numbers of participants (Group A and Group B). Ask people to sit in their groups, at opposite corners of the room. Give each group an envelope with a set of cards, a sheet of A3 paper and a worksheet with the appropriate instructions.

2) Tell participants to read the instructions on their worksheet and work as quickly as they can to carry out the task They need to place each card on the A3 paper in the appropriate column. For group A, they will place the cards according to whether they think each one is "masculine" or "feminine", and for Group B, according to whether society tends to regard the quality as "Positive / Desirable" or "Negative / Undesirable".

   Allow the groups 10 to 15 minutes to complete the task according to the instructions on the worksheet.

3) When they are ready, gather the whole group together again. Divide a piece of flipchart paper into two columns, and write 'Feminine' at the top of one, and 'Masculine' at the top of the other. Ask Group A to list the qualities they put into the "Feminine" column, and after each adjective, ask Group B if they placed that adjective in the Positive/ Desirable or the Negative/Undesirable column. Record this information beside each adjective using a plus (+) or minus (–) sign. Repeat the procedure for the "Masculine" column.

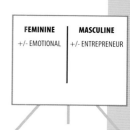

4) When Group A has listed all the adjectives, continue with the debriefing and evaluation.

Debriefing and evaluation

Ask participants some of the following questions:

- How did you feel during the activity? Looking at the flipchart paper, how do you feel about what you see?
- Does anything about the results surprise you? Explain why.
- In which column – feminine or masculine – are there more (-) signs next to the qualities? What does this tell you?
- Why are some (feminine of masculine) qualities less desirable ? How do you think this comes about?
- Do you consider this characterisation of "masculine" and "feminine" qualities to be an accurate classification, which would be true for all time and for all places?
- How do we learn gender stereotypes?
- In your opinion, how do gender stereotypes affect our behaviour, and how do they affect the way we treat or judge other people?

- What are some of the consequences of gender stereotypes for women, for men, and for non-binary people? Can you give examples from real life?
- How are gender stereotypes linked to discrimination, violence and hate speech? Can you think of examples of gender-based discrimination, violence or hate speech? What impact do these phenomena have on gender equality and the enjoyment of human rights?
- What can be done to avoid gender stereotyping? What can be done to avoid the negative consequences of stereotyping?

Tips for facilitators

By way of introducing the conclusion to the debriefing, you could inform participants that research has found that children as young as 5 or 6 years of age use gender related stereotypes.

The debriefing could also look at the fact that groups with "undesirable" characteristics are generally regarded as being less valuable, and they tend to have a lower status in society. This usually means that they are more often exposed to prejudice and to verbal or physical violence. You could ask participants to identify groups who have been affected by such problems in their local area and how they think these can be overcome. Try to link this with human rights and ask the group to identify human rights issues related to gender-based violence.

Suggestions for follow-up

If participants are interested in the topic, they may wish to raise awareness about gender stereotypes and gender-based violence and to prepare guidelines for their school or youth club. For this, you could use the activity "No violence in here".

Ideas for action

Support participants to carry out a research project about stereotyping in everyday life. If the members of your group attend school, discuss how they could research and document stereotyping in school over a period of time. On the basis of the results, your group could propose recommendations to the school authorities on how to address stereotyping, and the group could be involved as peer educators to raise awareness among other pupils. The same could be done in the youth club / organisation.

Developed by: Marietta Gargya, hotline worker at NANE Hotline for battered women and children, Hungary, on the basis of a research study by Broverman, I., Vogel, S. R. Broverman, D.M., Clarkson, F.E. and Rosenkrantz, P.S. (1972). 'Sex Role Stereotypes: A current appraisal'. Journal of Social Issues, 28. Blackwell. pp 59-78.

Set of cards:

DEPENDENT	**INDEPENDENT**
EMOTIONAL	**RATIONAL**
OBJECTIVE	**SUBJECTIVE**
SUBMISSIVE	**DOMINANT**
PASSIVE	**ACTIVE**
GOOD BUSINESS SKILLS	**POOR BUSINESS SKILLS**
COMPETENT	**INCOMPETENT**
UNDECISIVE	**DECISIVE**
AMBITIOUS	**UNAMBITIOUS**
DIPLOMATIC	**UNDIPLOMATIC**

Instructions for Group A

Headings: Feminine - Masculine

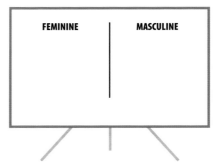

Certain characteristics are considered to be more feminine, while others are thought to be more masculine. Place the cards in the column where you think they belong. Work as quickly as you can, without thinking about it too much.

Instruction for Group B

Headings: Positive/Desirable - Negative/Undesirable

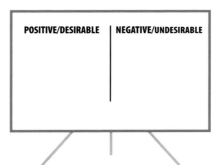

Certain characteristics are considered to be more positive and desirable, while others are thought to be negative and not desirable. Place the cards in the column where you think they belong. Work as quickly as you can, without thinking about it too much.

> "Nobody objects to a woman being a good writer or sculptor or geneticist if at the same time she manages to be a good wife, a good mother, good looking, good-tempered, well-groomed and non-aggressive."
>
> *Leslie M. McIntyre*

Greater Expectations?

Level 1

15 to 30

90 minutes

Complexity: Level 1

Group size: 15 to 30

Time: 90 minutes

Overview: This activity uses brainstorming to help participants understand the different expectations towards and demands on girls/ young women and boys/young men in contemporary society. It allows participants to explore concepts of gender equality further.

Objectives:
- To learn how to recognise society's differing expectations towards girls and boys, and young men and young women
- To reveal and discuss the gender expectations and norms which individuals face
- To discuss how gender norms affect people's human rights

Materials:
- Five sheets of flip chart paper
- a large wall
- masking tape
- a marker for each participant

Preparation: Hang six pieces of flipchart paper on the wall. Each paper should be marked with one of the following typical settings:

· School · Workplace · Family · Friends · Society · Partner

Divide each piece of flipchart paper into two columns: one should have the title 'boys / young men', and the other should have the title 'girls / young women'.

Instructions

1) Stick the prepared pieces of flipchart paper on the wall before the activity. Tell participants they should take a few minutes to think about what they believe is expected or demanded from girls and boys in the different settings identified on the posters. Allow them to walk around or sit down and think, and stress that they should do this part of the activity individually. They should write their ideas on the pieces of flipchart paper (in the appropriate box or column).

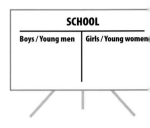

2) Once this phase has been completed, divide the participants into six sub-groups and place each group next to one of the pieces of paper. Tell them to discuss their setting with others in the group. They could use the following guiding questions to support the discussion:

   · Which differences can you identify between expectations and demands placed on girls, and those faced by boys?
   · What would you like to change?
   · How do you think this can be changed?

   Allow about 20-30 minutes for this part of the activity.

3) Bring the group together and ask each small group to report back briefly on their discussion to the whole group. Ask the other participants for initial reactions to the results: how do they feel about them, and does anything surprise them?

4) After the presentations, move to the debriefing and evaluation and continue discussion of the group work, focusing on how people can challenge existing gender norms and expectations.

Debriefing and evaluation

Start by asking participants how they felt doing the activity and if there was anything that they found difficult. You can then use the following questions to run the discussion:

• How did you find the exercise? How did you feel during the exercise?
• Was it easy to identify gender expectations in the first part of the activity?
• Where do people's gender expectations come from? Who establishes them?
• Is it easy for boys and girls / young men and young women to fulfil these expectations? What are the difficulties?
• Who helps to promote these expectations?
• How do we ourselves promote them (whether consciously or unconsciously)?
• Have you ever felt pressured by gender expectations? How did it feel? How did you react?

- Have you ever pressured others to conform to gender expectations? How do you think it would have made those others feel?
- Have you ever challenged gender expectations or norms? How was your challenge taken? Were there any consequences?
- Can gender expectations or demands violate human rights? Which rights, and how are they violated?
- How could we or our organisation work to address damaging gender stereotypes and expectations? What could be done to promote gender equality among young people?

Tips for facilitators

While this is a classic brainstorming and discussion activity, the topic of gender expectations can be controversial. Expectations relating to gender are also partly a matter of perception. As a result, this activity may cause disagreement: some participants may see gender expectations as perfectly reasonable, while others may see them as oppressive and demanding. How expectations are perceived is also likely to be linked to cultural and societal values. You could address some of these issues in discussion.

Please note that this exercise has been deliberately based around binary gender norms, however it is highly likely that it will trigger discussion of issues linked to diverse gender identities. If you feel it is important to challenge binary gender norms in the activity, you could add an extra space on the flipchart for 'other genders' besides 'girls / young women' and 'boys / young men'. You will need to adapt some of the questions in the debriefing.

Suggestions for follow-up

This activity can be a good starting point for exploring the concept of gender-based violence and learning about its different forms. The activity "Understanding gender-based violence" looks at different examples of gender-based violence, and participants discuss the consequences for individuals and society.

Ideas for action

Suggest that participants conduct longer-term observations of expectations relating to gender, focussing on different settings. This could be done over a week or a month. The results of their observations could be compared to a survey of young people of different genders in real settings (for example, school) about their perceptions of the expectations placed on different genders. You can initiate a discussion of the similarities and differences between the perceptions resulting from the survey and those resulting from individual observation.

Source: This activity was developed on the basis of an activity developed by the Intercultural Center, Foundation of Women's Forum, Sweden.

> "Human behaviour flows from three main sources: desire, emotion, and knowledge."
>
> *Plato*

The Impact of Gender-Based Violence

Level 2

8 to 30

60 minutes

Complexity: Level 2

Group size: 8 to 30

Time: 60 minutes

Overview: The participants look at various examples of gender-based violence and discuss the consequences for the individuals concerned and for society as a whole.

Objectives:
- To understand the meaning of gender-based violence recognise and be able to recognise different types of gender-based violence
- To discuss the impact of gender-based violence on those affected by it and on society as a whole
- To consider the question of personal responsibility in relation to occurrences of gender-based violence

Materials:
- Copies of stories (one story per group)
- Flipchart paper

Preparation: Make copies of the stories that can be found at the end of this activity. Prepare two pieces of flipchart paper, with the headings "Consequences on victims" and "Consequences on society". You may also want to read Section 3 of Chapter 1, where different types of gender-based violence are described.

Instructions

1) Ask participants if they have heard of gender-based violence. Discuss this briefly with the group, exploring the different examples of gender-based violence which exist. You may also provide participants with a definition of gender-based violence.

2) Tell participants that they will work in small groups of 4-5 people to discuss a brief story. They should read the text and answer the questions at the end. Hand out one story to each group and give them about 20 minutes to discuss the cases.

3) Once this part of the work is completed, ask the groups to come together and present their answers. They should begin by reading the story aloud. Allow other groups to comment on the group's results. If the groups are unclear about the types of gender-based violence present in the story, you may need to provide the answers yourself.

4) When the groups present their answers to the questions about the impact of violence on the victims and on society, write these down on the pieces of flipchart paper. After each presentation, read the summarised answers back to the whole group and ask if they would like to add or change anything.

Debriefing and evaluation

Begin this part of the activity with participants' general impressions of the activity and then discuss the consequences of gender-based violence and what participants can do to prevent it.

- What do you think about the activity? How did you feel doing it?
- Had you heard about all the different types of gender-based violence presented in the stories? Was there anything surprising for you?
- Was there anything common to different groups' responses to the impact of gender-based violence?
- Why does gender-based violence have consequences for the whole of society?
- What causes gender-based violence? Who is to blame?
- Which human rights are violated in case of gender-based violence?
- What can be done to put an end to such violence, and who can help to bring such a change about?
- What can you do to prevent this type of violence, and how can we all act against it?

Tips for facilitator

This activity is based on an activity from *Bookmarks* – Understanding hate speech. The stories in this activity can easily be modified, and facilitators are encouraged to adapt them to local context, where necessary. Some stories include more than one type of violence (e.g. Story 4 – verbal violence, hate speech, physical violence, hate crime).

Pay attention to this when explaining the types of violence: very often different types happen together at the same time. Try also to address the issue of intersectionality, when someone suffers from violence and discrimination on multiple grounds – as in the first story (gender and disability). You can read more about this in Chapter 4.

Participants are deliberately not introduced to different types of gender-based violence at the beginning of the activity: the discussions aim to explore what they already know on the topic. If you think this will be too difficult for participants, you could make a list of different types of gender-based violence on the flipchart and show this to them before they work on the stories.

We use the word "victim" in this activity, which is a word with certain negative connotations. Some people prefer to use other terms, such as: person targeted by violence or affected by violence. However, the word victim is used in several international human rights instruments, for example in the Council of Europe Convention on preventing and combating violence against women and domestic violence. The Explanatory report to the Convention specifies:

"The term 'victim' refers to both victims of violence against women, and victims of domestic violence, as defined in Article 3 (a) and Article 3 (b) respectively. While only women, including girls, can be victims of violence against women, victims of domestic violence may include men and women as well as children."

Make sure to emphasise that the only person responsible for violence is the perpetrator. It is never the victim's fault!

Suggestions for follow-up

If you want to explore further the question of violence in relationships, you could try the activity "Kati's story". Violence in online gaming is addressed in the activity "Changing the game" from *Bookmarks*, in which participants devise a small campaign against sexism in online games. Or you could explore further the topic of economic violence, using an activity in *Compass* called "Different wages". This is a simulation activity that confronts people with the realities of the labour market, addressing issues such as different wages for the same job, discrimination in the workplace and policies of low pay for young workers.

You could also present key points from the Council of Europe's Convention on Preventing and Combating Violence Against Women and Domestic Violence. You can find a shortened version of the Convention in the Appendices.

Ideas for action

On the basis of answers provided by the participants to the last question of the debriefing, ask participants what they would like to do as a group in order to prevent or act against gender-based violence. Develop a plan together, and then carry out the action.

Stories

Story 1

Martha moves using an electric wheelchair. She lives with her partner in a small apartment, in a small town. They have been together for 6 years. Steven, her partner, has always been a great support to her in carrying out daily activities. However, recently he has been under great pressure to work very long hours. Martha is at home alone and there are days when she does not eat for more than 8 hours. Last Monday, Steven returned home in the morning after a night shift and found that she had been unable to put herself to bed and had tried to sleep in her wheelchair. When Martha asked Steven to work from home in the evenings, he said this was not possible. Martha has no relatives locally, so it is difficult for her to call on anyone else. She also has few friends, as the couple rarely go out. Once when Martha told Steven she was hungry he told her: 'Come on, you are a woman! Make an effort and cook something for yourself or call for a take-away!".

Which examples of gender-based violence can you identify in this story? Who is the victim and who is the perpetrator? What are the likely consequences of violence for the victim? What are the possible consequences for society as a whole?

Story 2

Bernadette works as an accountant in a large company. She has recently received numerous missed calls from an unknown number. When she tried to call back, there was no response. She did not worry until recently, when she received several text messages from a different number. These made her feel uncomfortable, as the texts were very explicit: they called her a slut, suggested that she loves sex and described her body in detail. The last message was even threatening: "I dream about raping you and I will do it one day. You'll love it!". She did not know what to do so she told her friend about the messages, but the friend suggested that she calm down. However, she did offer to drive Bernadette to and from work every day. Bernadette felt slightly relieved, but recently, she noticed an unfamiliar man near her block of flats, looking at her. The same thing happened on the next day.

Which examples of gender-based violence can you identify in this story? Who is the victim and who is the perpetrator? What are the likely consequences of violence for the victim? What are the possible consequences for society as a whole?

Story 3

Linda, who is 17, is a passionate online gamer. In her free time, she plays a lot and she has even made some good friends online. Gaming has always been her passion and she is very good at it, especially at strategic online games. Last time she played her favourite game, one of the male players commented on her avatar (containing her picture) saying: 'God, you are so f… hot! I wish I was near you to show you what a real man is'. Linda did not react, although she felt a little uncomfortable: after all, it was only a game, and just a stupid comment. Two weeks later, she did not do very well in a game she was playing, and some of the players started to send her private messages: 'Go to the kitchen and bring me a beer, woman', 'Get some sex and come back again', 'Playing in a team with women always ends up like this. Never again!'. She decided she would not play the game for the next month.

Which examples of gender-based violence can you identify in this story? Who is the victim and who is the perpetrator? What are the likely consequences of violence for the victim? What are the possible consequences for society as a whole?

Story 4

Jan and Ivan have been in a relationship for 2 years. They decided to spend New Year's Eve at their friends, in a town about 100 km away. After the party, at 6 o'clock in the morning, they were going back to the hotel holding hands. They were close to the bus stop when they saw a group of young men walking towards them. One of the men started shouting: 'Look at those fags! You deserve to die! You are a shame to our country'. Jan and Ivan were scared. Three of the men started to run towards them. They kicked Jan in the belly and punched Ivan in the face. Jan and Ivan cried out for help, but then the bus arrived and the three men got on. Jan asked the driver for help, telling him that those men had just violently beaten him and his friend. They shouted back: 'they are fags!' The bus driver refused to help and shut the door in Jan's face.

Which examples of gender-based violence can you identify in this story? Who is the victim and who is the perpetrator? What are the likely consequences of violence for the victim? What are the possible consequences for society as a whole?

Story 5

Martina (16) met Sasha (17) at school. She had always liked him, so she couldn't have been happier when he asked her for a date. After two dates, she was sure she was in love. On the third date Sasha invited her home and started telling her how beautiful she was, and at one moment he touched her leg. Martina said nothing, but when he started to stroke her, she removed his hand. He suggested that they should undress and make love. She said it was too soon for her and that she wanted to wait until they knew each other better. He insisted and started to undress her. She wanted to leave but he forced her onto the bed by force and started to undress her, touching her in between the legs. She screamed and tried free herself, but Sasha was too strong.

Which examples of gender-based violence can you identify in this story? Who is the victim and who is the perpetrator? What are the likely consequences of violence for the victim? What are the possible consequences for society as a whole?

Story 6

After the birth of her second child, Samantha decided to go back to work as soon as her maternity leave was over. She discussed it with her husband, who asked her to wait to make this decision until her maternity leave was coming to an end. As this time approached, she submitted a number of job applications and was invited to an interview, and was then offered the job. She was very happy and shared the news with her husband. He was less happy and started asking about the job, identifying difficulties and problems, such as that the children would need to go to nursery school, there would be problems with picking them up, the family would need to eat out more often, etc. After two hours of very intense discussion, he asked: 'Don't you have enough money? I always give you money when you go shopping. You don't need more. You are a woman and need to take care of our children'.

Which examples of gender-based violence can you identify in this story? Who is the victim and who is the perpetrator? What are the likely consequences of violence for the victim? What are the possible consequences for society as a whole?

Story 7

The government of country X pushed a new law through parliament which decriminalised marital rape, on the grounds that rape is "not possible" between people who are married. The government also passed a law removing sexual orientation from the list of factors classified as leading to hate crime.

Which examples of gender-based violence can you identify in this story? Who is the victim and who is the perpetrator? What are the likely consequences of violence for the victim? What are the possible consequences for society as a whole?

Story 8

Melinda, a high school teacher, wrote a letter to colleagues informing them that in a few months' time, she would be undergoing sex reassignment surgery from male-to-female. Melinda had worked in the school for 5 years, and twice had been chosen by students as the best teacher of the year. Just one month after Melinda's surgery had begun, at a meeting for all parents of the school the school board made an announcement about Melinda's status. About 20 parents wrote in to protest, requesting that Melinda be removed from the staff. The school board decided to dismiss Melinda in September, on the basis of parents' complaints. Melinda decided to fight for her rights and lodged a legal complaint against the school.

Which examples of gender-based violence can you identify in this story? Who is the victim and who is the perpetrator? What are the likely consequences of violence for the victim? What are the possible consequences for society as a whole?

> "I'm the one you love to hate."
> *Rob Halford*

Kati's Story

Level 4

10 to 20

60 minutes

Complexity: Level 4

Group size: 10 to 20

Time: 60 minutes

Overview: This short simulation activity helps to build empathy towards victims of interpersonal or relationship violence and demonstrates that leaving a violent relationship generally takes place in stages. Participants listen to a story and use blankets to symbolise different stages of entering and leaving an abusive relationship.

Objectives:
- To identify the stages of a typical abusive relationship and to develop understanding about the process of leaving a violent relationship
- To build empathy towards victims of interpersonal or relationship violence
- To discuss the role of third persons (friends, family members, professional helpers, etc.) in helping a person to remove themselves from a violent relationship

Materials:
- An enclosed space, with doors that can be closed, and large enough for the whole group to stand in a circle around a chair
- One chair for the middle of the room
- Eight light blankets or bed sheets, large enough to cover an adult fully

Preparation

- Before running the activity, familiarise yourself with the issue of violence in relationships, including physical violence. Chapter 1 of this manual will be helpful in clarifying the differences between various kinds of violence, particularly the sections dealing with domestic violence and abuse.
- Make sure you have a co-facilitator – ideally someone who has already worked with this group. If you are facilitating alone, ask a participant to act as co-facilitator.
- Before running the activity, approach a participant you believe to be "emotionally strong" and ask them whether they would agree to take on the role of Kati. Talk them through the entire activity before asking them to decide, and make sure they understand that the blankets will be placed over them. Make sure that they do not suffer from any form of claustrophobia or anxiety.
- Prepare the room by placing one chair in the middle and create a space so that everyone can sit in a circle around the chair or in a semi-circle in front of it. Put the blankets in a pile nearby.

Instructions

The activity illustrates the different stages of entering and leaving a violent relationship.

As facilitator, your task will be to read aloud the story of Kati (see the handout below), leaving a pause after each episode of the story.

The story is divided into two parts: part one describes the different stages of the abusive relationship, and part two deals with leaving it. In part one, after the first paragraph, your co-facilitator will put the blanket over Kati. The blanket symbolises an event that is likely to lead to or be the result of abuse or violence. After this, participants should understand what they are expected to do after each episode in the story.

In the second part of the story, your co-facilitator will remove the blanket from Kati, to symbolise a stage of leaving the violent relationship. Participants should follow accordingly. To maintain the surprise effect, it is better not to tell the whole group straight away about the meaning of putting blankets over Kati or removing them.

1) Explain that the aim of the activity is to build empathy towards victims of interpersonal or relationship violence, using a symbol to represent the highly limited space and possibilities available to battered women.

2) Ask the participant that you have prepared to take on the role of Kati to come forward. Introduce the participant to the group. Tell everyone else that s/he will have a difficult task, but that s/he will be safe during the activity. Ask the volunteer to sit on the chair in the middle of the room. Then introduce your co-facilitator to the group. Explain that this person will assist you in running the activity. Pass around the blankets or sheets among participants evenly (1 for every 2 or 3 participants). The co-facilitator should have one.

3) Explain to participants that you are going to read out a series of statements. There will be a short pause between each statement. Participants should follow the story closely and pay particular attention to the pauses, as each of them will have a task during the pauses. Also tell them to pay attention to the co-facilitator, as during the first pause s/he will demonstrate what participants will need to do later. Explain to participants that the person playing 'Kati' has been briefed thoroughly, is fully aware of what is going to happen and is happy to accept the challenge.

4) Ask participants to be silent during the reading of the story, and tell them that if they have questions, they should keep them until this part of the activity is over. Tell them to take note of their feelings as the activity proceeds. If they have questions of clarification, ask them to raise these now, before the main part of the activity begins.

5) Start reading the story slowly. At the first pause, signal to the co-facilitator to put the first blanket over Kati. Make sure that the co-facilitator knows in advance to cover Kati completely. Continue reading the story. At the next pause, encourage participants to put on another blanket over Kati. If participants are hesitant, you can look up, nod your head or signal to the co-facilitator to guide a participant in putting on another blanket.

When you get to the part of the story where you ask Kati questions, read even more slowly.

When you get to the first pause in the second part, signal to the co-facilitator to come forward to remove the first blanket. Again, signal to participants that they should follow the example of the co-facilitator at the next pause. Participants do not normally hesitate to remove the blankets, but if they do, signal to the co-facilitator to guide them.

6) After all blankets have been removed, thank the participant who played Kati, and ask them to sit back in the circle. Allow participants a moment to settle before beginning the debriefing.

Debriefing and evaluation

Begin the debriefing by asking for a round of impressions, to get an idea of how everyone feels. It is important to remember that this can be an emotionally challenging activity, and participants may feel upset or uncomfortable. Remind them that they have the right not to say anything. Offer the participant who played Kati the possibility to speak first about their feelings. Continue with others who indicate that they want to speak. During the debriefing, keep the paper with Kati's story close at hand, so that you can refresh participants' memories of any aspects of the story, as necessary.

The following guiding questions can help you to develop the discussion:

• How did it feel to put the blankets on Kati? How did it feel to watch others cover her?

- How did you feel about the removal of the blankets?
- Did you notice the reaction of other participants during the covering and the removal? Were there differences?
- Who is responsible for Kati having been covered by so many blankets? Is it Kati, her husband, or other people in the story?
- Why were the blankets removed in stages? Why did we not just remove them all at once?
- In your opinion, what were the different roles and responsibilities of the people in this story for ending the abuse? Could they have played their roles differently?
- What, in general, is the responsibility of "third parties", i.e. to individuals not belonging to either side? What is the responsibility of society?
- Which human rights are violated in cases of domestic violence? How does it affect the struggle for gender equality?
- What do you think that young people, youth workers and youth organisations can do to prevent or stop violence in abusive relationships?

Tips for facilitators

This activity needs a particularly safe environment. It is not an activity that can be run with a group that has only recently come together. If your group works together regularly, this is an activity for when they already know and trust you, as facilitator, and each other. If your group has come together for a one-off residential activity, it is suggested that you run this activity only after the group has worked together for a few days. Trust in the facilitator is just as important as trust in each other for the success of this activity.

Make sure that no one disturbs the storytelling: avoid any coming and going at this stage. If you are running this activity after a break, make sure that everyone is back in the room before you start.

It is strongly suggested that before the activity, you explain to the volunteer playing Kati that s/he will be covered fully by several blankets. The volunteer must be claustrophobia-free and ready to experience some physical hardship during the activity. You may also decide that Kati should be played by a co-facilitator. This is advisable if you have not, by this point, had the chance to build a high level of trust and safety in the group.

Some participants may be hesitant about putting the blanket over Kati, or may prefer to put it on Kati's lap rather than over her head. The facilitator and co-facilitator should stay silent during the activity: try to encourage participants to perform the act of covering Kati fully by using eye contact and guidance. Bring into the debriefing stage any hesitations or unwillingness on the part of participants, according to how they have performed the act of covering Kati.

Remember that you cannot necessarily know "who is in the room". Any of the participants may have experienced an abusive relationship, and you should avoid putting any pressure on such people to disclose things they do not want to speak about.

Try to formulate the questions you ask in the debriefing in a non-personal manner, so that even if participants have experience of such matters, they do not feel the need to answer by referring to their experience directly. Be aware that such experiences may be painful for participants to be reminded of, and that as a facilitator it will be your responsibility to deal with the emotional consequences of running the activity in your group. In other words, and in practical terms, if a participant gets upset or starts to cry, you need to be prepared to deal with that both on a one to one basis, and with the whole group. This may be as simple as taking a break, asking the participant if they want to go to their room to freshen up, and telling the rest of the group that the person needed some time out and will speak about it when he/she/they are ready; or it may involve addressing the reasons for the participant getting upset in a discussion with the whole group - with their prior consent, of course.

Variations on this activity exist. You can alter the story to fit the environment you are working in. You could also make 6 to 8 steps rather than 9. Be sure, however, that you have an equal number of story steps for both the first phase and the second phase of the activity (i.e. putting on and taking off blankets). Do not go above eight steps; staying under the blankets is no fun!

Suggestions for follow-up

It is possible to work with variations on this activity by using a different 'story' to illustrate Kati's situation.

Have a look at the activity 'Domestic Affairs' to develop the theme of domestic violence and 'Power Station' to develop the theme of how power and violence are related. Both activities are from *Compass – manual for human rights education with young people*.

Ideas for action

Consider providing information about domestic and relationship violence to your own target group. If you have not been active in the field of gender-based violence before, consult an NGO dealing with these issues for advice on how best to inform your target group about the problem, and support them to understand how they can help themselves or others affected by it. Involve your group in the preparation of the resource materials (e.g. flyers, blog, etc.). Check the Internet or local organisations offering crisis intervention to battered women or other people exposed to ongoing relational violence. Find out what support they give to victims. If possible, invite the representative of such an organisation to explain what they do to help in 'removing Kati's blankets'.

KATI'S STORY

<u>PART I</u>

Kati is 28. She married Jan when she was 20 and he was 23. They have two children, who are 3 and 7 years of age.

When Kati was a child, she often saw her father beating her mother. It happened several times a week. Kati remembers that sometimes her mother had to go to the hospital because of her injuries.

(Pause)

Co-facilitator covers "Kati" with first blanket.

Immediately after they get married, Jan tells Kati that he will take care of the family income, because Kati does not know how to save. He tells her she will get from him only enough money to buy food and household items. He tells her she will have to show him receipts to prove that she spent the money on what she asked the money for and that he approved.

(Pause)

Kati gets pregnant in the first year of their marriage. Jan starts to tell Kati regularly that she does not know how to run a household and that she is very lucky to have him, because nobody else would want her for a wife.

(Pause)

After the birth of their first child, Jan starts to beat Kati. He accuses her of loving the child more than him.

(Pause)

Kati goes to her mother and tells her about being beaten by Jan. Her mother tells her that this is part of marriage and she should learn to put up with it. According to her mother, "a woman has to stick with her husband".

(Pause)

As their first son grows older, Jan threatens and beats him too. Kati is worried, but at the same time she believes that it can be very harmful to children to separate them from their fathers.

(Pause)

Kati tells one of her co-workers that she is regularly beaten by Jan, and that she needs help. Her colleague tells the others at her workplace, and now everybody is talking about her.

(Pause)

Kati is increasingly absent from work without a proper excuse and she is laid off. Now she does not have a job or an income of her own.

(Pause)

PART II

(Question to the person in the middle and to mark the transition from covering to uncovering Kati)

Kati, why do you have to live like this?

(Pause)

Why don't you leave your husband?

(Pause)

Kati reads a story in a magazine about a battered woman who manages to leave an abusive relationship. The article contains the phone numbers of hotlines, shelters, and drop-in centres for abused women. Kati decides that she cannot bear being abused any longer. She called a hotline where she had a long discussion with a woman who told her that she is one of many women experiencing domestic violence.

(Pause)

Co-facilitator removes one blanket

For the first time Kati has an open discussion with her older son about their shared fear of their violent husband and father.

(Pause)

After a few weeks of thinking and planning, Kati calls her sister and asks her whether she could move to her place with her sons for a short period. Her sister had long given up hope that Kati would ever leave her violent husband and now she is very glad to be of help. (Pause)

One afternoon Kati packs up their everyday belongings and moves with her sons to her sister's place.

(Pause)

She starts to look for a job. Her sister helps by asking friends if they know of any opportunities, and they look through the job advertisements together.

(Pause)

Kati visits a lawyer to get information about custody and child visitation issues and advice about how the truth about Jan's violence towards them can be revealed. They also discuss divorce procedures.

(Pause)

Kati finds a job she likes, and moves into a rented apartment with her sons. She visits Child Welfare Services and finds out that her older son can enrol in a support group for children who have fled from violent homes.

(Pause)

Kati finds a self-help group of women who have survived domestic violence. Through sharing and listening she learns to understand how and why her romantic relationship developed into an abusive one. She decides that once she feels she is back on her feet, she will join a group to support battered women herself.

(Pause)

> "If you think you are too small to have an impact, try going to bed with a mosquito in the room."
> *Anita Roddick*

The Knight in Shining Armor

Level 3

10 to 20

60 minutes

Complexity: Level 3

Group size: 10 to 20

Time: 60 minutes

Overview: This short role play introduces the difficulties of recognising abuse and looks at early warning signs to identify potential abusers. It provides a good basis for discussion on how society romanticises relationships which may involve violence and oppression.

Objectives:
- To discuss the boundaries of a safe and equal relationship
- To learn to recognise the early warning signs of an abusive relationship
- To discuss the role of education and / or youth work in helping to prevent violence in intimate relationships

Materials:
- Copies of the story of the Knight in Shining Armor for Susie, the narrator and the knight

Preparation

- Familiarise yourself with the issue of violence in relationships before running this activity. Chapter 1 of this manual, especially the sections dealing with domestic violence and abuse, is particularly helpful for clarifying the differences between various kinds of gender-based violence and for identifying potential human rights concerns.
- Select two participants or a small team to help you with co-facilitating this activity. Brief them in advance about what will happen during the activity. Give each of them a copy of the story of the Knight in Shining Armor. If possible, the person that plays Susie (and is 'courted') should be female. If you do not think that any participant is appropriate for the role, ask a (female) team member to be Susie. The other participant or team member should be the narrator. You (the facilitator) should play the knight.
- Prepare the working area so that all participants can sit in front of the actors, in such way they can observe all the action clearly.

Instructions

1) Explain to participants that they will hear a short story about a knight on a white horse, and that afterwards there will be a discussion of the issues raised and the feelings evoked.

2) The actors move to the middle of the room. You (the facilitator) are the knight. You kneel in front of Susie, or sit next to her, and hold her hand. It is preferable for you to act out the 'courting' scenes by heart, rather than reading, so if possible, try to learn the dialogue in advance. The narrator stands to the side and reads aloud their parts of the story.

3) After the 'courting scene' and story have been completed, look at the faces of participants for reactions or emotions. If they seem a little shocked or upset, ask for a moment of silence for them to reflect on and take note of their feelings.

Debriefing and evaluation

Begin the debriefing by asking the person who played Susie to share her feelings and impressions about the role play. Then continue by asking everyone the following questions:

- How did the story make you feel? Why?
- What do you think about this relationship?
- At which point do you think Susie should have realised that this is a dangerous relationship?
- What are the signals that indicate that this relationship is becoming abusive?
- What can we understand about romantic relationships from this story?
- Where does a genuinely equal relationship end and an abusive one begins?

- From where do we get our ideas about what relationships should be like? How realistic are these ideas or stories?
- Which human rights are violated in cases of domestic violence?
- How do romanticised views of relationships affect young people?
- What can you do to raise awareness of young people about gender equality?

Tips for facilitators

This activity can be very emotional for some participants: it needs to be run in a safe environment. This is not an activity that can be run with a group that has only recently met. If your group has come together for a one-off residential activity, it is suggested that you run this activity only after the group has worked together for a few days. Participants need to be able to trust the facilitator as well as other members of the group.

Bear in mind that you do not necessarily know "who is in the room". Someone may have experienced, or be experiencing, an abusive relationship. You should make sure that no-one feels under any pressure to disclose things that they are not ready to speak about. Try to formulate the questions you ask in the debriefing in a non-personalised manner, so that even if they participants have relevant personal experiences, they do not feel that they have to answer by referring to these experiences directly.

Be aware that such experiences may be painful for participants and that as a facilitator it will be your responsibility to deal with any emotional consequences of running the activity in your group. If a participant gets upset or begins to cry, you need to be prepared to deal with that both on a one to one basis and in the whole group.

Suggestions for follow-up

Run the activity Kati's story" with the same group to develop further the theme of domestic violence and abuse. You could use some of the information in Chapter 1 to provide further information on domestic violence. You could also use chapter 3 in this manual to explore with participants ways of acting against gender-based violence, including domestic violence.

Ideas for action

Participants could get in touch with a local hotline or shelter for women experiencing domestic violence to understand the extent of the problem in their community. You could also arrange a meeting with people working in relevant organisations. Alternatively, participants could conduct research online, or by making enquiries with the police, into existing measures for addressing domestic violence. They could design a resource for young people which explains domestic violence and outlines the support that exists for victims in the local area. If such support services do not exist, participants could design a campaign to for them to be established.

The knight in shining armor

Knight: Wow Susie! You are so beautiful! I love your style so much! You are such an individual, and I love that about you…!

Narrator: Susie is very happy and feels attracted to the knight

Knight: I've never felt so close to anyone. You are the only one I trust, the only one I can share my problems with, the only one who understands me. It is so good to be with you. I love you so much…

Narrator: Susie feels that she is very important to the man. She feels safe.

Knight: I feel I have found my other half. We have been created for each other. We don't need anybody else, do we?

Narrator: And Susie indeed feels that the Knight is her whole world. Every minute they spend away from each other is is painful.

Knight: You are so beautiful, so pretty. But don't you think that your skirt is a bit daring? I'm worried about you: I think you should wear something else. That would make me feel better. We belong together, don't we? You are mine.

Narrator: And because Susie loves him and would not want to argue about such an insignificant thing, she changes the way she dresses to suit his wishes.

Knight: You spend too much time with your girlfriends. We have such a great time together: am I not enough for you? I don't think you should put so much trust in them. I think they have a bad influence on you: I don't like the way you talk about them and the things you do together. I don't like the way you talk to me when you come back from being with them.

Narrator: And because Susie wants to be nice to him, she begins to see less and less of her friends. Soon they have been left behind altogether.

Knight: I do like your parents, but why do we have to see them every Sunday? I'd like to spend more time with you alone. Anyway, they do not seem to like me. All they do is criticise me. I'm not even allowed to relax on Sundays! They can't wait for us to break up. I wish you didn't want to spend so much time with them.

Narrator: Susie is worried about their relationship. She does not want to threaten it, so she spends less time with her family. Now there is peace… Or is there?

> "You can chain me, you can torture me, you can even destroy this body, but you will never imprison my mind."
>
> *Mahatma Gandhi*

N vs Sweden

Level 4

Any

190 minutes

Complexity: Level 4

Group size: Any

Time: 190 minutes

Overview: This simulation activity looks at issues surrounding women seeking asylum, using a case brought to the European Court of Human Rights.

Objectives:
- To reflect on the issues facing women seeking asylum
- To develop critical thinking skills, logical argumentation, and a sense of justice
- To develop an understanding of the role of the European Court of Human Rights

Materials:
- Copies of the case
- Copies of role cards
- Additional information for the facilitator

Preparation: Prepare the role cards, making sure that you have enough copies for participants.

Ensure that there are separate spaces for the 3 groups to work at the preparation stage, and a plenary room where the court hearing can take place.

Instructions

1) Tell the group that the session will be devoted to a case which came before the European Court of Human Rights. Ask participants what they know about the Court and the European Convention of Human Rights.

2) Inform them that the case deals with the rejection of an asylum claim made by an Afghan woman to the Swedish government. Depending on the group, you may need to clarify some of the terminology relating to migration (e.g. asylum seeker, migrant, refugee).

3) Hand out copies of the case for participants to read individually. Give them about 10 minutes to read this in silence.

4) Tell participants that the question they are to consider in the trial is: "Would deporting N. be a violation of article 3?". Make sure that everyone understands this question, in broad terms.

5) Divide the participants into 4 groups:

   Group 1 represents N.

   Group 2 represents the Swedish Government

   Group 3 represents the European Court of Human Rights

   Group 4 represents experts from UNHCR

   Give each group the appropriate role card and explain that they have 30 minutes to clarify their positions. Groups 1 and 2 should prepare their arguments to put to the court, while Group 3 should prepare questions for both sides. Group 4 needs to be ready to present information about conditions facing Afghani women claiming asylum, without taking sides in this particular case.

6) After 30 minutes, invite the participants for the Court hearing.

   The Court hearing is presided over by the judges and should last 30 minutes. Groups 1, 2, and 4 each have 5 minutes to present their main arguments. After the main arguments have been presented the judges should put questions to the different parties.

7) Each of the judges should then come to an individual decision. Allow them about 5 minutes for reflection. Bring the group back together and ask the judges to present their individual decisions and the arguments.

8) Inform the participants about the real decision of the European Court and the reasoning behind it. Ask for their reactions and then proceed to the debriefing and evaluation.

The verdict:

The Court had to establish whether the applicant's personal situation was such that her return to Afghanistan would contravene Article 3. (…) The court found that as the applicant had resided in Sweden since 2004, she might be perceived as not conforming to the gender roles ascribed to her by Afghan society. Moreover, she had attempted to divorce her husband and had demonstrated a real and genuine intention of not living with him. However, if the spouses were deported to Afghanistan, separately or together, the applicant's husband might decide to resume their married life together against her wish. The new Shiite Personal Status Law required women to comply with their husbands' sexual requests and to obtain permission to leave the home, except in emergencies. (…) The Court could not ignore the general risk indicated by statistics and international reports. As regards the applicant's extramarital relationship, she had failed to submit any relevant and detailed information to the Swedish authorities and she has not even tried to explain why she failed to do so. Nevertheless, should her husband perceive the applicant's filing for divorce or other actions as an indication of an extramarital relationship, adultery was a crime under the Afghan Penal Code. Should the applicant succeed in living separated from her husband in Afghanistan, women without male support and protection faced limitations on conducting a normal social life, including the limitations on their freedom of movement, and lacked the means of survival, which prompted many to return to abusive family situations. (…) There were no strong reasons to question the veracity of the applicant's statement that she had had no contact with her family for almost five years and therefore no longer had a social network or adequate protection in Afghanistan. In the special circumstances of the present case, there were substantial grounds for believing that if deported to Afghanistan, the applicant would face various cumulative risks of reprisals from her husband, his family, her own family and from the Afghan society which fell under Article 3[1].

Accordingly, the Court found that the implementation of the deportation order against the applicant would give rise to a violation of Article 3 of the Convention.

Debriefing and evaluation

You can use this activity to support participants understand more about the concerns of women seeking asylum and the gender issues relating to migration. The activity can also be used to raise awareness of the work of the European Court of Human Rights. Depending on your focus and the composition of your group, use some of the questions below to run the debriefing.

- Did you find the issues raised by this case easy to resolve? If not, which ones were most difficult for you?
- Did you find your role difficult to play? If so, what was difficult?
- Do you think the judges made the right decision?

- *Ask the judges*: What were the important factors for you in making the decision?
- *Ask everyone*: In the real case, the European Court felt that there was a risk of Article 3 being violated. How did they justify this decision?
- What are the aspects of this case which are specific to women?
- Why it is important to adopt a gender perspective on migration issues?
- N.'s credibility and consistency was questioned during the trial. How do you explain this, and was it fair?
- Have you heard of this case before? Are you aware of anything like this in your country?
- This case presents the risks faced by N. in the event of deportation back to Afghanistan. Which other risks do asylum seeking women face - both while fleeing, and in the 'host' countries?
- Does your country respect international standards with respect to protection of asylum seekers and refugees?
- What is the general attitude of people in your country towards asylum seekers? Does the attitude differ towards female asylum seekers?
- What kind of support is available to asylum seekers/refugees/migrants in your community?
- Certain rights, such as the freedom from torture, cannot be restricted or limited. Why do you think this is the case?
- Why do we need the European Court of Human Rights? Who can take a case before the Court?

Tips for facilitator

You could adapt the simulation in various ways. Instead of having a big trial, you could set up mini-courts, each with its own mini-trial. You would ideally have equal number of members in each group.

You should encourage participants to use their time in working groups to clarify the case and to prepare opening statements, or to prepare questions for all sides, in the case of the judges.

You could use this activity to further explore the connection between gender and migration. Refer to the ECHR database to find court cases brought against your country (*http://hudoc.echr.coe.int*). Make sure you have prepared yourself beforehand on the role and functioning of the court, and on issues surrounding women refugees or asylum seekers.

Be aware that the activity may stir up islamophobic views or beliefs about cultural superiority. These often arise when discussing women of Muslim faith. Ensure that judgements about the particular situation in Afghanistan do not lead participants to make generalisations about how women are treated or viewed by the Islamic faith.

Suggestions for follow-up

You could follow up this activity in various ways:

Explore the issue of women in armed conflict by engaging participants in research and discussion. This is one of the main areas of action identified by the Beijing Declaration and Platform for Action. (*http://beijing20.unwomen.org/en/in-focus/armed-conflict*).

The activities "3 things" and "Can I come in?" from *Compass* also address issues concerning refugees.

You could explore further the position of women of Muslim faith in your country/ community, including the challenges they face.

In *Bookmarks*, you can find further ideas and activities that look at hate speech against refugees and migrants, such as "The stories they tell".

Ideas for action

Participants could research cases brought against their country at the European Court of Human Rights and/or the current stance of their government with respect to asylum seekers and refugees. The HUDOC database provides access to the case-law of the Court (hudoc.echr.coe.int/). Participants could also investigate the support services available to asylum seeking women and LGBT+ persons.

Organise a Living Library together with participants and invite refugees and immigrants as books. The Living Library works in the same way as a normal library, but instead of books there are people. It aims to break down prejudices, by allowing members of the public who may have a preconceived idea about individuals from particular communities to meet and talk and listen. The Council of Europe publication "Don't judge the book by its cover"[2] offers helpful advice for setting up a living library project.

The manual *We Can! Taking Action against Hate Speech through Counter and Alternative Narratives* provides ideas on how to take action online and offline to challenge hate speech against refugees in the media, and how to promote respect for their human rights.

1. Source: European Court of Human Rights / Information Note no. 132 – July 2010
2. *https://rm.coe.int/16807023dd*

N. Vs Sweden

This case came before the European Court of Human Rights. It concerns N., a woman born in Afghanistan and living in Fagersta, Sweden.

13 August 2004 – N. and her husband, X., arrive in Sweden, illegally helped by a smuggler.

16 August 2004 – N. and X. apply for asylum and residence permits. They state they have been persecuted since 1996 because of X.'s involvement in the Communist party. This had also led to his arrest on 2 occasions, and to the couple's relocation to Kabul. X claims poor health: sleepiness, anxiety and aggressive behaviour. N. claims that her political stance was well known in Afghanistan, as she was a teacher for women: this was not accepted by the leading elite in Kabul.

29 March 2005 - the Migration Board rejects the couple's application. It argues that the situation in Kabul is better than in other parts of the country and questions the claim that the couple's lives will be in danger if they return to Afghanistan. The Migration Board rules that the information provided is too vague, and that poor mental health is not grounds for asylum.

2005 - The couple appeals the decision. In addition to the claims above, N. also informs the court that she has separated from her husband, lives alone and intends to pursue a divorce, even if X opposes it. This puts her at risk of serious persecution in Afghanistan as she would be considered to have brought dishonour both on X and on her family. She believes that X's family will seek revenge and that at best, she will become a social outcast. She also claims that she was not able to obtain a divorce in Afghanistan, pointing that the punishment for adultery in Afghanistan would be death by stoning.

19 March 2007 - The appeal is rejected. The court rules that X has failed to demonstrate that he would be of interest to the resistance groups in Afghanistan. With respect to N., the court points out that the former ban on education of women has now been replaced by a policy of affirmative action, and that a considerable time has passed since N. was involved in women's education. With respect to her private life, the court remarks that N. was not formally divorced, and according to her statement, she had not had an extra marital affair - so she would not be in danger of being punished for adultery. The court also notes that N. has not demonstrated that her family has rejected her, so she does have a network in Afghanistan.

4 September 2007 – N. appeals again, receives a refusal, which makes the decision final and the deportation orders enforceable.

27 October 2007, 28 January 2008 – N. invokes new circumstances and twice applies for a residence permit. She is refused.

February 2008 – she petitions the Court in Sweden for a divorce from X and intends to invoke the divorce as grounds to stop her deportation. X informs the court that he opposes the divorce.

19 November 2008 - The Court rejects the petition, claiming it has not competence, because the couple are not legal residents in Sweden.

17 October 2008 – N. requests a review of the asylum claim, and a stop to the deportation. She points to a worsening of the situation in Kabul, and a well-founded fear of persecution, as she has since started a relationship with a Swedish man and therefore risks the death penalty in Afghanistan. She claims to have had no contact with her family since 2005. The re-evaluation is rejected.

17 February 2009 – All attempts to appeal this decision are rejected and the case is transferred to the police for enforcement of deportation.

28 April 2009 – N. brings the case to the European Court of Human Rights (ECHR). To the information presented above, she adds a letter from a Swedish man that confirms that they have been in a relationship since 2008 and have been living together in his apartment since April 2009. The Government declares that this information was not presented before by N., even though it might have been relevant to her asylum claim. The Government also says that N.'s mail address has not been changed to the man's apartment . The European Court notifies the government that is not advisable to enforce the deportation orders while the trial is ongoing.

 N vs Sweden

Role card for Judges

Your role is to decide whether the deportation of N. to Afghanistan would constitute a violation of Article 3. You are also responsible for presiding over the Court hearing. You need to ensure that each party presents their main arguments in no more than 5 minutes, and you need to prepare questions for each of the parties involved. The questions should be designed to give you the information that you need to make the decision. At the end of the hearing, each of the members of your group should present their decision and the arguments supporting it.

Information on conditions facing women in Afghanistan

From UNHCR Eligibility Guidelines for Assessing the International Protection Needs of Afghan Asylum-Seekers (July 2009)

In view of the serious and widespread human rights violations and ongoing armed conflict in many parts of the country, the UNHCR considers that a significant number of Afghan asylum seekers are in need of international protection. Applications by Afghan asylum-seekers should be determined on an individual basis, according to fair and efficient refugee status determination procedures, including the right of appeal. Favourable consideration should be given to the specific groups identified in these Guidelines, including, but not limited to (i) persons perceived as contravening Sharia law and members of minority religious groups; (ii) ethnic minority groups; (iii) persons associated with or perceived as supporting the Government, including civil society members; (iv) actual or perceived supporters of armed anti-Government groups; (v) journalists; (vi) persons associated with the People's Democratic Party of Afghanistan or other left-aligned political parties; (vii) women; (viii) children; and (ix) persons at risk of becoming victims of blood feuds.

Women are at particular risk of ill-treatment if perceived as not conforming to the gender roles ascribed to them by society, tradition and even the legal system. Ill-treatment occurs in a variety of forms and may be inflicted by several actors, including family members. Such treatment includes domestic violence, excessive custodial sentences and degrading and inhuman treatment. The Shiite Personal Status Law (2009) requires women to comply with their husbands' sexual requests, and to obtain permission to leave the home, except in emergencies. The code has yet to be implemented and is currently under review as a result of international pressure.

Cases of physical violence perpetrated against women and girls in Afghanistan have increased by about 40% in the period from March 2007 to March 2008. Existing figures indicate that currently up to 80% of Afghan women are affected by domestic violence.

Afghan women, who have adopted a less culturally conservative lifestyle, such as those returning from exile in Iran or Europe, continue to be perceived as transgressing entrenched social and religious norms and may, as a result, be subjected to domestic violence and other forms of punishment ranging from isolation and stigmatization to honour crimes for those accused of bringing shame to their families, communities or tribes.

Unaccompanied women or women lacking a male "tutor" (mahram) continued to face limitations on conducting a normal social life. They include divorced women, unmarried women who are not virgins, and women whose engagements to be married have been broken. Unless they marry, which is very difficult given the social stigma associated with these women, social rejection and discrimination continue to be the norm. Many Afghan women are prevented from leaving the family compound without a burqa and a male companion, who has to be a husband or a close relative. Women without male support and protection generally lack the means of survival, given the social restrictions on women living alone, including the limitations on their freedom of movement. Unable to live independently, they face years of quasi-detention, prompting many to return to abusive family situations. The results of such "reconciliation" are generally not monitored and abuse or honour crimes committed upon return are often done with impunity. Furthermore, women's rights activists face threats and intimidation, particularly if outspoken about women's rights, the role of Islam or the behaviour of commanders.

European Convention on Human Rights

Article 3 - Prohibition of torture
No one shall be subjected to torture or to inhuman or degrading treatment or punishment.

Role card for N.

You have 30 minutes to discuss the case and prepare your opening statement, which needs to prove that the deportation of N. to Afghanistan would result into a violation of article 3.

N.'s claim is that:

She faces a real risk of being persecuted or even sentenced to death as she has been separated from her husband and is now involved with another man

She risks being subjected to inhuman and degrading treatment as her family has disowned her, and she has no social network or male protection in Afghanistan

She believes that both her family and her husband's family will have been informed about her attempt to divorce her husband

She is not able to divorce her husband in Afghanistan as she needs two witnesses to support her claim. Even so, she is still at risk of inhumane and degrading treatment.

European Convention on Human Rights

Article 3 - Prohibition of torture
No one shall be subjected to torture or to inhuman or degrading treatment or punishment.

Role card for the Swedish Government

You have 30 minutes to discuss the case and to prepare your opening statement, which needs to prove that the deportation of N. to Afghanistan would not result into a violation of article 3.

You are claiming that:

While international reports confirm the very difficult conditions for women in Afghanistan, the situation in Kabul is slightly better, compared to the rest of the country.

The applicant did not provide sufficient proof that she is at real and concrete risk of being subjected to ill treatment, either by the government and/or at the hands of private individuals.

N.'s general credibility is in question, as her story was vague and lacked detail, particularly with respect to her extramarital affair. There is no indication that this affair is known to the Afghan authorities, or to her and her husband's family.

Legallyl, she is still married, and there is no indication that the Afghan authorities or the families are aware of her attempt to get a divorce in Sweden. It is still possible, under certain circumstances (e.g. if her husband is ill and that it endangered the wife) for her to divorce in Afghanistan.

European Convention on Human Rights

Article 3 - Prohibition of torture
No one shall be subjected to torture or to inhuman or degrading treatment or punishment.

Role card for UNHCR Experts

You represent the UN Refugee Agency and your role is to provide the judges with an expert opinion on conditions facing asylum seekers from Afghanistan, particularly women. You have 30 minutes to prepare a 5 minutes input on the main points relevant to the case. You should not take the side of either of the parties but should be ready to provide an objective and expert opinion for the court.

The UNHCR is mandated to lead and co-ordinate international action to protect refugees and resolve refugee problems worldwide. Its primary purpose is to safeguard the rights and well-being of refugees. It aims to ensure that everyone can exercise the right to seek asylum and find safe refuge in another state, with the option of returning home voluntarily, integrating locally, or resettling in a third country.

Additional information

From the *UNHCR Eligibility Guidelines for Assessing the International Protection Needs of Afghan Asylum-Seekers* (July 2009)

In view of the serious and widespread human rights violations and ongoing armed conflict in many parts of the country, UNHCR considers that a significant number of Afghan asylum seekers are in need of international protection. Applications by Afghan asylum-seekers should be determined on an individual basis, according to fair and efficient refugee status determination procedures, including the right of appeal. Favourable consideration should be given to the specific groups identified in these Guidelines, including, but not limited to (i) persons perceived as contravening Sharia law and members of minority religious groups; (ii) ethnic minority groups; (iii) persons associated with or perceived as supporting the Government, including civil society members; (iv) actual or perceived supporters of armed anti-Government groups; (v) journalists; (vi) persons associated with the People's Democratic Party of Afghanistan or other left-aligned political parties; (vii) women; (viii) children; and (ix) persons at risk of becoming victims of blood feuds.

Women are at particular risk of ill-treatment if perceived as not conforming to the gender roles ascribed to them by society, tradition and even the legal system. Ill-treatment occurs in a variety of forms and may be inflicted by several actors, including family members. Such treatment includes domestic violence, excessive custodial sentences and degrading and inhuman treatment. The Shiite Personal Status Law (2009) requires women to comply with their husbands' sexual requests, and to obtain permission to leave the home, except in emergencies. The code has yet to be implemented and is currently under review as a result of international pressure.

Cases of physical violence perpetrated against women and girls in Afghanistan have increased by about 40% in the period from March 2007 to March 2008. Existing figures indicate that currently up to 80% of Afghan women are affected by domestic violence.

Afghan women, who have adopted a less culturally conservative lifestyle, such as those returning from exile in Iran or Europe, continue to be perceived as transgressing entrenched social and religious norms and may, as a result, be subjected to domestic violence and other forms of punishment ranging from isolation and stigmatization to honour crimes for those accused of bringing shame to their families, communities or tribes.

Unaccompanied women or women lacking a male "tutor" (mahram) continued to face limitations on conducting a normal social life. They include divorced women, unmarried women who are not virgins, and women whose engagements to be married have been broken. Unless they marry, which is very difficult given the social stigma associated with these women, social rejection and discrimination continue to be the norm. Many Afghan women are prevented from leaving the family compound without a burqa and a male companion, who has to be a husband or a close relative. Women without male support and protection generally lack the means of survival, given the social restrictions on women living alone, including the limitations on their freedom of movement. Unable to live independently, they face years of quasi-detention, prompting many to return to abusive family situations. The results of such "reconciliation" are generally not monitored and abuse or honour crimes committed upon return are often done with impunity. Furthermore, women's rights activists face threats and intimidation, particularly if outspoken about women's rights, the role of Islam or the behaviour of commanders.

European Convention on Human Rights

Article 3 - Prohibition of torture
No one shall be subjected to torture or to inhuman or degrading treatment or punishment.

> "In order to carry a positive action, we must develop here a positive vision"
>
> *Dalai Lama*

No Violence Here

Level 4

10 to 30

120 minutes

Complexity: Level 4

Group size: 10 to 30

Time: 120 minutes

Overview: This is a simulation activity, in which participants devise a policy on preventing and acting against gender-based violence in their school.

Objectives:
- To understand that gender-based violence is a human rights violation
- To explore the concept of restorative justice as a means of addressing cases of gender-based violence
- To develop discussion skills and the ability to draw up policy statements

Materials:
- Role cards for each group and the card describing the concept of restorative justice

Preparation:
- Make sure you have enough space for four groups to work separately.
- Prepare a flipchart or a slide with a definition of gender-based violence. You can use the definition of gender-based violence from Chapter 1.
- Make copies of the handouts: the story and role cards for each group; restorative justice cards for 3 of the 4 groups

Instructions

1) Ask participants what they understand by gender-based violence. Collect a few answers from the group and if necessary, show them the definition on flip-chart paper or a slide, allowing some time for questions or clarifications. You will find the definition in Chapter 1.

2) Tell participants that the activity will involve a simulation. They will need to imagine that they are members of a school community, in which there have been several cases of gender-based violence. They should listen to the story first, and then in groups, will make decisions about how to address gender-based violence at school. Start reading the story, which you can find in the end of this activity

   Once the story has been read out, show participants the timeline of the activity:

   · Preparation – 30 minutes (with a possibility for groups to consult experts after 15 minutes)
   · Meeting of the school community – 40 minutes (by the end of which, policy guidelines will have been drawn up)
   · Debriefing and evaluation: 50 minutes

3) Explain that the results of the small group work do not have to be in final written form. Groups can just make a list of points of items that need to be included in the school policy against gender-based violence.

4) Split the group into 4 smaller groups and assign roles to them: students, teachers (incl. school management), parents, and independent experts. The group of experts can be smaller than the other groups.

   Give each group a role card and allocate a space for each one to work. The card explaining the concept of restorative justice should be given to all groups except the group of parents. After 15 minutes, announce that from this time on, the groups are able to consult the experts.

5) After 30 minutes of group work, call participants back into plenary and start the meeting. The meeting should be run by the experts and should include:

   • Welcome address, outlining the aim of the meeting
   • Short presentations from each of the other groups (students, teachers and parents) – 3 minutes each
   • Question and answer session: 10 minutes
   • Open discussion: 15 minutes (optional)
   • Discussion and finalising guidelines: what should be in the guidelines (list all items on the flipchart)
   • Closure of the meeting

6) Take participants out of role. You could do this by asking participants to stand with their eyes closed and telling them that they are leaving the school now

and coming back to this room and tactivity. Move to the debriefing and evaluation, using some of the questions below.

Debriefing and evaluation

As the activity may have been very emotional for some participants, start by inviting them to share their emotions, and then continue with the more detailed questions on what participants have learnt, and what can be done in cases of violence occurring. Use some of the following guiding questions:

- How did you feel during the activity? Did these emotions change during the activity?
- What was the most difficult part of the activity? Why? Which difficulties did you encounter in the preparation phase, and then during the meeting?
- Does gender-based violence happen at school or in your organisation/youth club? How is it normally dealt with?
- How does gender-based violence affect people who suffer from it personally? How does it affect a whole school community or a youth organisation?
- Have you heard of the concept of restorative justice before? Do you think it could be useful when addressing certain cases of gender-based violence? Explain your answer.
- Do you think it makes sense to introduce policies about gender-based violence or violence in general in places where young people are (school, youth club, etc.)? What should such policies include? Does your school or organisation have such a policy?
- How does gender-based violence affect gender equality? Which human rights are likely to be violated in cases of gender-based violence?
- Do we have a personal responsibility to address cases of gender-based violence? What is this responsibility?

Tips for facilitators

The activity may be difficult for some groups, especially groups that have never seen policy guidelines before. You could start by asking participants if they are familiar with their school rules, as an example of policy document.

The case described in the activity takes place in a school, but you could adapt it to a youth club or organisation context.

The simulation may provoke disputes and may also lead to potential conflict. Tell the 'experts' that you are there to support them: if conflicts arise during the discussions, be prepared to step in to help in resolving them.

Suggestions for follow-up

Working through this activity with participants may enable you to introduce them to human rights instruments, such as the Council of Europe Istanbul Convention or the Council of Europe Convention on the Protection of Children against Sexual Exploitation and Sexual Abuse (Lanzarote Convention), or the Committee of Ministers' Recommendation CM/Rec (2010)5 to member states on measures to combat discrimination on grounds of sexual orientation or gender identity. You can find information on all these documents in Chapter 1, and there are abbreviated versions in the Appendices.

If you think the topic of safety of LGBT+ people is an important issue to be explored further, try running the activity "Spaces and Places".

Ideas for action

If participants feel that their group or institution – e.g. their school or youth club/ organisation - needs a policy about gender-based violence, you could work with them on developing a proposal for how to ensure that one is adopted. Participants could start by developing a lesson plan on gender-based violence and organise an awareness-raising workshop with their peers.

The story

You are members of a school community. Several cases of gender-based violence have occurred in recent weeks, for example sexist comments on the school Facebook page, people making jokes about a student who identifies as transgender, and a girl who was beaten by her boyfriend. You all want to make sure that there is no place for gender-based violence in your school. For that reason, the school management,, in response to claims by a number of students, has decided to draw up a policy against gender-based violence in the school. To begin with, you will work in separate groups:

- students nominated by the school community
- teachers, including school management
- parents.

There will also be a group of independent experts to support you in devising such a policy. The task of each group will be to develop a short statement (about 3-5 points) outlining the most important things to be included in a policy against gender-based violence. Each group should also write a short paragraph (or series of bullet points) on how occurrences of gender-based violence should be addressed. You will have about 30 minutes to do this, and after 15 minutes, you will be given the chance to consult with some 'independent experts'. The experts will invite each group for a meeting, and the group will have 3 minutes to present the outcomes of their work and discuss their recommendations with the experts.

Role card: Parents

You are a group of parents at a school where there have been instances of gender-based violence. The school has decided to devise a policy against such violence, and you are in favour of such a move.

Your group's priorities are:

- The safety of your children is of the utmost importance
- The school should pay greater attention to respect for civic and family values among students
- You would like to have more influence on the teaching of so called 'controversial issues', such as LGBT

Prepare a short statement (about 3-5 points) outlining what you stand for and what you regard as the important things to be included in the policy against gender-based violence. Then write a short paragraph (or bullet points) on how occurrences of gender-based violence should be addressed.

You will have about 30 minutes for this task in your group. Half way through, after 15 minutes, you will be given the chance to consult with experts. You can use this to refine the points you wish to raise during the school meeting.

At the meeting, you will have 3 minutes to present your ideas and then discuss them with others. The meeting will be facilitated by a group of independent experts who will help to finalise the policy.

Meeting schedule

- Welcome address and aims of the meeting
- Short presentations from each group (students, teachers and parents) – 3 minutes each
- Question and answer session: about 10 minutes
- Open discussion: 15 minutes (optional)
- Agreement on the policy guidelines for the policy paper: what should be included (list all items on the flipchart)
- Closure of the meeting

The story

You are members of a school community. Several cases of gender-based violence have occurred in recent weeks, for example sexist comments on the school Facebook page, people making jokes about a student who identifies as transgender, and a girl who was beaten by her boyfriend. You all want to make sure that there is no place for gender-based violence in your school. For that reason, the school management,, in response to claims by a number of students, has decided to draw up a policy against gender-based violence in the school. To begin with, you will work in separate groups:

- students nominated by the school community
- teachers, including school management
- parents.

There will also be a group of independent experts to support you in devising such a policy. The task of each group will be to develop a short statement (about 3-5 points) outlining the most important things to be included in a policy against gender-based violence. Each group should also write a short paragraph (or series of bullet points) on how occurrences of gender-based violence should be addressed. You will have about 30 minutes to do this, and after 15 minutes, you will be given the chance to consult with some 'independent experts'. The experts will invite each group for a meeting, and the group will have 3 minutes to present the outcomes of their work and discuss their recommendations with the experts.

Role card: student representatives

You are a group of students who were nominated by the school community to help to devise a school policy against gender-based violence.

Your group's priorities:

- You are in favour of full gender expression: everyone has the right to be who they want, and this decision should be fully respected.
- LGBT+ people should be protected, and facilities should be created for transgender people, including gender-neutral toilets
- The values you would like to promote are: non-violence, non-discrimination, tolerance, equality
- You want to make sure everyone feels safe at school, regardless of their gender identity or sexual orientation

Prepare a short statement (about 3-5 points) outlining what you stand for and what you regard as the most important things to be included in the final policy against gender-based violence .

Then write a short paragraph (or bullet points) on how instances of gender-based violence should be addressed. You are in favour of restorative justice approach. You can read about this in the separate handout.

You will have about 30 minutes in total in your small group for this task. Half way through, after 15 minutes, you will be given the chance to consult with experts. You can use this to refine the points you wish to raise during the school meeting.

At the meeting, your group will have 3 minutes to present your ideas, and you can then discuss them with others. The meeting will be facilitated by the group of independent experts, who will help to finalise the policy.

Meeting schedule

- Welcome address and aims of the meeting
- Short presentations from each group (students, teachers and parents) – 3 minutes each
- Question and answer session: about 10 minutes
- Open discussion: 15 minutes (optional)
- Agreement on the policy guidelines for the policy paper: what should be included (list all items on the flipchart)
- Closure of the meeting

Restorative justice

Restorative justice can be used in all instances where something happens which causes harm to people, relationships, or the community.

The concept is based on 3 ideas:

- repair: violence causes harm, and restorative justice demands that the harm is repaired;
- encounter: the best way to determine how to repair the harm is to have the parties decide together; and
- transformation: repair can cause fundamental changes in people, relationships and communities.

Restorative justice is a way of dealing with cases of disruption or violence by addressing not just the wrongdoing, but also the damage caused. It maintains that the best way to do this is for all people concerned to meet and discuss the problem and to propose solutions. At such meetings:

- All parties are included (victims, perpetrators, and other people affected). The meeting should be facilitated by an impartial outsider
- Addressing the damage caused is an important part of any resolution.
- The resolution must be agreed upon by all parties at the meeting

In practice, such a process can look like this:

There is a group of people nominated by the school community that facilitates a meeting, at which both victim and perpetrator are present. Each side presents what happened and how they understand it. The victim can suggest how they believe justice can be restored, which might involve making demands on the perpetrator to repair the situation. Such a proposal can also come from the facilitator, but the victim has to be in agreement. The perpetrator then needs to agree to the measures proposed to repair the harm. The process of restoring justice is supervised by the facilitators or people nominated by the facilitators.

Restorative justice cannot be used in all instances of gender-based violence. Many types of gender-based violence constitute a crime and should be reported immediately to the law enforcement authorities, which should take legal action (which may involve restorative measures).

Based on: *http://restorativejustice.org/restorative-justice/about-restorative-justice/tutorial-intro-to-restorative-justice/lesson-1-what-is-restorative-justice/#sthash.wd1Bsy9t.dpbs*

The story

You are members of a school community. Several cases of gender-based violence have occurred in recent weeks, for example sexist comments on the school Facebook page, people making jokes about a student who identifies as transgender, and a girl who was beaten by her boyfriend. You all want to make sure that there is no place for gender-based violence in your school. For that reason, the school management,, in response to claims by a number of students, has decided to draw up a policy against gender-based violence in the school. To begin with, you will work in separate groups:

- students nominated by the school community
- teachers, including school management
- parents.

There will also be a group of independent experts to support you in devising such a policy. The task of each group will be to develop a short statement (about 3-5 points) outlining the most important things to be included in a policy against gender-based violence. Each group should also write a short paragraph (or series of bullet points) on how occurrences of gender-based violence should be addressed. You will have about 30 minutes to do this, and after 15 minutes, you will be given the chance to consult with some 'independent experts'. The experts will invite each group for a meeting, and the group will have 3 minutes to present the outcomes of their work and discuss their recommendations with the experts.

Role card: Teachers
(including school management)

You are a group of teachers and representatives of school management who have been selected by the school community to draw up a school policy against gender-based violence.

Your group's priorities:

- Student safety is of the utmost importance for you. The school should be free from violence, and students should feel that they are properly protected against violence, including knowing that measures will be taken when gender-based violence occurs.
- The school needs to put more effort into prevention of gender-based violence
- The values you would like to promote are: non-violence, non-discrimination, tolerance, equality

Prepare a short statement (about 3-5 points) outlining what you stand for and what you regard as the most important things to be included in the policy against gender-based violence .

Then write a short paragraph (or bullet points) on how instances of gender-based violence should be addressed. You are aware of the concept of restorative justice, but you are not sure if this is an appropriate response in cases of gender-based violence. You should discuss other ideas for tackling incidents of gender-based violence at school.

You will have about 30 minutes in total in your small group for this task. Half way through, after 15 minutes, you will be given the chance to consult with experts. You can use this to refine the points you wish to raise during the school meeting.

At the meeting, your group will have 3 minutes to present your ideas and you can then discuss them with others. The meeting will be facilitated by the group of independent experts who will help to finalise the policy.

Meeting schedule

- Welcome address and aims of the meeting
- Short presentations from each group (students, teachers and parents) – 3 minutes each
- Question and answer session: about 10 minutes
- Open discussion: 15 minutes (optional)
- Agreement on the policy guidelines for the policy paper: what should be included (list all items on the flipchart)
- Closure of the meeting

Restorative justice

Restorative justice can be used in all instances where something happens which causes harm to people, relationships, or the community.

The concept is based on 3 ideas:

- repair: violence causes harm, and restorative justice demands that the harm is repaired;
- encounter: the best way to determine how to repair the harm is to have the parties decide together; and
- transformation: repair can cause fundamental changes in people, relationships and communities.

Restorative justice is a way of dealing with cases of disruption or violence by addressing not just the wrongdoing, but also the damage caused. It maintains that the best way to do this is for all people concerned to meet and discuss the problem and to propose solutions. At such meetings:

- All parties are included (victims, perpetrators, and other people affected). The meeting should be facilitated by an impartial outsider
- Addressing the damage caused is an important part of any resolution.
- The resolution must be agreed upon by all parties at the meeting

In practice, such a process can look like this:

There is a group of people nominated by the school community that facilitates a meeting, at which both victim and perpetrator are present. Each side presents what happened and how they understand it. The victim can suggest how they believe justice can be restored, which might involve making demands on the perpetrator to repair the situation. Such a proposal can also come from the facilitator, but the victim has to be in agreement. The perpetrator then needs to agree to the measures proposed to repair the harm. The process of restoring justice is supervised by the facilitators or people nominated by the facilitators.

Restorative justice cannot be used in all instances of gender-based violence. Many types of gender-based violence constitute a crime and should be reported immediately to the law enforcement authorities, which should take legal action (which may involve restorative measures).

Based on: *http://restorativejustice.org/restorative-justice/about-restorative-justice/tutorial-intro-to-restorative-justice/lesson-1-what-is-restorative-justice/#sthash.wd1Bsy9t.dpbs*

The story

You are members of a school community. Several cases of gender-based violence have occurred in recent weeks, for example sexist comments on the school Facebook page, people making jokes about a student who identifies as transgender, and a girl who was beaten by her boyfriend. You all want to make sure that there is no place for gender-based violence in your school. For that reason, the school management,, in response to claims by a number of students, has decided to draw up a policy against gender-based violence in the school. To begin with, you will work in separate groups:

- students nominated by the school community
- teachers, including school management
- parents.

There will also be a group of independent experts to support you in devising such a policy. The task of each group will be to develop a short statement (about 3-5 points) outlining the most important things to be included in a policy against gender-based violence. Each group should also write a short paragraph (or series of bullet points) on how occurrences of gender-based violence should be addressed. You will have about 30 minutes to do this, and after 15 minutes, you will be given the chance to consult with some 'independent experts'. The experts will invite each group for a meeting, and the group will have 3 minutes to present the outcomes of their work and discuss their recommendations with the experts.

Role card: Experts

You are the group of experts which was invited to help the school draw up a policy against gender-based violence. Your task is to support the students, teachers and parents in drafting the policy and help them make sure it is as inclusive as possible.

You should make sure the policy includes:

- Measures to ensure the safety of all students, including LGBT+ people
- The promotion of such values as: non-violence, non-discrimination, tolerance, equality
- Provision for education on gender-based violence (prevention)
- Measures to be taken in case gender-based violence occurs (you are in favour of a restorative justice approach. You can read about it in the accompanying paper)

You will have about 15 minutes to discuss how you are going to support the groups. After this time, the groups may call you and ask for guidance.

After the preparation phase, you will facilitate the meeting with teachers, students and parents, which should result in the final policy guidelines for the policy statement, including the measures to be taken when gender-based violence occurs. You do not have to finalise the paper during the meeting.

Meeting schedule

- Welcome address and aims of the meeting
- Short presentations from each group (students, teachers and parents) – 3 minutes each
- Question and answer session: about 10 minutes
- Open discussion: 15 minutes (optional)
- Agreement on the policy guidelines for the policy paper: what should be included (list all items on the flipchart)
- Closure of the meeting

Restorative justice

Restorative justice can be used in all instances where something happens which causes harm to people, relationships, or the community.

The concept is based on 3 ideas:

- repair: violence causes harm, and restorative justice demands that the harm is repaired;
- encounter: the best way to determine how to repair the harm is to have the parties decide together; and
- transformation: repair can cause fundamental changes in people, relationships and communities.

Restorative justice is a way of dealing with cases of disruption or violence by addressing not just the wrongdoing, but also the damage caused. It maintains that the best way to do this is for all people concerned to meet and discuss the problem and to propose solutions. At such meetings:

- All parties are included (victims, perpetrators, and other people affected). The meeting should be facilitated by an impartial outsider
- Addressing the damage caused is an important part of any resolution.
- The resolution must be agreed upon by all parties at the meeting

In practice, such a process can look like this:

There is a group of people nominated by the school community that facilitates a meeting, at which both victim and perpetrator are present. Each side presents what happened and how they understand it. The victim can suggest how they believe justice can be restored, which might involve making demands on the perpetrator to repair the situation. Such a proposal can also come from the facilitator, but the victim has to be in agreement. The perpetrator then needs to agree to the measures proposed to repair the harm. The process of restoring justice is supervised by the facilitators or people nominated by the facilitators.

Restorative justice cannot be used in all instances of gender-based violence. Many types of gender-based violence constitute a crime and should be reported immediately to the law enforcement authorities, which should take legal action (which may involve restorative measures).

Based on: *http://restorativejustice.org/restorative-justice/about-restorative-justice/tutorial-intro-to-restorative-justice/lesson-1-what-is-restorative-justice/#sthash.wd1Bsy9t.dpbs*

> "The limits of my language are the limits of my world."
>
> *Ludwig Wittgenstein*

Our Daily Sexism

Level 2

60 to 20

45 minutes (Part one) 120 minutes (Part two)

Complexity: Level 2

Group size: 6 to 20

Time: 45 minutes (Part one), 120 minutes (Part two)

Overview: In this activity, participants need to decide how they would respond to different examples of sexist hate speech online. They then develop an online action that they could implement to act against examples of gender-based violence.

Objectives:
- To learn to recognise sexist hate speech and the consequences it has on the people targeted
- To develop an online action against sexist hate speech
- To identify different ways of responding to sexist hate speech online

Materials:
- Flipchart paper, markers and masking tape
- Copies of the Action cards (at least one for each group)

Preparation: Make 4 signs on pieces of flipchart paper and stick each one in a different corner of the room. The signs should read:

- Nothing
- Respond to the person who did it
- Report the behaviour
- Something else

Make sure there is enough space for participants to move around the room.

Instructions

This activity is done in two parts.

<u>Part 1 (45 minutes)</u>

1) Ask participants if they know what hate speech is, and whether they have come across hate speech online. Provide participants with a definition of sexism:

   Sexism means perceiving and judging people only on the basis of the particular sex/gender category they are thought to belong to. Sexism involves unequal treatment of the person on the same basis. It applies to both men and women; however, women are normally considered to be more frequent targets of sexism. Extreme sexism includes sexual harassment, rape, female genital mutilation and other forms of sexual violence. However, everyday sexism takes different forms, sometimes not easily recognisable – for example, telling jokes about blond girls, commenting on the female body (objectifying women), reacting to the way women are dressed ("what does she wear? She's asking to be raped"), giving women easier tasks in online games ("she is a woman, she won't manage the next level"), or objectifying women in advertising, etc.

2) Tell participants that in this activity they will look at examples of sexist hate speech. Point out the signs in the corners of the room and explain that you will read out several different scenarios. Participants should choose which of the following options best fits what they would do:

   · Nothing
   · Respond to the person who did it
   · Report the behaviour
   · Something else

3) Explain that after each scenario has been read out, participants should go to the corner which is closest to the way they would probably respond. Tell them to be honest about what they think they would do!

4) Read out the first scenario and give participants time to select their corner. Once they have taken a position, ask a few in each group to explain why they chose that response. Then read out the next scenario and continue until you feel enough cases have been discussed.

5) Ask participants how sexist hate speech affects people who are targeted, how it affects bystanders (people who witness it) and how it affects society generally. You could also ask specifically: how does sexist hate speech affect women/men/LGBT+?

6) You may want to continue with the first part of the Debriefing and Evaluation (see below) or move immediately to part 2.

<u>Part 2 (120 minutes)</u>

1) Tell participants that in this part of the activity they will work in smaller groups to develop an online action, aimed at raising awareness about sexist hate speech and the ways of dealing with it.

2) Split participants into 3 groups and give them the Action Cards that can be found at the end of this activity. Different groups will have different tasks:

· Group One will develop a mini-campaign addressing the issue of sexist hate speech online

· Group Two will develop a script of a video clip against sexist hate speech to be posted online

· Group Three will develop counter narratives against sexist hate speech online

3) Tell the groups where they will be working. Allow about 60 minutes for this part of the activity.

4) After the participants have finished developing their actions, bring them back into plenary and ask to present their work.

5) Help participants to plan the actions that each group designed. They should think about such things as:

Who will be in charge of taking the action forward?

When, and how will it be done?

6) Move to the debriefing and evaluation.

Debriefing and evaluation

This part of the activity can be done in two parts. You could use the first set of questions after Part One of the activity:

• How did you find the activity? Which scenarios did you find it most difficult to respond to and why?

• Have you ever come across sexist hate speech online – either as a person targeted by hate speech, or as a witness? How did you feel?

• Should people have the right to say whatever they want on the internet? If not, what should be the limits?

• Which human rights are violated by hate speech?

• How can you help to prevent or act against sexist hate speech online?

• After Part two, you could ask the following questions:

• Are you happy with the results of your work? What was the most difficult part of the task for you?

• Do you think it is important to act against sexist hate speech online? Why?

• How easy will it be to carry out the actions you have developed?

• Do you need supporting in order to implement them?

• What do you hope will be the result of your action?

Tips for facilitators

The activity can be run in a single session, or part 2 could be run at a later date. You could also run either of the two parts without the other: just the responses to sexist hate speech, or just the action planning. This will depend on the learning needs of your participants and the aims you want to set for the activity.

As the activity is conceived (in two parts), participants are first able to explore different ways of reacting to sexist hate speech, and they then go on to draw up plans for action. This order allows them to see that anyone can work to bring about change and fight against hate speech online; and to recognise that it is everyone's responsibility to do so.

The second part may be challenging for participants. Allow them to be creative, and try not to limit them in their ideas, but be available for support, and remind them – if necessary - not to be too ambitious, but to stay focussed. If three actions seem to be too many, select just one of the cards for participants to work on.

The group working on alternative and counter narratives may need additional support: you could recommend that they choose about 3 examples of sexist hate speech, and brainstorm ideas for how they could respond to these. For further information on using counter narratives, refer to the manual *"WE CAN! Taking Action against Hate Speech through Counter and Alternative Narratives"* which can be found online.[1] The web site of the Council of Europe's campaign against hate speech also offers inspiring examples of actions against hate speech online, as well as educational strategies for addressing the problem: *https://www.nohatespeechmovement.org*.

Suggestions for follow-up

If participants are interested in exploring further the topic of gender-based violence in the media, you could run the activity "Digital media bash", in which participants use research and observation techniques to address the problematic use of violence in the digital media.

You could also work further on alternative and counter narratives against hate speech. Using the manual WE CAN! Taking Action against Hate Speech through Counter and Alternative Narratives, prepare a workshop on how to develop narratives against hate speech.

Ideas for action

Help participants to finalise their actions and carry them out online. Think about how they can evaluate the impact of their actions.

1. "WE CAN! Taking Action against Hate Speech through Counter and Alternative Narratives", Council of Europe, 2017: *https://rm.coe.int/wecan-eng-final-23052017-web/168071ba08*

Source: This activity is adapted from the activity "Confronting Cyberbullying" in: *Bookmarks – Combatting Hate Speech Online through Human Rights Education*, Council of Europe 2014

Scenarios

A boy from your school commented on one of your photos on Facebook, saying: "You look hot. I would not mind putting my tongue into your mouth"

Someone posted a photo of you on snapchat. The picture had been taken secretly, while you were taking a shower after a sports lesson.

In a discussion on social network, your brother boasts about how many girls he shagged. He also says that all women are just "bitches".

A girl in your class told you that she has received nasty text messages calling her "pervert tomboy", "disgusting lesbian" and "ugly pig", and making fun of her "big tits". Some boys from your class have been pulling her hair and laughing at her in school.

Your best friend put the following post onto his social network: "Women are made to stay at home and take care of children. History teaches us that they are good only at that."

You noticed that a person from your class is very unhappy and does not talk to anyone. During the break, you approached them and asked what the problem was. They told you that they had received messages on online messenger from classmates calling them: "a dirty bitch", "sissy with the vagina" and "a freak, neither a man nor a woman".

Your friend told you that she had been raped by her boyfriend. He also posted a photo of her online, with the comment: "I finally got her".

During an online game, other gamers sent you messages like: "you should cook something instead of being here" or "did you check your man has enough beer at home".

In an online discussion about refugees, in which you tried to explain why it is important to receive them in your country, a person you do not know said: "I can see you fantasise about being raped. You do not need refugees. I can provide you with that, with pleasure".

Your friend regularly posts online jokes picturing women as inferior to men and as "sex machines".

ACTION CARD

Group 1: Mini-campaign against sexist hate speech

You will develop a mini-campaign to be carried out online that raises awareness about sexist hate speech online and motivates people to take action against it.

Online campaigns are usually meant to attract people's attention to a specific issue/problem. A good campaign needs to:

- Be clear about what it wants to communicate
- Ideally, be about just one issue: keep it focussed!
- Engage the public in a conversation/discussion
- Be interesting, both in form and content
- Include visuals (photos, memes, etc.)
- Happen over a period of time (e.g. once a week, over the period of a month)

You do not need to prepare everything immediately. Focus on developing a general idea for a mini-campaign. The following questions may help you:

- What is your aim? E.g. you could aim to raise awareness of different responses to sexist hate speech online, or responses or strategies for victims of sexting.
- Who is your campaign addressed at? e.g it might be addressed at pupils in your school, or at the general public
- What would you like to communicate and how? Will you use visuals? What could they show, and which medium will you use (photos, drawings, etc.)?
- How will you engage your audience in the conversation?

ACTION CARD

Group 2: Video against sexist hate speech online

You need to develop an idea for a video against sexist hate speech online. The video should aim at raising awareness about sexist hate speech online and motivate people to take action against it. Do not make the video itself, but think about what should be included and how it can be done. The following points will help you to plan:

- Choose the issue that you would like to present in the video, for example stereotypes about women
- Think about who your video is addressed to: e.g. your friends, pupils at school, etc.
- Decide on the way you want to present it and the message you want to communicate
- Think about how the video will be made – e.g. in the form of a role play, cartoons, photos with a voiceover, etc.
- Develop a detailed script – scene by scene
- Think about timing: the best and strongest videos are short!
- Where will you post the video?

If you have enough time, try to make the film itself.

ACTION CARD

Group 3: Alternative and counter narratives against sexist hate speech

Your task is to develop alternative and counter narratives against sexist hate speech online. Counter and alternative narratives combat hate speech by discrediting and deconstructing the narratives on which they are based. They also propose (alternative) narratives based on human rights and democratic values, such as openness, respect for difference, freedom and equality. New narratives may be effective by providing alternative and accurate information, by accounting for different perspectives and views, or by using humour and appealing to emotions (without discrediting the person who posted the hate speech. Two examples of alternative and counter narratives are given below:

1) Message posted on social media

Message	Alternative or counter narrative
Men deserve better. We should be complaining - not these stupid sensitive bitches (women). We get called rapists a lot of the time when most of us haven't done anything.	Men being called rapist is just as unacceptable as women being called stupid sensitive bitches. None of this should be condoned: there should be respect for all genders.

2) Hate Destroyer - An action run by the Finish National Committee of the No Hate Speech Movement Campaign used creative art to challenge hateful images. The activity challenged a racist, homophobic and neo-nazi graffitti, expressed in symbols and words on a wall. The challenge used the same space to paint new symbols and words next to, and over the original paintings. The new symbols and words proposed a different narrative - of love, and respect for diversity and human rights. A video is available at *https://www.youtube.com/watch?v=V4Pc4uY0HiE*

You can use examples of sexist hate speech from the earlier examples, or propose your own. When developing these narratives, think about the following:

• What is the best way to approach these specific examples of sexist hate speech?
• What do you want to say, and how would you frame the response – e.g. providing accurate information, using humour etc.
• How or where would you disseminate the message online, so that other people can learn from your example?

> "It is hard to fight an enemy that has outposts in your head"
>
> *Sally Kempton*

Safety in My Life

Level 2

8 to 20

60 minutes

Complexity: Level 2

Group size: 8 to 20

Time: 60 minutes

Overview: This activity uses brainstorming to reflect about what people do to avoid violence and to identify common threats to safety according to sex. It highlights gender differences in relation to violence, and addresses the absence of appropriate information for young people on the nature of interpersonal violence

Objectives:
- To recognise the differences in safety levels and concerns for men and women, and for boys and girls
- To discover the information gap for young people on the realities of gender-based violence
- To identify some ways for youth work to play a role in filling this gap

Materials: Flipchart paper and markers for each of the small groups

Preparation: Set out a circle of chairs in the middle of the room for the introduction to the activity. Put flip chart paper and markers in each of the spaces allocated for working groups.

Instructions

1) Explain that this activity is about sharing and compiling ideas for what people can do in order to stay safe. Participants will work initially in single sex groups: these will create lists of their own, which will then be shared and discussed with others.

2) Form small groups, with not more than four or five people in each. These should be single-sex groups.

3) Ask each group to go to one of the prepared working spaces. Ask the groups to share ideas on the subject of 'staying safe': they should think about and share things they do to avoid violence and stay safe. The groups should also discuss threats to their safety that they face on a regular basis. Give them about 20 minutes for the sharing exercise and tell them they should list their actions and threats on the flip chart paper.

4) Get the groups back together and ask each one to report back. Hang the flipcharts so they can be seen by everyone, and place lists from groups of the same sex next to each other.

Debriefing and evaluation

Ask for participants' first impressions of the activity and the results. A good way to begin this discussion is to ask if anyone is surprised by any of actions or items on the different lists, in particular by any striking differences or similarities between the women's group/s and the men's.

- What do you think about the differences in actions for protection by men and by women? Where do these differences come from?
- Are the lists of threats representative of the actual dangers boys and girls, men and women face in their daily lives? Why, or why not?
- Which dangers might be missing from the lists? Why do you think that such dangers did not feature in your discussions?
- Can you identify the dangers in your local context?
- What information do we receive about violence and safety from violence?
- Where does such information come from? Is it credible? Do young people take it seriously?
- Whose job is it, or should it be, to inform young people and children about violence and precautions for staying safe? How could you or your organisation contribute to making a change in this respect?
- What are the main challenges to gender-based violence in your community / country?
- Which human rights are violated in cases of gender-based violence?

Tips for facilitators

This activity requires a certain level of awareness from participants on what violence is, the forms that exist, and how these are defined. Make sure that you read the information about violence in Chapter 1 of this manual in preparation for running the activity, so that you can help participants clarify any confusion that may exist around the different types of violence that can be observed in daily life.

Lists made by participants often focus heavily on precautions against violence from complete strangers, even though there is evidence that violence is most often perpetrated by someone known to the victim.

Be aware that if most participants believe that they are safe from violence, this can often manifest itself in attitudes of victim blaming, and the activity may even strengthen prejudiced attitudes towards victims of violence. Discussions about taking precautions against violence or actively defending one's own safety might lead to some participants placing blame on victims for not having done enough to ensure their own safety. You may need to reinforce the message that perpetrators of violence are always responsible for their own actions. Violence is not caused by insufficient information or inadequate awareness of safety concerns, nor is it caused by finding oneself in a vulnerable position. People who do not manage to ensure their own safety do not "decide" to become victims. Perpetrators, on the other hand, actively decide to use violence.

Explain that violence is a social phenomenon; keeping safe from violence demands learned social skills. Make sure that you focus the discussion on the extent to which society, including social institutions from family to school, prepares young people for the most typical forms of violence they are likely to encounter.

Most of this activity is carried out in single sex groups. Pay special attention to this fact and be sensitive about people who do not identify themselves as men or women. You may even want to create a third group – OTHER GENDERS – if you feel this is necessary and will be safe for transgender people.

Suggestions for follow-up

The publication *Young People and Violence Prevention – Youth Policy Recommendations*, edited by Gavan Titley and published by the Council of Europe, provides an easy-to-understand guide to the issue of violence in the everyday lives of young people, and some ideas on how to combat it. This book is available for downloading at *http://book.coe.int/youth*.

If you want to pursue the topic further, try the activity "Power Station" from *Compass*, in which participants brainstorm acts of violence that are common in their daily lives and then look for creative ways of dealing with them. If you want to explore further the topic of gender-based violence, try using the activity 'Understanding gender-based violence', in which participants analyse different examples of violence.

Ideas for action

Suggest to the group that they research programmes that exist in the local area which are engaged in violence prevention with young people, and that they contact those involved to find out more about what they do and how. Discuss with your group how you could collectively contribute to violence prevention efforts.

Suggest to the group that they review school programmes to explore the extent to which they address these issues as part of the curriculum. If there is an obvious lack of violence prevention programmes in a given school, suggest that the group considers developing a project in cooperation with a specialised organisation to initiate a violence prevention or human rights education programme with a gender focus in the school.

Source: Adapted from Adams, M., Bell, L.A. and Griffin, P. (Eds.) (1997). Teaching for Diversity and Social Justice. Routledge, p. 122.

> "Labels are for clothing. Labels are not for people"
>
> *Martina Navratilova*

Sex Sells?

Level 2

10 to 30

60 to 75
minutes

Complexity: Level 2

Group size: 10 to 30

Time: 60 to 75 minutes

Overview: This activity addresses several issues concerning public perceptions of gender, sex and sexuality. Participants analyse how different genders are depicted in advertisements in newspapers and magazines using a special tool for analysis.

Objectives:
- To identify gender stereotypes projected through the media
- To reflect upon and discuss the social construction of gender roles
- To raise awareness of inequality of opportunity between genders

Materials:
- Newspapers and magazines
- Scissors, glue
- Flipchart paper and "post-its" in two different colours
- Copies of the grid for analysis for each group (see handouts)

Preparation:
- Collect various newspapers and magazines, rich in advertisements and with pictures
- Read through the instructions carefully and study the grid that participants will use in the second part of the activity (see handouts)

Instructions

1) Introduce the activity. Start by referring to daily life and common perceptions of different gender roles in society: remind participants that it is almost impossible to find aspects of life where gender issues are absent. Even with basic questions, such as who washes the dishes at home, how girls and boys sit in schools, or where women and men are generally employed, gender is present. Explain that advertisements in the media very often reflect and magnify the different characteristics, stereotypes and prejudices relating to gender that exist in society.

2) Hand out the newspapers and magazines, with a selection of "post-its", and ask participants to look through them and select one advertisement to analyse individually. The selected advertisement should convey something about gender roles and expressions (e.g. it might contain pictures of women, men, or other genders)

   Using the grid (see handouts), each participant should then identify and note down the different parties in the advertisement they have chosen, the direct (obvious) messages and any possible hidden messages, and the use made by the advertisement of gender stereotypes.

   In addition to filling out the grid, ask participants to write down the attributes of men and women they find in the advertisement on post-its of different colour. Specify at the beginning of the activity which colour they should use for attributes of men, and which for attributes which apply to the women portrayed.

3) Once participants have filled out their grid (give them about 20 minutes for this task, to include time for reflection), ask them to get together in pairs to share their advertisements, grids, and gender analysis (the different post-its with attributes of men and women). Give participants about 20 minutes for this task as both participants in the pair will need time to present and share.

4) When participants have finished the work in pairs, ask them to present the attributes assigned to different genders to the whole group. They should stick all the post-its describing women onto one piece of flip chart paper, and all those for men onto another.

Debriefing and evaluation

Ask participants to comment on the attributes on the post-its, particularly relating to the differences between those applying to men and those to women. They may refer to the advertisements, but this is not essential.

Use some of the following questions to explore the issues in greater detail:

- How do you feel about the lists of male and female attributes which were to be found in the advertisements you analysed?
- Do these attributes accurately describe men and women you know, or men and women in general? Explain your answer.
- Is there anything problematic or unethical about the way men and women were portrayed in these advertisements?

- How are attributes such as those you identified reflected in the context where you live?
- How does the way that women and men are portrayed in advertising affect the way that young women and men see themselves and others?
- How do you think advertising could avoid the use of stereotyped and negative portrayals of women and men?
- How might advertising contribute to forms of gender-based violence?
- Are there any consequences of such adversitisng practices on human rights, how they are perceived and respected?
- How can you / your organisation contribute to the creation of more gender equitable advertising practices?

Tips for facilitators

Be aware that advertising often uses overtly sexual images or covert sexual messages about women or men to "sell" the product they are advertising. This needs to be addressed but be aware that any discussion relating to sex may be uncomfortable for some participants.

You can decide to include additional colour for 'other genders' if you feel it is important to tackle the issue related to transgender people. If you decide to do it, adapt the questions in the debriefing accordingly.

Suggestions for follow-up

The topic of media and gender could be explored further. The activity "Digital media bash" uses research and observation techniques to look at the use of violence in the digital media.

This activity can also be used to initiate discussion on homophobic or sexist online hate speech. In the activity "Saying it worse" from *Bookmarks*, participants have to rank different examples of anti-gay hate speech according to which they think are 'worse'. In this manual, the activity "Our daily sexism" involves participants in the process of deciding how they would respond to different examples of sexist hate speech online. They also need to develop an online action that they could carry out to address sexist hate speech.

Ideas for action

Ask the group to develop a code of ethics for media professionals working in advertising and marketing to guide them on the presentation of gender in the media.

Contact local media professionals, especially those working in marketing and advertising, to discuss the issue of the presentation of gender in the media. If your group has already worked out a code of ethics, ask for the media professionals' comments. Alternatively, invite media professionals to come and meet the members of your group and organise a panel discussion on the presentation of gender in the media. Consider inviting feminist activists with strong views on the issue to take part in the discussion.

Grid for Analysis

Look at the picture you have chosen and describe it:

1) What roles people have in the picture, e.g. husband, wife, partner, parent, etc.

2) What are people actually doing?

3) What is their behaviour: active or passive, smiling or being sad, showing aggression, taking initiative, etc.

Once you identify the roles, activities and behaviours, assign them to a concrete person (write it down in the "Who?" column), e.g. husband (role) - man (who?)

In the "(In-)appropriate?" column decide if you consider the connection between the person (who?) and the role they have, the activity they do and their behaviour appropriate or inappropriate.

In the "Why?" column justify why you consider this connection appropriate or inappropriate.

Once you finish your analysis, write down different attributes assigned to people of different genders in your picture. These attributes should be written on post-its of different colour (your facilitator will tell you which colours to use). Attributes are usually qualities or features of a person, such as: dominant, self-confident, strong, weak, etc.

The picture

	What?	Who?	(In-)Appropriate?	Why?
Role				
Activity				
Behaviour				

> "The safety of the people shall be the highest law"
> *Marcus Tullius Cicero*

Spaces and Places

Level 2

10 to 30

40 to 60 minutes

Complexity: Level 2

Group size: 10 to 30

Time: 40 to 60 minutes

Overview: This activity looks at the safety of LGBT+ young people in different everyday settings. Participants position themselves along the length of a wall, according to how safe or unsafe they think it is for LGBT+ people to be "out" in particular settings.

Objectives:
- To raise participants' awareness of the fact that openly LGBT+ young people may feel unsafe when entering (public) spaces
- To reflect on what it means to be safe when your gender identity or sexual orientation is not accepted by society
- To discuss the human rights threats faced by LBGT+ people

Materials:
- A large empty wall, with space for the participants to move along it
- Three large pieces of paper with the headings: 'SAFE', 'UNSAFE', 'I DON'T KNOW'

Preparation: Prepare three large pieces of paper with 'SAFE', 'UNSAFE', 'I DON'T KNOW' written on them. Stick the first two onto opposite ends of a large empty wall making sure that there is plenty of space between them.

The poster with 'I DON'T KNOW' written on it should be placed in a corner or a different side of the room facing the "Safe" – "Unsafe" wall.

Instructions

1) Ask participants to imagine that the room is a giant opinion scale, with one end of the room representing 'SAFE', the other end 'UNSAFE'. Indicate the posters on the wall and clarify that those who have no idea about how to answer can choose the 'I DON'T KNOW' space.

2) Explain to participants that they will need to imagine the safety levels for LGBT+ people to be 'out' at various events or locations, and to position themselves on the scale accordingly

   Read aloud each of the events or locations below, allowing time between reading each one for participants to position themselves in silence:

   · at a gay or lesbian bar
   · during a classroom discussion at school
   · during a music festival
   · during a discussion at school where racist, homophobic and xenophobic remarks are made
   · at a gay or lesbian bookstore
   · at the work place
   · in a local youth club in a culturally diverse urban area
   · at the pharmacy when asking for condoms
   · at a football match or any other sports event
   · at a youth conference or training course where homophobic remarks have been expressed by participants

3) After each statement ask participants to explain the position they have taken by asking individual participants why they think a setting is safe or unsafe for LGBTs+ to show they are "out". Encourage participants to engage in discussion with others who have a different view, but try to ensure that they provide relevant, evidence-based arguments, or that they speak from a position of personal experience. Participants should outline their own opinion rather than disputing the opinion of others, but they may make references to arguments put by other people.

   Make sure to invite also the participants who opted for "I don't know" to share anything they may want to share or to check if they are better informed now and could thus place themselves in the safety scale.

   Repeat this procedure for some or all of the settings on the list. Decide in advance how long you would like to devote to the discussion of each setting (5 to 10 minutes, recommended). This will give you an idea of how long you need for the whole activity.

4) Invite the participants for the debriefing.

Debriefing and evaluation

Start by inviting participants to share how they feel after the activity.

- Was there anything surprising in any of the positions taken or arguments made?
- Were there differences in perception concerning the safety of these settings for LGBT+ people who are "out"? Why?
- Based on the activity, what are some of the characteristics of settings considered to be 'unsafe' for LGBT+?
- What are some of the characteristics of settings considered to be 'safe' for LGBT+?
- Can you identify settings from your local context which are 'safe' or 'unsafe'?
- What are some of the dangers facing young LGBTs+ who are 'out' in your local context?
- Are there other aspects of identity - other than belonging to LGBT+ - which might lead to someone feeling unsafe in your local context?
- What do you think that people in these settings can do to help LGBTs+ who are 'out' to feel safe? Give examples from the different settings
- What precautions can young LGBTs+ take to improve their own safety?
- Why do some people have difficulties in imagining the level of safety of some places (the "I don't know" positions)?
- What are some of the human rights threats facing LGBT+ people in your community / country? Can these be overcome? How?

Tips for facilitators

You need to give consideration to the right time to run this activity with your group, depending on the group itself and the specific objectives you have. You might not want to use this activity at the beginning of a training, if participants do not already know each other and do not feel safe to challenge each others' views or speak about their personal experiences. You should ensure that participants have a minimal understanding of the terminology and what is involved in coming out. You can find more information on these questions in Chapter 4, in the section on LGBT+.

Depending on the composition of your group and the experiences of participants, the activity may lead to some of them sharing personal experiences involving violence and insecurity. You should be prepared to deal with such experiences and the emotions that might arise as a result of sharing them. However, you should also make it clear to participants at the beginning of the activity that they should not feel compelled to share anything that they are not comfortable with.

It may be useful to run this activity together with a co-facilitator who can support you by taking notes or supporting participants who may need to take a break from the activity.

Especially when working with a local group, it is useful to be aware of any instances or settings where there has been violence against LGBT+. Awareness of any such issues will be helpful when facilitating the discussion among participants.

When working with a group that has limited awareness and experience with LGBT+ you might be faced with a situation where 'I DON'T KNOW' is the most common answer. To avoid this, you can take the option away, pushing people to make a choice between 'SAFE' and 'UNSAFE'.

The list of settings provided is not exhaustive. You could revise it to make it more relevant to your group's reality.

It may be useful for the debriefing if the facilitator or a co-facilitator has made a note of the results for each setting, and these are displayed for participants, so that they can recall how many people thought the setting was unsafe or safe, etc. It may also be useful to make a note of some of the arguments used by participants, so that you can refer to these later on during the discussion.

The issue of safety in public spaces is also important for women, as well as from an intersectional point of view. You could develop a list of roles for participants to play, and ask them to position themselves according to their perceived level of security. Such a list could include such roles as being a young woman, young LGBT+ from an ethnic community, etc.

Suggestions for follow-up

You could try the activity "Where do you stand?" from *Compass*, using statements adapted to the themes of gender and gender-based violence.

The activity could also be followed by looking at private instances of gender-based violence – e.g using 'Kati's story' or 'Understanding gender-based violence' from this manual.

Ideas for action

You could work further with participants on the question of safety and inclusion within their organisations and groups. They could conduct an 'inclusivity analysis' of your group, or another organisation they belong to. Such an analysis can be carried out by reviewing organisational policies and practices to check whether they are safe, welcoming and open to LGBT young people. Be aware that this type of review requires a large measure of openness to criticism on your part and on the part of others in your organisation.

You could also suggest that young people conduct some research in the local community, identifying places where violence targeting LGBT+ has occurred. They could work to raise awareness of such issues in the community by organising a silent march to highlight instances of violence, or create collaborative online maps that illustrate the extent of the problem and indications about available support services in the community.

You could also invite law enforcement representatives to discuss with the group the measures they adopt (or do not adopt) to prevent and follow-up on instances of violence against LGBT+.

> "Compassion is the basis of morality"
> *Arthur Schopenhauer*

Stella

Level 2

5 to 30

120 minutes

Complexity: Level 2

Group size: 5 to 30

Time: 120 minutes

Overview: This activity uses ranking methods to expose the differences in participants' moral values, and to open discussion on questions of gender inequality and socialisation into gender-based stereotyping

Objectives:
- To enable participants to reflect on their own values and priorities in relation to gender issues
- To analyse the sources and influences which lead to different moral positions or priorities
- To understand how individuals become socialised into gender-based stereotyping and prescribed gender roles

Materials:
- A copy of Stella's story for each participant

Preparation: Make sure you have enough space for participants to work individually, in small groups of 3 to 6, and in plenary.

Instructions

1) Introduce the activity and its objectives. Ask them to read the story individually and to rank the behaviour of each character (Stella, Vitali, Ralf, Stella's mother and Goran) along a scale from 'best' to 'worst'. For example, they might decide that Stella's behaviour was the worst, Goran's was the next worst, Ralf's was next – and so on. Give participants 10 minutes for this task.

2) When everyone has decided on their individual ranking, ask participants to get together in small groups (between 3 to 6 people) and compare and discuss their results with others. The task of the small groups is to come up with a common ranking – a list that everyone in the small group can agree on. The group should create a common ranking on the basis of shared understanding and consensus, rather than using, for example, a majority voting.

3) Optional: After the small groups have agreed a common ranking, you could repeat this phase by bringing two small groups together to form medium size groups. However, if you do include this phase, groups in the first round should not be larger than 4 people.

4) Ask each group to present the results of their discussions to the plenary. Groups should give brief arguments for their commonly agreed ranking.

Debriefing and evaluation

Use some of the following questions to debrief the activity:

- When you worked individually, how did you decide what was good and what was bad behaviour?
- Was it difficult to agree on a ranking that suited everyone?
- What were the challenges or blocks which made agreement difficult?
- What role do personal values play in such a process?
- Where do personal values, such as those reflected in this activity, come from?
- Can you identify any prescribed gender roles in the story?
- Which gender related concerns or dilemmas are raised by this story?
- Are any of these concerns present in the context where you live? How do issues such as these affect young people?
- Which human rights issues can you identify in the story? Do you think human rights are useful when dealing with moral dilemmas related to gender? Explain your answer
- How can we support young people to deal with social pressures relating to morality and gender?

Tips for facilitators

It is important that you establish an open atmosphere in which every ranking of the story is seen to be acceptable, and where you do not start 'blaming' people for arguments you might consider strange or bad yourself.

The activity can be adapted in a number of ways. One possibility is to run it as described, and then to repeat it with a changed story, in which all the women become men, and vice-versa. Do participants' rankings remain the same? If not, why does the change make a difference? You could also include the ages of characters in the story, and experiment in other ways: for example, by making them all have the same gender, or by including a character's ethnic or national background. It would then be interesting to look at how the changes in the story make a difference to the ranking, and why.

Suggestions for follow-up

You could follow this activity with other activities that explore gender stereotyping and gender socialisation, for example: "Gender-in-a-box" or "Good, better, best".

You could also explore gender-based violence and intersectionality through activities such as "Understanding gender-based violence" or "About Maria".

Ideas for action

Suggest to your group that they explore the question of values, as these relate to gender, in different settings or communities. You could do this in several ways, for example: conducting a series of interviews using different audio-visual methods with representatives of different religious and cultural communities, or inviting women and men from the communities you are interested in knowing more about to come to meet the members of your group and to discuss values related to gender.

Stella's Story

Somewhere in a far-off land lives a beautiful girl called Stella. She is in love with the handsome Vitali, who lives on the other side of an enormous river. Earlier in the year, all the bridges across this river were swept away by a terrible flood, and all the boats except one were damaged or destroyed. Stella asks Ralf, the owner of the only remaining boat, to take her to the other side of the river. Ralf agrees, on one condition: he insists that Stella sleep with him. Stella is confused. She does not know what to do and runs to her mother to ask for advice. Her mother tells her that she does not want to interfere in Stella's private business. In desperation, Stella sleeps with Ralf, who then takes her across the river. The joyful Stella rushes to Vitali to embrace him and proceeds to tell him everything that happened. Vitali pushes her away roughly, and Stella runs off, sobbing. Not far from Vitali's house, Stella meets Goran, Vitali's best friend. She tells him everything that has happened. Goran punches Vitali for what he has done to Stella, and then walks away with her…

> "Saying NO can be an ultimate self-care"
> *Claudia Black*

Too Hard to Respond

Level 3

6 to 30

60 minutes

Complexity: Level 3

Group size: 6 to 30

Time: 60 minutes

Overview: This activity uses brainstorming and role-playing to address ways of responding to unwanted sexual advances, sexual bullying and harassment.

Objectives:
- To identify different forms of sexual bullying and harassment commonly faced by young people
- To practice different reactions to unwanted sexual advances or bullying
- To understand the dangers for young people, particularly women, of vague or ambiguous sexual overtures and responses

Materials:
- Flipchart and markers

Preparation: Read through the instructions carefully, study or research about sexual bullying and harrassment (see also chapter 4). If you know some people in the group, consider preparing one or two to volunteer in order to start the role-playing.

Instructions

1) Introduce the activity by asking participants if they have heard of cases of about sexual bullying or harassment. Ask them to give examples of different kinds of of sexual bullying and harassment on the flipchart.

2) When the group has drawn up a list, ask participants to brainstorm ideas for how they might react to different forms of sexual bullying or harassment. Note these responses down on the flip chart next to the forms of bullying / harassment. If participants come up with responses that suggest using physical violence, ask them to think about other possible ways to respond in a non-violent way.

3) Ask for at least two volunteers who would like to role-play a reaction to unwanted sexual advances, bullying or harassment. Give them some examples of possible scenarios, if necessary. These might include: making unwanted comments about people's appearance or looks, pressuring another person to do something they do not want using emotional blackmail (e.g. "you would do that if you loved me"), or name calling and insulting another person using homophobic language.

4) Give the volunteer pairs a few minutes to choose and prepare their sketch. If they have difficulty choosing a scenario, give them one yourself (see Tips for facilitators for ideas).

5) Ask the volunteers to act out their scene to others in the group.

6) Then ask the couple to play the same scene again, inviting other participants to step in and propose their own responses to the dialogue. They could do this by calling out "Freeze", at which point those playing the scene should stop, and the person calling "Freeze" should step in to replace one of the characters in the dialogue. The scene continues, with a different proposal for resolving the problem. In this way, the dialogue can be moved on in a different, perhaps more effective, or more assertive, direction. This offers a way for the spectators to play an active role in proposing alternative ways of asking for and refusing sexual intercourse.
Continue with one sketch until there are no further suggestions from the audience, or until players have been replaced a maximum of three times.

7) Move on to the next volunteer pair and repeat the procedure. Try to offer all participants who wish to take part in the dialogue the opportunity to do so, obviously within the limits of the time available to you. After that, continue with debriefing and evaluation.

Debriefing and evaluation

Ask participants to share with the rest of the group some of the things they feel they have learned from the activity.

- How did you feel during the activity? Was it hard to enact examples of sexual bullying and harassment? Why?

- Was it easy to respond to bullying? Why, or why not?
- Why do some people engage in sexual bullying or harassment? What do they want to achieve?
- Were any of the responses proposed violent in nature? Is this ever a good idea?
- Why is it difficult for some people to react to sexual bullying / harassment?
- Why do some people decide not to report extreme forms of sexual harassment, such as rape or sexual assault?
- What impact can sexual bullying / harassment have on young people?
- Who or what could help you in responding to unwanted sexual advances or reacting to sexual bullying / harassment and, if necessary, reporting it?
- Have you ever heard of self-defence classes / training for people who want to protect themselves from violence (e.g. Krav Maga)? What do you think about such an idea?
- Sexual bullying and harassment are forms of gender-based violence. What other forms of gender-based violence do you know?
- Which human rights are violated when people experience sexual bullying and harassment?
- What can young people do to raise awareness among their peers about sexual bullying / harassment and ways of reacting to it?

Tips for facilitators

In the first part of the activity, when you ask participants to brainstorm different forms of sexual bullying / harassment, it is important to focus on examples that are relevant for young people. You may want to help participants with this task, asking them, for example, if they have ever witnessed someone commenting on another person's appearance, or someone making sexualised comments about other people.

When young people propose a violent response to sexual bullying or harassment, ask them if it would be possible in those particular cases to react differently – without using violence – as violence has a tendency to escalate. Be aware that in some extreme cases, when harassment threatens people's lives, violence may be the only option people have at a particular moment.

Suggest that participants choose scenes to role-play which do not represent violent and extreme cases of sexual harassment (do not ask them to enact a case of rape!), but rather focus on "lighter" forms, for example:

- someone makes comments about the way you look (using sexualised language) and you react firmly saying: "It is none of your business what I wear. And… I will never accept the language you are using, so please stop, otherwise I will have to report it".

- someone wears clothing which depicts (pictures, words, drawings…) inappropriate sexual behaviour or language, and you decide to ask two friends to join you and approach the person, in order to draw their attention to the inappropriate content and asking them never to wear it again.
- someone touches you without your consent and you ask them not to, while also informing them you intend to report this to the school management.

You may also decide to focus on how to respond assertively to unwanted sexual advances. In other words, how to say NO, taking care of your own personal space and human rights, and at the same time, not using offensive words or actions.

It is sometimes difficult to recognise sexual bullying. Certain forms of communication, particularly non-verbal forms such as body language or eye contact, are often subject to very different interpretations. Even where verbal communication is involved, misunderstandings may arise – for example, a meeting between two people might be interpreted by one as a friendly chat and the other as a romantic date.

This activity may raise a lot of emotions, especially when there is a participant in the group who has experienced sexual bullying. Make sure you run this activity with a co-facilitator, so that they can take care of such a person, if this becomes necessary.

Suggestions for follow-up

Follow up by using the activity "Let's talk about sex" from *Compass*, to explore further attitudes to sexuality, including homophobia.

You might also want to further explore issues of domestic violence through "Kati's Story" and "Knight in Shining Armor".

Ideas for action

Check whether there have been any information campaigns related to sexual rights, sexual violence, or date and acquaintance rape in your neighbourhood or country. Try to obtain materials (posters, flyers, free-cards) for your school or youth club, or get together and make your own campaign materials. Use the different resources to initiate a discussion on what kind of campaign would be effective, and how to prepare it. If you do establish your own campaign, whether on prevention or raising awareness, do not forget that it will be seen by any victims and survivors that attend your school or live in your community. Make sure that you provide information about services (hotlines, drop-in centres) for victims of different forms of sexual abuse or gender-based violence.

Check if there are any self-defence trainings in your neighbourhood for people who want to protect themselves from violence. If there are, ask them if you can get a demonstration training.

> "Love is about giving freedom and power, not about gaining control or possession."
>
> *Jeffrey Fry*

What to Do?

Level 2

6 to 30

60 minutes

Complexity: Level 2

Group size: 6 to 30

Time: 60 minutes

Overview: This activity explores opinions in the group on common dilemmas relating to sex, sexuality, relationships and violence.

Objectives:
- To identify and discuss dilemmas related to sex, sexuality and violence that young people face as they enter the adult world
- To discuss and explore different approaches to dealing with these dilemmas
- To learn about sexual and reproductive rights within the human rights framework

Materials:
- The handout "Dilemmas" (for reading aloud by the facilitator)
- A large enclosed working space with four corners or four separate spaces.

Preparation: Familiarise yourself with the dilemmas and make signs for each corner: A, B, C and Other.

Instructions

1) Invite participants to stand in the middle of the room and tell them that you will read aloud a number of stories which present dilemmas related to sex, sexuality, violence and relationships. For each dilemma, participants should select one of the possible options (A,B,C, or Other) and take a stand by choosing a corner of the room which corresponds to their preferred response. Indicate the different corners and read out the first dilemma.

2) When everyone has selected a corner and is standing in place, allow participants to discuss their response with others around them. Ask participants from each corner to give a reason for why they are standing there.

3) Repeat the process for each of the dilemmas, or as many as you wish to present. Then move on to the debriefing and evaluation.

Debriefing and evaluation

Begin by asking participants for their impressions of the activity, and then continue the discussion to focus on the dilemmas young people have relating to sexuality, sex, violence and relationships. Use some of the following questions:

- How did you feel during the activity? Why?
- Was there anything surprising in the responses or positions of other participants?
- Do you consider that these dilemmas are representative of those faced by young people today?
- How do you think young people make a decision when faced with such a dilemma?
- When you have a dilemma (large or small), how do you go about resolving it?
- Where can young people faced with such dilemmas get support from if they need it?
- Which human rights can you identify which are relevant to human sexuality?
- What challenges do young people face in exercising their rights related to sexuality? What are some of the challenges related to gender equality?

Tips for facilitators

You can adapt the dilemmas to suit the group you are working with, by changing the sex, age, sexuality, nationality or other characteristics of the persons described, or by changing the scenarios. Remember that it is not always possible to know 'who is in the room' and that you should avoid using the personal stories of participants.

If you have digital projector, it may be helpful to display the options on each dilemma on the screen.

Suggestions for follow-up

Explore the activity 'Look who's coming to dinner!' in the Education Pack All Different – All Equal, to broaden the perspective of participants on relationship dilemmas, and to explore the effects of other people's opinions on the relationship choices and self-determination of young people.

Ideas for action

Find out whether any form of support (counselling, anonymous help-line, etc.) exists for dealing with the concerns of young people in your local area. If none exist, consider whether your group could initiate a project to provide relevant peer support services.

Ranja's dilemma

Ranja is 14 and is in love. Her girlfriend feels the same way. They have been together for two months, but Ranja's parents don't know this. She is sure they would forbid her to go on seeing her girlfriend. What should Ranja do?

A. Stop seeing the person she is in love with

B. Take her girlfriend home and present her to her parents

C. Continue to meet her in secret

D. Something else (Other corner)

Barry's dilemma

Barry is 16. He is gay, but no one in his family or circle of friends knows this. He likes a boy in his class and would like to have a relationship with him. However, he is not sure if the boy will be open to the proposal, and he is worried that the boy might tell other people in the class and that his parents might find out. What should Barry do?

A. Drop the whole idea and forget about the boy

B. Tell his parents and friends that he is gay, and ask the boy out on a date and just see what happens

C. Try to get to know the boy better, to check whether he has similar feelings, before revealing his own

D. Something else (Other Corner)

Jenny's dilemma

Jenny is 15. The coolest guy in the school asks her home after the disco, telling her his parents are away. Jenny likes him, but doesn't really know him. She has heard that he has slept with lots of girls at school. She doesn't want to have sex with him yet. What should she do?

A. Say no

B. Say yes

C. Say yes, but only if a few friends go too

D. Something else (Other corner)

Nasrine and Eddie's dilemma

Nasrine and Eddie are 18 and 19 respectively. They have been together for more than a year. They have just found out that Nasrine is pregnant. They were not planning on having kids but had been thinking about getting married. Nasrine wants to tell her parents. Eddie is sure they will not approve and might even try to break them up. They don't know what to do, because Nasrine is still finishing school. What should Nasrine and Eddie do?

A. Go to a counsellor for advice

B. Get married quickly and secretly and then announce the pregnancy to Nasrine's parents

C. Tell Nasrine's parents and ask for their support in planning the next steps

D. Something else (Other corner)

Ingrid's dilemma

Ingrid and Shane are both 17. They have been going out together for 2 years. One night they are out at a disco and Shane gets drunk. Ingrid decides to go on to another disco without Shane and he gets very angry, starts shouting at her and pushes her to the ground. What should Ingrid do?

A. Stay with Shane for the rest of the night and forget what happened

B. Leave the disco without Shane and tell her friends what just happened

C. Hit back, until Shane stops shouting

D. Something else (Other corner)

Alina's dilemma

Alina was born intersex, but the doctors took the decision to operate surgically to make them a woman. Their parents were not informed about the decision, and no additional follow up on Alina's condition was ever made. Alina was raised as a girl, not knowing what being intersex means. By the time Alina reached puberty, they started to develop several health issues, and certain markers of masculinity. At the last medical consultation, the doctors revealed to Alina and their parents the original cause of the issue and proposed further hormonal treatment to force female characteristics. Alina's parents were very much in agreement with the doctors' proposal. What should Alina do?

A. Allow her parents and the doctors to decide, because they know better

B. Ask for more information and further options, while taking only the medication necessary to mitigate health risks

C. Sue the doctors and institutions that were responsible for the situation

D. Something else (Open corner)

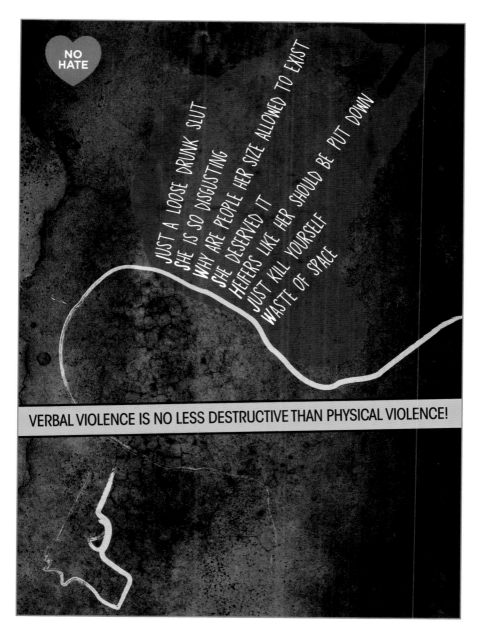

Poster created by the No Hate Ninjas (Portugal) for the No Hate Speech Movement youth campaign.

CHAPTER 3
Taking action against gender-based violence

Taking action against gender-based violence

In this chapter, we look at some of the ways that young people can take action for human rights and against gender-based violence.

1. Protecting the victims/survivors

The first priority when responding to gender-based violence must be to respond to the needs of victims/survivors, and ensure that they are properly protected. A number of different institutions and organisations may play a role in offering this protection – e.g. social services, the police, and the courts. The state officially has a responsibility for support services, but in many communities they will be provided by third parties such as civil society organisations and in particular by women's organisations.

Responses to gender-based violence need to ensure:

- A victim-centred approach;
- Accessibility for all victims;
- Confidentiality and privacy for victims and survivors;
- The safety and well-being of victims/survivors (and any accompanying children);
- Full accountability for perpetrators;
- Effective access for victims/survivors to legal remedies and legal aid, free where possible;
- That power imbalances and gender inequality are taken into account when designing further support systems for victims/survivors, including possible empowerment strategies.

Some practical measures to respect these principles might include:

- Round-the-clock free telephone lines providing information, support and counselling;
- Immediate points of contact so that victims/survivors can easily access medical and legal services
- Provision of safe accommodation, for example: safety houses and shelters, opportunities for victims to keep using their home, with continual assessment of risk, relocation support for long term needs, etc.;
- Access to gender sensitive primary health care and specialist gender-based violence services;
- Advocacy and legal support, including free legal assistance, advice, advocacy, and court support services for victims/survivors.

- Accessible information about rights and entitlements, including free access to qualified and impartial interpreters and the translation of legal documents, where necessary or where requested;
- Emergency barring orders in cases of domestic violence;
- Access to counselling, both short and long term, including access to support groups;
- Facilitating the economic independence of victims/survivors from their abusers;
- Support for the professional and social reintegration of victims/survivors, focusing on ensuring their capacity to make decisions about their lives. This may include training, support finding work, support finding long-term accommodation, and assistance building a social network of support.

Prosecution of perpetrators needs to be built into policy measures to address gender violence. However, in addition to prosecution and punishment - where appropriate -work with the perpetrators of gender-based violence can also help to reduce the chances of their returning to patterns of violence. It is worth noting that in some cases of domestic violence, victims choose to return home and resume relationships. In such cases it is important that there are services available which work with perpetrators to reduce violent behaviour.

Such services might include the provision of counselling to address the root causes of violence, or training and education on gender-based violence. Work with men only groups is often helpful.

National helplines

The Secretariat of the Istanbul Convention maintains a list of national helplines available in Europe.
https://www.coe.int/en/web/istanbul-convention/help-lines

Essential Services for Women and Girls Subject to Violence

The United Nations Joint Global Programme on Essential Services for Women and Girls Subject to Violence has developed service delivery guidelines for services to be provided by the health, social services, police and justice sectors as well as guidelines for the coordination of essential services and the governance of coordination processes and mechanisms.

http://www.unwomen.org/en/digital-library/publications/2015/12/essential-services-package-for-women-and-girls-subject-to-violence

2. Prevention of gender–based violence

Prevention plays a central role in efforts to eradicate and remove the root causes of gender-based violence. Youth work and human rights activism can make an important contribution to such preventative work.

This might include:

- Work to change attitudes, or questioning gender roles and stereotypes that make gender-based violence acceptable in society. This can be done through organising campaigns, training, peer-to-peer education, or by including a gender equality dimension in all aspects of education policies;
- Providing accessible information about what gender-based violence is, about its different forms, possible remedies and existing support measures. This might include producing leaflets or websites, working on social media campaigns, creating TV spots, or making information available in youth centres and schools;
- Training professionals to be able to identify, address and respond to gender-based violence. This might include providing training for teachers, youth workers, social workers, trainers, the police, the justice system, health care providers, etc.;
- Revealing the scale of the problem: gender-based violence is rarely discussed, and data at a local or regional level is often not available, or is incomplete. Many victims choose not to report incidents, and certain forms of violence (e.g. sexist hate speech) may not be punishable by law. It is very important that the extent of the problem is made clear;
- Awareness raising campaigns and policies to address gender inequality and gender-based violence can also help to raise the importance of the problem in the public eye. Such campaigns might use traditional means, such as posters, leaflets and websites, but might also utilise social media and flash mobs, for example;
- Empowerment programmes which strengthen the self-esteem and autonomy of those sections of the population which are more likely to be at risk of violence;
- Furthering gender equality and human rights education for everyone.

The four campaigns below are meant to be examples of global actions anf initiatives which may support local action by strengthening the global dimension of the issues and the action.

Voices against violence

UN Women, in partnership with the World Association of Girl Guides and Girl Scouts (WAGGGS) has developed a global non-formal education curriculum to engage young people in efforts to prevent and end violence against girls and women. "Voices against Violence" is a co-educational curriculum designed for various age groups, from 5 to 25 years. It provides young people with the tools and expertise to understand the root causes of violence in their communities, to educate and involve peers and others in the community to work to prevent such violence, and helps them to to learn where they can access support, if they experience violence.

http://www.unwomen.org/en/what-we-do/ending-violence-against-women/prevention

International Day against Homophobia, Transphobia and Biphobia

Since 2005, 17 May has been observed around the globe as the International Day against Homophobia, Transphobia and Biphobia. It marks the date when, in 1990, the World Health Organization removed homosexuality from its list of mental disorders. 17 May has become an annual landmark, drawing the attention of decision makers, the media, the general public, commentators, local authorities, and others to the risks and difficulties faced by Lesbians, Gays, Bisexuals, Transgender or Intersex people, and by others who do not conform to majority sexual and gender norms. Coordinated by the IDAHO Committee 17 May is marked around the globe with political statements, street marches, parades, festivals, art and educational activities.

http://www.dayagainsthomophobia.org

#metoo (including names in other languages)

#Metoo is a hashtag which began in October 2017 and has since spread virally on social media. It has acted both to highlight the prevalence of gender-based violence and harassment in the workplace, on a global level, and to offer solidarity and support. #Metoo arose after a series of public claims of sexual misconduct arose, against a well-known American film producer. The hashtag has been used widely in many European countries, and denunciations cover different professions and areas of life: politics, sport, finance, cinema etc. The movement is reported to have extended to more than 85 countries, expanding the scope of the initial discussion and prompting the European Parliament to hold a special discussion on sexual harassment on 25 October 2017, calling, among other things, for the ratification of the Istanbul Convention by the European Union and its member states.

16 days of activism against gender-based violence

This is an international campaign, which runs each year from the 25th November - International Day for the Elimination of Violence against Women - to the 10th December, International Human Rights Day. It is seen as a time to galvanise action to end violence against women and girls around the world. The campaign originates from the first Women's Global Leadership Institute, coordinated by the Center for Women's Global Leadership, in 1991. Each year the campaign takes a theme – either a new one, or a continuation of a previous theme. Throughout the 16 days of the campaign, numerous organisations and movements run events dealing with particular areas of gender inequality, in order to bring attention to these issues and help to bring about change.

https://16dayscwgl.rutgers.edu

3. Building a human rights culture

Effective action requires not only responding to incidents of gender-based violence and working to prevent individual instances, but also building a culture based on alternative principles and values to those which underlie gender-based violence and discrimination. Human rights offer a set of values to inform our daily lives, and they establish minimum standards for full equality and a life in dignity. Effective work with young people and communities against gender-based violence also requires working for human rights.

Working towards a human rights culture with a gender perspective can take many forms. It may involve advocating and building support for strong institutions and for adequate state responses or mechanisms to address human rights violations and gender-based violence. Actions that could be taken include advocating for your country to sign and ratify the Istanbul Convention, and implementing its legal and political requirements.

Other possible actions might include advocating for the signature and implementation of the Lanzarote Convention, or the abolition of sterilisation as mandatory for sex reassignment, or forbidding the 'sex normalising' surgeries that exist in some countries and which operate on new born intersex without information being given to those involved, and sometimes without their consent.

Working for gender equality demands measures that will lead to substantive equality. Such work can involve empowering women and girls, and LGBT+ communities, to take part in community life, including creating spaces and opportunities for them to participate in decision making and policy design.

4. Gender in youth work and youth organisations

Where there are people, there are gender issues; and where there are people, there is the potential for gender-based violence. When young people work, organise, socialise and engage in education together, there will always be a gender dimension, and this needs to be taken into account.

Youth initiatives can play a role in responding to gender-based violence, from supporting young people's access to proper information about gender-based violence, to advocating for the change of laws and policies. However, youth organisations also need to inspect their own work, to see how, and to what extent, gender issues are addressed.

The best way to start this process of self-reflection is to analyse the ways in which gender features in the work of particular organisations and, generally in organisations or institutions delivering youth work. Gender mainstreaming does not mean simply counting numbers of young women and young men, nor does it necessarily demand running special activities for these groups, although this may be important. The following section invites you to reflect alone, or together, on gender matters in relation to your community and the organisation you work with. It should help you to take stock and provide you with ideas about what you could do more effectively to address gender in your work.

a) Community level

Reflect

- Is there widespread social and political recognition that gender-based violence is an issue?
- Are there laws in your country that protect victims of gender-based violence and punish perpetrators?
- Are these laws successfully applied? What are the enforcement mechanisms, and who collects the data?
- How are the issues of gender and gender-based violence reflected in local and national media?
- Who else works on gender-based violence? Are there other organisations carrying out work on the topic that you could learn from, or cooperate with?
- Are the issues of violence and gender-based violence addressed in schools?

Take action

Join coalitions and networks of organisations working on gender-based violence. There is no point in duplicating the work of other organisations, and work is often more effective when people and organisations cooperate. If you are just starting to address gender-based violence in your work you could benefit from joining a coalition, giving you access to other organisations' knowledge and expertise, contacts, training, and research. You could offer a contribution based on providing a youth perspective on the issues discussed, and on expanding the outreach of the coalition.

b) Organisation level

Reflect

- How does your organisation address gender-based violence? How does it work on prevention (e.g. it reports cases of gender-based violence, it runs awareness-raising campaigns, etc.)?
- Who is involved in the decision making structures of your organisation? Are men and women equally represented? Can LGBT+ young people openly assert their identity and take part in your organisation? Are they part of any decision making structures?
- Do you consider the effect of decisions on different groups – e.g. on men, women, and those who identify as neither?
- Are you aware of gender-based violence experienced by young people in your organisation/group? Are such instances documented/acted upon/discussed? Are there mechanisms in place for reporting or supporting victims?
- Is gender equality viewed through a human rights lens, with a clear understanding that gender equality is not about "special rights", but about promoting everyone's dignity and rights to freedom and equality?
- Have the youth workers and youth leaders within the organisation been trained to recognise gender-based violence, and are they able to address it in their youth work, including by providing victims with information about rights and services they can access?
- Are your activities accessible to everyone? How is gender reflected in your selection processes and in communication with participants?
- What kind of resources do you use in your activities? Do these reflect and reproduce gender stereotypes and roles in the society – or do they question them?
- Is there provision for equality of opportunity and participation both with respect to participants, but also for teams or experts invited?
- Do you have a policy for addressing harassment or gender-based violence incidents that might occur in youth work contexts? Is this policy, including any contact persons, made explicit to participants?

Take action

Draft a gender policy document containing (a) statements of principle relating to gender equality (b) specific regulations about how these will be monitored and (c) mechanisms for safeguarding gender equality. The drafting of strategies and policies to promote gender equality can be an important process in itself, even before any strategy or policy is implemented. In participatory environments, such processes and documents need to be dynamic, and open to consultation and revision.

Domination techniques

In training, and in organisational contexts, it is important to consider the ways in which power relationships and gender norms are maintained. To highlight and analyse how the relationship between the sexes can be linked to power, the Norwegian social psychologist Berit Ås developed an analysis of domination techniques which incorporates the following points:

a) *Making invisible*: If nobody listens to what you say, you can easily stop talking.

   Marginalising people can be done through individual actions but can also be the effect of an environment, where it is difficult to make one's voice heard.

b) *Ridiculing*: Ridicule can be expressed in comments, insults and jokes, or in non- verbal communication which hints at the other's inadequacy. People may often play along with these dynamics to avoid being the subject of ridicule.

c) *Withholding information*: Those who hold important information may exercise power and influence. If information is not shared evenly among people in the same position, or if decisions are taken without involving everyone concerned, there is an inequality of power. It may be that important issues are discussed in informal groups, or that decisions have already been taken informally when the official body meets.

d) *Double punishment*: Double punishment means that whatever you do is condemned, or seen as wrong. A girl who is not involved in discussion may be seen as passive, boring and avoiding responsibility. On the other hand, if she gets involved, she may be pointed out for taking too much space and wanting to be "everywhere".

e) *Shame and guilt*: Creating feelings of shame and guilt is a powerful tool of oppression. Among boys, it may involve accusing someone of being 'girly', or not sufficiently manly. In families, feelings of shame and guilt may be used to control children's habits or actions, where these are likely to disrupt or where they conflict with established values. In youth contexts, people may be shamed for such things as not taking part, or sharing a joke.

f) *Objectification*: Objectification is normally associated with the kinds of sexualised images that circulate in the popular media. However, people can be objectified in organisational contexts, for example by being referred to in terms of their physical appearance, or by being included merely tokenistically because of their perceived identity.

g) *Violence and the threat of violence*: The fear of being subjected to violence is a strong restraint on people's behaviour and freedom of movement. For example, having to take a longer route home in order to avoid violence, and not daring to go out at night for fear of violence are everyday realities for many young people.

c) Language

Reflect

- Do you use a gender binary system of reference in application forms or in communication with young people?
- Do you use gender normative titles such as Ms/Mr in documents?
- Are you able to detect sexist language, and respond appropriately?
- Do you explain choices, such as using gender-neutral pronouns, to participants and youth workers?

Take action

Review and, if necessary, create a series of template documents for your organisation, by removing all gender normative titles and including gender sensitive language. This may be difficult to do in some languages, so you may need to see if any such attempts have already been made by others, and discuss possible solutions with colleagues.

d) Safe environments and facilities

Reflect

- If you work in a youth centre, have staff been trained on questions of gender equality - including any staff involved in providing services? If you work in a school, or are holding sessions in another establishment, have you discussed such issues with those with responsibility for the establishment?
- When running residential projects, do you take into account the comfort of participants - in terms of accommodation, sharing of rooms, the safety and security of venues and the local neighbourhood?
- Do you accommodate for specific needs (e.g. by allowing someone to accompany a participant, if necessary)?
- Have you developed a code of conduct with participants?
- Do you have emergency contacts for participants? Are you aware of any particular issues you may need to take into account when communicating with emergency contacts? For example, in the case of an LGBT+ participant, do you know if they are "out" to the emergency contact?
- In the case of minors, are you aware of what it may be appropriate or inappropriate to communicate to parents?
- Is there an allocated "trust member" of the educational team that participants can either seek advice from, or appeal to, in cases of discrimination? Is the allocated person aware of issues which might require recourse to legal action?

Take action

Work with "single sex" groups in youth work is often used to help young people to address prejudice, stereotypes, and questions about gender norms, and to provide a space for them to explore issues such as sexuality and gender identity. Such groups can help to bridge the gap between society's expectations and self-realisation. You could also think of these groups in terms broader than gender: a girls-only group should include transgender girls, if they want to join. You could also organise support groups for young intersex people, or for young lesbian and gays. The same principle should apply: to provide a safe space, where questions relating to gender identity and gender-based violence can be discussed.

An effective group should provide members with a feeling of belonging, with tools to deal with problems and conflicts that might arise in everyday life, and with increased self-awareness.

Project examples

The Youth Department of the Council of Europe has adopted a set of Guidelines on integrating and mainstreaming gender equality into the intercultural activities of the Council of Europe and its partners: https://www.coe.int/en/web/youth/gender-equality-guidelines

In Chapter 2, the activity 'No Violence in Here' can be used to support you to devise a policy for action, and to prevent gender-based violence in school. You could adapt the activity to start a similar discussion in your organisation.

The International Lesbian, Gay, Bisexual, Transgender and Queer Youth Student Organisation (IGLYO) has developed a toolkit on addressing norms with young people, *Norms Criticism*, with the aim of supporting young people to deconstruct norms affecting their lives and identities, and to be able to self-identify and express themselves independently of sexual orientation, gender identity, gender expression, sex characteristics or bodily diversity, and without violence and hatred.

A similar resource, **Break the norm!** is also available at https://www.coe.int/en/web/youth/gender-equality - courtesy of the Living History Forum and RFSL Ungdom (Sweden)

Amnesty International's 'My Body, My Rights' campaign promotes sexual and reproductive rights for everyone around the world. The campaign advocates for governments to stop using criminal law to control people's sexuality and reproduction and ensure that people have easy access to sexual and reproductive health services, education and information. It also advocates for the empowerment of people to make decisions over their bodies and the prohibition of all forms of discrimination and violence. The campaign involves research, awareness raising through online and offline actions, petitions, and other advocacy efforts: *https://www.amnesty.org/en/get-involved/my-body-my-rights/*

Giuvlipen (feminism in Romani language) is a feminist Roma theatre company from Bucharest. They have produced and staged theatre plays and performances that explore the intersection of racism and sexism in the experience of Roma women, with the aim of breaking down stereotypes and prejudice both in the Roma community and in society at large. *www.Giuvlipen.tumblr.org*

'Phenja – Violence has no colour' was a project implemented by the Association for Roma Women Rights Promotion (E-Romnja) in the period 2014-2016, focusing on working with Roma communities in Romania to explore and expose gender-based violence against Roma women. *www.e-romja.ro*

LGBT Youth Scotland provides online support to young people through a LiveChat feature of their website, providing the opportunity to chat with trained youth workers in real time about questions of sexual identity, coming out, relationship issues, bullying, and sexual health. *https://www.lgbtyouth.org.uk/yp-online-support*

5. Developing an initiative or a strategy addressing gender-based violence

Any action requires planning. Planning should be carried out together with the members of your group/organisation, to ensure that you focus on what your group wants, what they are able to do, and the best ways of achieving this. The section below offers a simple way of structuring a plan and organising work with a group in order to help them achieve their aims effectively.

Step 1: Know yourselves

You can use the reflection questions above to reflect critically on the work of your group or organisation on gender and gender-based violence. However, before beginning, you may also want to review the knowledge and skills that exist in your group, as well as on participants' interests.

A SWOT analysis is an effective way of doing this. Such an analysis also looks at the circumstances outside the group which might influence what you may be able to do.

The acronym SWOT stands for:

Strengths: things the group is good at doing

Weaknesses: things the group is less good at doing

Opportunities: possibilities existing outside the group that might be utilised to benefit the action

Threats: things outside the group that might get in the way of the aims of the action.

Step 2: Make choices

How does a group choose which issue to work on? In most cases, people in the group will have issues that they think are important and want to work on. The main difficulty may be in arriving at a common agreement about which issue to choose, and about the best way to approach it.

You will need to keep all members of the group behind the final decision, so do not rush a discussion about issues: give them plenty of time to air preferences and talk through the advantages of choosing one rather than another. Remind them that there may be opportunities to address other concerns later on. Remind them also that the most important thing is that the group stays together to work through an action - so if one person is strongly against a particular choice, it may not be worth pursuing. Try to reach consensus in the group, rather than going for a majority decision.

Knowing the problem

A problem tree provides a useful tool for analysing the issue you will be working on. This is a method of breaking down an issue, looking at causes and consequences, and placing it in the context of other problems in society. A problem tree can be useful both in providing a better understanding of an issue for the group, and in helping to approach a solution in a more strategic way. You can find an example of a problem tree at the bottom of this chapter.

This is the procedure a group would use to draw up a problem tree for their own issue:

- Start by writing down the problem that you wish to tackle in the middle of a large sheet of paper.
- Underneath it, write down all the things that contribute to the problem, and link these up to form the roots of the original problem. Take each root at a time and think about its causes, writing down the things that contribute to this 'root'. Keep tackling each root until you can take the exercise no further. Be aware that the tree may have deeper roots than you think!
- You may also want to extend the "branches" of the tree in the same manner: these will be the consequences of your original problem. You may find that what you began with as your main concern is actually the root or branch of a different tree.

When you have finished, take a look at your tree:

- Should you tackle the task you originally set yourself or one of its contributing factors first?
- Has the tree helped you to think of ways to go about tackling this problem?

Step 3: Identify the solution(s)

It is important to know what you would like to happen as a result of your action! What would count as a success? Get the group to think about what they are trying to achieve, and how they will measure whether or not they have been successful. They may find it useful to go back to the problem tree and use this to identify concrete solutions. In general, attacking the roots will lead to solutions further up the tree.

Be mindful that changes in policy are often difficult to bring about, but not impossible. The group needs to be realistic about what it can hope for: remind them that even a "small" result can be an invaluable contribution to resolving a larger problem. Effective campaigns are nearly always built up from exactly such "small" actions, and anything achieved by your group can either be built on later on, or picked up by other activists concerned about the problem.

It may be helpful for the group to brainstorm some general reasons for taking action. This may help them to pick out those which are most relevant to their own issue, and to identify a number of specific objectives that they feel it is realistic to achieve.

Step 4: Planning your action

Your group has now decided on an issue and has an idea of what they might be trying to do. It is time to decide on the methods they will use to achieve their aim.

a) Which problem do you want to address?

This step is simple: it will be the result of the problem tree exercise that the group carried out. If you did not carry out the problem tree activity, try to get the group to formulate the problem they want to address as accurately as possible.

b) What is your target audience?

Unless you are hoping to resolve the problem immediately, the target audience for your action may not be the person or people who can make the final change that you are looking for. Your action is quite likely to be no more than a step towards making the change; for example, you may be trying to alert the public to an issue, in order to put pressure on the government. Or you may be trying to set up a local group so that the group can work on the issue you are concerned about. Your target audience may consist of more than one group of people.

c) Which changes do you hope to see?

This question again relates to your action, but not necessarily to the final change you might be aiming for. You may be able to generate interest in the problem, which will encourage others to take action in different ways, and that, in turn, may be enough to bring about a change in company policy or in government regulations applying to those companies.

In this box you need to think about what the action is meant to achieve, and how you will know whether or not you have succeeded.

d) How is change expected to come about?

This question is not yet about the mechanism that the group decides to use, it is about how the action is supposed to work, and will often relate to the psychology of changing people's minds or making people realise that they need to do something differently. It is a very important question that is often forgotten, and ignoring it could affect the impact of your action.

e) What means will you use to influence your audience?

In this stage you should decide on the exact course of action to be taken by the group. The choices will have been narrowed down by moving through the previous steps. The group should now be able to draw up a list of possible actions which could help to bring about the transition identified in the previous box. Encourage them to think creatively, and look back at some of the suggestions in this chapter. Try again to reach consensus over the final choice.

Step 5: Getting organised

There is one final stage before taking the ideas of the group out onto the public. It is highly recommended that the group draws up an action plan to decide on organisational matters. Although this may not be essential for a simple action, it is a useful habit for any group, and will ensure that tasks are divided out equally, according to skills and preferences. It should also ensure that nothing is forgotten!

They will need to decide:

- Which tasks need to be carried out?
- Who is going to undertake the different task(s)?
- When are they going to be done?

Step 6: Monitoring and evaluation

It is vital to take some time after the action is finished to debrief the group and assess what went well, and what could have gone better. If we are talking about a more complex project, you might want to ensure a monitoring mechanism and regular group meetings to assess how things are going, what could be changed and done better. This can be done at the end of each action in the project.

The following questions may be useful as a framework for conducting an evaluation discussion with your group:

- What are your feelings after the day of action? (This can be done as a brief run round the group.)
- What did you feel went well?
- Was anything more difficult than you had imagined it to be?
- Was there anything unexpected?
- Do you think there are any lessons we could learn for next time?
- Did we achieve what we set out to do?
- Did we achieve anything else that perhaps we had not foreseen?
- Do you feel satisfied with yourselves, and would you like to try something like this again?
- What shall we do next?

The problem tree[1]

You may use the example of this problem tree to explore the realities of gender-based violence in your community or organisation and strategise your campaigns, action or education activities.

You may also use the problem tree to as an educational tool to work with young people to create a deeper understanding of gender-based violence:

- Explain that in order to understand and respond to gender-based violence, we need to see it as a problem with numerous connections to socialisation and power relations in society. It can thus be useful to look at the underlying causes of gender-based violence.
- Show participants the "Gender-based violence tree" and tell them that they will be working in groups to identify some of the things which lead to gender-based violence (the "roots"of the tree), and some of its the effects (the "branches").
- Explain the logic of the tree image. Every box which leads up the tree to another box is answering the question "why?". This is true for the branches as well as the roots. You could take an example of gender-based violence to illustrate this in more detail, such as "domestic violence is a private matter of the family" leads to / is renforced by "reports of domestic violence are not followed-up by the police". It is also possible to discuss how some of these causes and effects nourish or justify each other.

The roots: when participants work down the tree, starting from gender-based violence itself, they are exploring answers to the question "why does this happen?". They should fill the "roots" with as many reasons as possible. Give them an illustration of how one "cause" will have its own causes. For example, ask them why sexist jokes abound. Prompt with questions about where we "learn" negative things we believe about LGBT+ people or "feminists".

The branches: here participants need to explore the possible consequences of items lower down the branch. Ask them what could happen to an individual or to a group which is victim of gender-based violence. Ask them what might happen as a result of that.

- Divide participants into groups and give them a piece of flipchart paper to draw their tree on. Tell them to write the following text, or an example of your own, in the 'trunk' of the tree and then to complete as many branches and roots as they are able to. You can provide this example has been posted on the Internet: *We need to concentrate on curing gays, not tolerating them!* Or this one from a news headline: *One woman in ten is victim of violence in her own home*[2].
- Give the groups some 20 minutes to complete their trees. Ask the groups to present their results and show their trees to the others.
- Debrief the activity, focusing on the relations between trees and branches , how difficult it was and where it is possible or necessary to introduce change. You may also want to address "vicious circles" in the tree: for example, mistrust in the police forces results in fewer reports of violence, which reinforces the feeling of impunity and superiority… where to stop the circle?

Endnotes

1 This activity is adapted from the activity "Roots and branches" in Bookmarks, the manual to combat online hate speech through human rights education, Council of Europe, 2016.
https://www.coe.int/en/web/no-hate-campaign/bookmarks-connexions

2 Le Monde, 17 January 2019

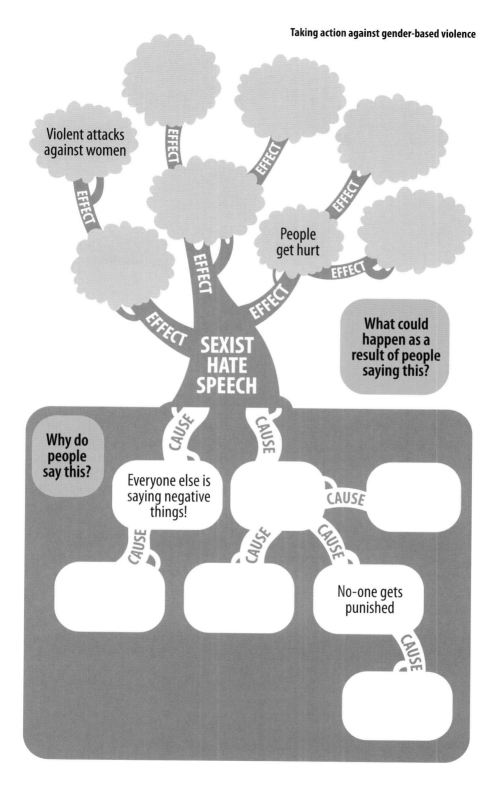

CHAPTER 4
Themes related to gender and gender-based violence

Themes related to gender and gender-based violence

This chapter provides users and readers of Gender Matters with additional useful information on a few topics which are likely to be raised in the discussion, especially in the debriefing, of the activities in chapter 2. They serve thus to prepare facilitators by presenting some essential information on five themes:

- Feminism and Women's Rights Movements
- Intersectionality and Multiple Discrimination
- LGBT+
- Masculinities
- Sexuality

The choice of these themes was determined by their connection with the activities and by the fact that many of them are subject to controversy, often resulting from misunderstanding, if not outright misinformation. Each of them is indeed complex and the object of intense debate and opposing views among experts, scholars, activists and young people. It is not the intention of this manual to either limit or "fix" the debates to what is in this chapter. Instead, these pages should be seen as starting points or anchors for non-experts. We hope that they will inspire readers to seek more information, expand their knowledge and develop their own opinion and points of view. The authors have endeavoured to be as neutral and factual as possible, an almost impossible aim as we all have our own experiences, views and preferences. The text should therefore be interpreted as a non-prescriptive proposal to learn more or to recall essentials.

Feminism and women's rights movements

There are people who believe that we do not need feminism today, but nothing could be further from the truth. Women have struggled for equality and against oppression for centuries, and although some battles have been partly won - such as the right to vote and equal access to education – women are still disproportionally affected by all forms of violence and by discrimination in every aspect of life.

It is true that in some areas and on certain issues, there have been improvements: for example, in Saudi Arabia women were allowed, for the first time, to vote and run for office in 2015(!). However, on other issues there has been little or no progress: for example, there have been insignificant reductions in cases of violence against women. Women continue to receive lower pay for the same work as men in all parts of the world; there are still countries that do not have laws against marital rape, and still allow child brides; and practices such as "honour" killings and female genital mutilation still exist.

Jokes about feminism and stereotypes about feminists persist, and many of these are also homophobic and assume that being lesbian is something 'bad'. In fact, being a feminist is not something particular to any sex or gender: there are women and men who consider themselves feminists, some are gay or lesbian, some heterosexual, bisexual or transgender - and some may identify differently.

The concept of feminism reflects a history of different struggles, and the term has been interpreted in fuller and more complex ways as understanding has developed . In general, feminism can be seen as a movement to put an end to sexism, sexist exploitation and oppression and to achieve full gender equality in law and in practice.

Women's movements and the history of feminism

There have been many extraordinary women who have played an important role in local or world history, but not all of these have necessarily been advocates of women's issues. The women's movement is made up of women and men who work and fight to achieve gender equality and to improve the lives of women as a social group. In most societies, women were traditionally confined to the home as daughters, wives and mothers, and we are often only aware of women in history because of their relation to famous men. Of course many women throughout history did in fact play an important role in cultural and political life, but they tend to be invisible. An organised women's movement only really started in the 19th century, even though women activists and the struggle for equality have always been part of all human societies.

One of the early pioneers, who thought and wrote about women as a group, is the Italian writer Christine de Pizan, who published a book about women's position in society as early as 1495. Christine de Pizan wrote about books she had read by famous men, who wrote books about the sins and weaknesses of girls and women, and questioned whether women were really human beings at all, or whether they were more similar to animals. Christine de Pizan's work offers a good example of the early stages of the struggle for women's equality. However, she was very unusual in being able to read and write, which was not at all common for women of that time.

In later history, women took part in the French revolution from the very beginning: the demonstrations that led to the revolution started with a large group of working women marching to Versailles to demand not only food to feed their families, but also political change. However, the French Revolution did not lead to proper recognition of women's rights. For that reason, in September 1791, Olympe de Gouges wrote the Declaration of the Rights of Woman and of the Female Citizen, in response to the Declaration of the Rights of Man and of the Citizen, and with the intention of exposing the failure of the French Revolution to recognise gender equality. As a result of her writings de Gouges was accused, tried and convicted of treason, resulting in her immediate execution.

The women's movement began to develop in North America, mainly because women there were allowed to go to school earlier than in Europe - and women who can read and write, and who are encouraged to think for themselves, usually start to question how society works. The first activists travelled around North America and fought for the end of both slavery and women's oppression. They organised the 'First Women's Rights Convention' in 1848, and continued to campaign to improve the social position of all women. The movement also began in Europe with the same broad aims: activists collected signatures demanding that working women should receive their own wages and not their husbands', that women should be able to own a house and have custody of their children.

The fight for women's right to vote in elections is known as the 'suffragette movement'. By the end of the 19th century, this had become a worldwide movement, and the words 'feminism' and 'feminist movement' started to be used from that point on. This **first wave of feminism** activism included mass demonstrations, the publishing of newspapers, organised debates, and the establishment of international women's organisations. By the 1920s, women had won the right to vote in most European countries and in North America. At around the same time, women became more active in communist, socialist and social democratic parties because increasing numbers of women began to work outside the home in factories and offices. Women were first allowed to go to university in the early 20th century, having both a career and a family. In certain countries, when fascist parties gained power the feminist movement was banned. Women started organising again after the end of the Second World War, and they soon gained equal political rights in most European countries, with women's emancipation becoming an important aim and most women being allowed to take on full-time jobs, divorce their husbands and go to university.

In Western Europe and the USA, the feminist movement was resurgent by the 1970s. Although this **second wave of feminism** aimed to achieve 'women's liberation', different groups had different ideas about how this should be done. Liberal feminists wanted better equality laws and reform of institutions such as schools, churches and the media. Radical feminists argued that the root cause of women's inequality is patriarchy: men, as a group, oppress women. They also focused on violence against women by men, and started to talk about violence in the family, and rape. Socialist feminists argued that it is a combination of patriarchy and capitalism that causes women's oppression. The second wave of feminism also resulted in new areas of science: women's studies became a discipline to be studied at university, and books began to be published about women's achievements in literature, music and science, and recording women's previously unwritten history. Finally, the women's movement played an important role in the drafting of international documents about women's rights, such as the Universal Declaration of Human Rights and the Convention on the Elimination of all Forms of Discrimination Against Women (CEDAW, 1979).

The **third wave of feminism** mainly refers to the American movement in the 1990s, and was a reaction to the **backlash** of conservative media and politicians announcing the end of feminism or referring to 'post-feminism'. The term 'backlash' was popularised by Susan Faludi in her book "Backlash. The Undeclared War against Women", published in 1991, and describing the negative reaction of the patriarchal system towards women's liberation. This was hardly a new phenomenon: women's movements had always been met with antagonism. However, in the 1980s, institutionalised forms of attacks on women's rights grew stronger. The third wave of feminism can be characterised by an increased awareness of overlapping categories, such as race, class, gender, sexual orientation. More emphasis was also placed on racial issues, including the status of women in other parts of the world (global feminism). This was also a moment when a number of feminist non-governmental organisations were established, but focusing on specific feminist issues, rather than claiming to represent general feminist ideas. Third wave feminism actively uses media and pop culture to promote its ideas and to run activities, for example by publishing blogs or e-zines. It focuses on bringing feminism closer to the people's daily lives. The main issues that third wave feminists are concerned about include: sexual harassment, domestic violence, the pay gap between men and women, eating disorders and body image, sexual and reproductive rights, honour crimes and female genital mutilation.

Cyberfeminism and networked feminism (fourth-wave feminism)

The term cyberfeminism is used to describe the work of feminists interested in theorising, critiquing, and making use of the Internet, cyberspace, and new-media technologies in general. The term and movement grew out of "third-wave" feminism. However, the exact meaning is still unclear to some: even at the first meeting of cyberfeminists "The First Cyberfeminist International (FCI)" in Kassel (Germany), participants found it hard to provide a definition, and as a result of discussions, they proposed 100 anti-theses[1] (with reference to Martin Luther's theses) on what cyberfeminism is not. These included, for example, it is not an institution, it is not an ideology, it is not an –ism. Cyberfeminism is considered to be a predecessor of 'networked feminism', which refers generally to feminism on the Internet: for example, mobilising people to take action against sexism, misogyny or gender-based violence against women. One example is the online movement #metoo in 2017, which was a response on social networks from women all over the world to the case of Harvey Weinstein, a Hollywood producer who was accused of sexually harassing female staff in the movie industry.

Sexism

This term is very often present in feminist literature as well as in the media and everyday life, and it is an important concept in understanding feminism. Sexism means perceiving and judging people only on the basis of their belonging to a particular sex or gender. It also covers discrimination of a person on the same basis. It is important to note that sexism applies to both men and women, however, women are more affected by sexism than men in all areas of life. Everyday sexism takes different forms, sometimes not easily recognisable – for example, telling jokes about girls, commenting on the female body (objectifying women), reacting to the way women are dressed, assigning women easier tasks in Internet games or objectifying women in advertising.

The literature mentions three types of sexism[2]:

- **Traditional sexism:** supporting traditional gender roles, treating women as worse than men, employing traditional stereotypes which portray women as less competent than men.
- **Modern sexism:** denying gender discrimination ('it is not a problem anymore'), having a negative attitude towards women's rights, denying the validity of claims made by women
- **Neosexism:** This notion refers to ideologies that justify discrimination towards women on the basis of competences – "men are effectively better competent for some things" – for example in managerial or leadership positions, and not on a direct discrimination of women. Defenders of these ideas tend to ignore or deny the difficulties faced by women in society as having an influence on "competences".

If it is true that the situation of women's human rights has improved in recent years, this does not mean that sexism has ended.

In March 2019, the Committee of Ministers of the Council of Europe adopted Recommendation CM/Rec(2019)1 on preventing and combating sexism. The Recommendation defines sexism as

> any act, gesture, visual representation, spoken or written words, practice or behaviour based upon the idea that a person or a group of persons is inferior because of their sex, which occurs in the public or private sphere, whether online or offline, with the purpose or effect of:
>
> - Violating the inherent dignity or rights of a person or a group of persons;
> - Resulting in physical, sexual, psychological or socio-economic harm or suffering to a person or a group of persons;
> - Creating an intimidating, hostile, degrading, humiliating or offensive environment;
> - Constituting a barrier to the autonomy and full realisation of human rights by a person or a group of persons;
> - Maintaining and reinforcing gender stereotypes.

The Recommendation stresses that sexism is a manifestation of historically unequal power relations between women and men, which leads to discrimination and prevents the full advancement of women in society. The Committee of Ministers asks Governments of member states to take measures to prevent and combat sexism and its manifestations in the public and private spheres, and encourage relevant stakeholders to implement appropriate legislation, policies and programmes.

Women's rights are human rights

Why do we need women's rights, when these are simply human rights? Why do we need human rights treaties about women's rights, when we have already general human rights instruments? Almost everywhere in the world, women are denied their human rights just because of their sex or gender. Women's rights should not be seen as special rights: they are human rights enshrined in international human rights treaties and other documents, and include such rights as freedom from discrimination, right to life, freedom from torture, right to privacy, access to health, right to decent living conditions, right to safety, and many others. However, there are also human rights instruments that take into account the specific situation of women in society with regards to accessing or exercising their human rights, or which aim to protect them from violence.

The Convention on the Elimination of All Forms of Discrimination against Women (CEDAW) – was adopted in 1979 by the UN General Assembly, and is often described as an international bill of rights for women. The document calls on all member states of the UN to adopt measures against discrimination of women in all spheres of life and protect them from any kind of violence. The Convention establishes the Committee on the Elimination of Discrimination against Women, which is the body that monitors States parties' compliance with the Convention. The Committee receives and considers complaints from individuals or groups within its jurisdiction.

The UN Security Council resolution 1325 on women, peace and security (2000) recognises the fact that armed conflicts or wars affect women differently than men, and highlights the specific role of women in peace building processes. This resolution was followed by 7 other resolutions subsequently adopted in 2008, 2009, 2010, 2013, and 2015.

At the level of the Council of Europe, **the European Convention on Human Rights** obliges member states to respect and promote all human rights in the Convention without discrimination on any grounds, including sex (Article 14 of the Convention). A further treaty, **the Revised European Social Charter** (1996), provides for equality between women and men in education, work and family life, and calls for positive measures in order to ensure equal opportunities and the right to equal remuneration.

The Council of Europe Convention on Action against Trafficking in Human Beings (2005) aims at preventing and combating trafficking in women, men and children for the purpose of sexual, labour or other types of exploitation. It is also designed to offer protection to victims and to ensure that traffickers face prosecution. This Convention includes a non-discrimination provision in Article 3, and obliges state signatories to promote gender equality and to use gender mainstreaming in the development, implementation and assessment of measures for implementing the Convention.

The Council of Europe Convention on Preventing and Combating Violence against Women and Domestic Violence (Istanbul Convention, 2011) is the most far-reaching international treaty to tackle violence against women in all its forms. You can read more about this treaty in the first chapter of this manual and in the appendices.

Recommendation No. R (79)10 of the Committee of Ministers concerning women migrants, calls on member states to ensure that national legislation and regulations concerning women migrants are fully adapted to meet international standards. It also recommends that measures should be taken to provide relevant information to women migrants, to prevent discrimination in their working conditions, to promote their socio-cultural integration and to improve their access to vocational guidance and training. The Council of Europe Gender Equality

Strategy for 2018 – 2023 foresees the review and update of this Recommendation.

Recommendation No. R (90)4 of the Council of Europe Committee of Ministers, on the elimination of sexism from language, calls on member states to promote the use of language reflecting the principle of equality between women and men, and to take appropriate measures to encourage the use of non-sexist language, taking account of the presence, status and role of women in society. The Recommendation also calls on member states to bring terminology used in legal documents, public administration and education into line with the principle of equality, and to encourage the use of non-sexist language in the media.

Recommendation No (2012)6 of the Council of Europe Committee of Ministers on the protection and promotion of the rights of women and girls with disabilities asks member states to adopt appropriate legislative measures and to undertake other positive actions likely to encourage the participation of women and girls with disabilities in all areas of life. Noting that women and girls with disabilities may suffer multiple discrimination, the proposed measures cover areas such as education and training, employment and economic status, health care, access to social protection, sexual and reproductive rights, motherhood and family life, access to justice and protection from violence and abuse, participation in culture, sport, leisure and tourism, and raising awareness and changing attitudes.

Recommendation CM/Rec(2019)1 of the Council of Europe Committee of Ministers on preventing and combating sexism asks member states to take measures to prevent and combat sexism and its manifestations in the public and private spheres, and encourage relevant stakeholders to implement appropriate legislation, policies and programmes. It also proposes specific measures to member states, including changes in legislation, education and awareness raising campaigns, programmes for children and young people on media literacy, development of online resources, research and integration of a gender equality perspective in all policies, programmes and research in relation to artificial intelligence.

Intersectionality and multiple discrimination

Discrimination

Discrimination is one of the most common human rights violations and is prohibited under human rights law. The principles of equality in rights and dignity, and freedom from discrimination were outlined in the first two articles of the Universal Declaration on Human Rights:

- All human beings are born free and equal in dignity and rights" (Article 1)
- Everyone is entitled to all the rights and freedoms set forth in this Declaration, without distinction of any kind.(Article 2)

Protection against discrimination in Europe can be found both within European Union law and within the Council of Europe treaty system, notably in the work of the European Court of Human Rights[3].

Article 14 of the European Convention on Human Rights and Fundamental Freedoms states that the rights and freedoms set out in the Convention should be secured *"without discrimination on any ground such as sex, race, colour, language, religion, political or other opinion, national or social origin, association with a national minority, property, birth or other status."* Protocol 12 to the Convention (2005) expanded the scope of the prohibition on discrimination, to cover all rights guaranteed at national level, regardless of whether or not they are rights within the Convention.

For countries in the European Union, the Charter of Fundamental Rights prohibits discrimination (Article 21) and is legally binding for all EU member states. EU institutions are legally bound to observe the Charter of Fundamental Rights of the European Union, including the provisions on non-discrimination. EU Member States must observe the Charter in relation to EU laws. In addition to the Charter, two EU Directives – the Employment Equality Directive and the Racial Equality Directive - prohibit discrimination in certain contexts, such as employment. It is complemented by a communication in 2009 stepping up the efforts of the EU to fight discrimination.

Discrimination occurs when a person is treated less favourably than other people in a comparable situation, only because they belong to or are perceived to belong to a particular group, and where such treatment cannot be objectively and reasonably justified. Several types of discrimination can be identified:

Direct discrimination is characterised by the intent to treat less favourably a person or a group. Indirect discrimination refers to cases where apparently neutral provisions or practices affect members (or perceived members) of a particular group in less favourable ways.

Structural discrimination is woven into the ways our societies function, and operates through norms, routines, patterns of attitudes and behaviour that create obstacles in achieving equal opportunities and real equality.

Multiple discrimination

People might be discriminated against because of one or more characteristics that are part of, or are perceived as part of their identity. People have multiple layers to their identity and may define themselves, or be defined by others, according to various criteria, including gender, sex, sexual orientation, nationality, ethnicity, social status, disability, religion and so on.

The concept of multiple discrimination recognises that discrimination can occur on the basis of more than one perceived characteristic. For example, a person who is discriminated on the grounds of their ethnicity may be also discrimination on the grounds of gender, sexual orientation, age, and so on. Such discrimination can, and often does, create *cumulative disadvantage*.

In 1995, the World Conference for Women, held in Beijing, drew attention to the fact that age, disability, social and economic status, ethnicity and race can create particular barriers for women. This led to the development of a framework for recognising multiple and coexisting forms of discrimination, which became part of the Beijing Platform for Action[4].

In her study on intersectionality in the European Union, Sandra Fredman proposes three main ways in which discrimination on more grounds than one can be conceptualised:

1) Sequential multiple discrimination – when a person suffers discrimination on different grounds on separate occasions. For example, a woman with a disability might suffer discrimination once because of her gender and on another occasion because of her disability. This type of discrimination is the easiest to deal with, because each incident can be assessed individually, and judged accordingly.

2) Additive multiple discrimination – when a person suffers discrimination on the same occasion but on two grounds, for example a gay woman is harassed because she is woman and gay. This type of discrimination is additive, because each of the grounds can be identified independently.

3) Intersectional discrimination – happens when two or multiple grounds operate simultaneously and interact in an inseparable manner, producing distinct and specific forms of discrimination. For example, a young Roma woman is discriminated in the labour market because she is Roma and is perceived to be 'dangerous', because she is a woman, and is therefore 'bound to have children soon', and because she is young and therefore unexperienced. In particular circumstances, the combination of these factors creates a negative synergy, so that the discrimination cannot be fully understood as the addition of criteria alone. In being considered

unexperienced and incompetent, the woman shares certain experiences of discrimination with young people; in being assumed to fit into a traditional role, she shares experiences with other women; and in being perceived as dangerous, she shares experiences with all Roma, including men. However, it is the particular intersection of all these factors that makes her case individual[5].

Multiple discrimination, including intersectional discrimination, are relatively recent concepts, which although now widely accepted, have not yet been fully reflected within the law and legal practice. Anti-discrimination law and its associated practice has traditionally taken a single-axis perspective, identifying and addressing single grounds in cases of discrimination.

Studies have shown an absence of data and legal mechanisms capable of dealing with intersectional discrimination at European level. Research into certain areas, for example women from disadvantaged communities, has produced some evidence that intersectional experiences of discrimination exist, and that policy and practice need to address all dimensions.

An intersectional approach to discrimination

Since the emergence of the term in 1989, intersectionality has been engaged in three main ways:

- applying an intersectional framework of analysis within research and teaching, particularly as applied to specific issues - for example, the interaction of disability and gender within the labour market;
- developing intersectionality as a theory and methodology;
- employing an intersectional lens to inform political interventions and advocacy work from NGOs and other campaigning organisations[6].

An intersectional analysis can be a useful tool for challenging the way that discrimination is perceived by society and at a legal level. It is primarily an analysis of the structures of power operating in context specific situations, and serves the purpose of making visible experiences of discrimination that would otherwise be lost within a single grounds analysis. An intersectional analysis can help to make the experiences of Muslim LGBT+ visible and the particular vulnerabilities they may face as Muslims exposed to islamophobia, as women exposed to sexism, as LGBT+ exposed to homo or transphobia.

What intersectional studies have revealed is that:

- Using a single grounds approach, victims are presented in essentialist terms, which can render minorities within a minority invisible in the public sphere - both in broader society and within the minority group. They are also likely to suffer from discrimination within the minority group;

- Victims are more likely to experience more instances of discrimination than shown by single grounds approaches;
- Victims are more likely to suffer from aggravated forms of discrimination, which are often more intense and make the person more vulnerable in society;
- Victims are more likely to suffer from structural inequalities in society, to be at risk of poverty, social exclusion and marginalisation.

Substantive equality ((also in the margin: substantive equality)) is understood as furthering equality of opportunity through four main functions:

1) Redressing disadvantage (the redistributive dimension)
2) Addressing stigma, prejudice, stereotyping and violence (the recognition dimension)
3) Enabling participation and giving a voice to those disadvantaged (the participative dimension)
4) Accommodating difference through structural change (the transformative dimension)[7]

Gender- based violence and intersectionality

Intersectional lenses can be very effective in dealing with gender-based violence, both in understanding the pervasiveness of the phenomenon, and in informing measures to address it. The personal and social resources used to cope with gender-based violence by survivors are influenced not only by gender, but also by the way that gender interacts with other aspects of identity and social position, such as ethnicity or disability or class. An intersectional approach to working with people who have experienced gender-based violence can provide for a more nuanced approach, by taking into account multiple forms of oppression and structural violence. Different forms of oppression accumulate over time and shape the sense of power, resilience and well-being of survivors, as well as affecting their capacity to deal with the trauma.

An intersectional approach can also better inform strategies for the prevention of gender-based violence by looking at the myriad of factors that lead to certain groups becoming more vulnerable and which limit their access to services and support.

An intersectional approach is also useful when understanding the causes of gender-based violence in relation to men, and in recognising that there are more ways of 'being a man' than traditional notions of masculinity allow - and that these should be acknowledged. You can read more about this in the sub-chapter on masculinities.

Working with young people on gender-based violence

The functions of substantive equality can also support measures in the field of youth work and youth policy, which is traditionally concerned with the recognition and participation of young people in society.

Discrimination on the grounds of age is a commonly acknowledged problem and a recurring factor in cases of gender-based discrimination and violence. Youth policies need to be analysed from an intersectional point of view, to see if they acknowledge those young people who may be particularly vulnerable both in their communities, and in youth policy generally. Giving such young people a voice and including them in the development of youth policy and in decision-making processes helps to respond to their need for participation and a voice, while also recognising the aggravated form of discrimination they are subjected to.

Youth work interventions which champion a human rights approach can also help to support and empower young people to learn about and act to defend their human rights.

Recommendation CM/Rec(2016)7 of the Committee of Ministers to member states, on Research on Young People's Access to Rights, calls on the member states of the Council of Europe to address the discriminatory practices faced by young people, on the grounds laid out in Article 14 of the European Convention on Human Rights or in any other form identified in case law of the European Court of Human Rights, with special attention to multifaceted identities and intersectionality of discrimination.

LGBT+

LGBT stands for lesbian, gay, bisexual and transgender/transsexual people. However, it is recognised that those four letters do not necessarily include all those whose sexuality is not heterosexual, or whose gender identity is not based on a traditional gender binary. The '+' symbol that is therefore used to include people whose identities do not fit typical binary notions of male and female, or who decide to identify themselves using other categories to describe their gender identity or their own understanding of their sexuality. This will include, for example, people who identify themselves as queer (a general term describing people not fitting into existing norms), questioning (people who explore their sexual orientation or/and gender identity), or pansexual (people who are attracted to all sexes and genders). It should be remembered, however, that some people may not want to identify themselves with any existing category.

Sexual orientations and gender identities

There is often confusion about what sexual orientation is, and how it is linked to gender identity.

Sexual orientation describes patterns of emotional, romantic and sexual attraction to other people. Traditionally, there are three sexual orientations: heterosexual (attraction to people of the opposite sex), bisexual (attraction to people of both sexes) and homosexual (attraction to people of the same sex). These three categories are by no means the only labels that describe the variety of sexual identifications. Sexual orientation should be seen on a continuum from heterosexual to homosexual, with many options in between. Furthermore, some people may decide not to identify themselves with a particular sexual orientation. There are men who have sex with men, or women who have sex with other women, but who do not see themselves as homosexual. They may, at the same time, engage in sexual relationships with people of the opposite sex, but do not want to be identified as bisexual. There is no agreement as to what determines sexual orientation: current research takes into account biological factors, such as genes, brain structure or hormones, as well as other factors, such as environment. Sexual orientation is not a matter of choice or preference and it cannot be altered at will. There are also other terms describing sexual orientation: monosexual (people who feel attracted to people of one gender) or plurisexual (people who are attracted to people of multiple genders).

Coming out

LBGT+ people may decide to make their sexual orientation and/or gender identity public. This process is called 'coming out' or 'coming out of the closet'. It usually starts with friends, acquaintances and family members. However, it is not obligatory to come out, and should always be a matter of personal choice whether to tell others, or not: no-one should be forced or pressured to do so. Coming out usually starts with acknowledging one's own sexual orientation and/or gender identity, and accepting it. LGBT+ people often live in environments that are hostile to people who do not conform to traditional norms. The coming out process can therefore be very painful, and is often associated with risks and fears of being rejected, ridiculed, bullied or even physically attacked. Hiding one's sexual orientation and/or gender identity and not being able to express one's own needs for a long time may be a very stressful and frustrating experience. Coming out allows people to overcome these negative feelings, and may lead to an experience of relief for many, especially when the response is positive and accepting. However, it may also be connected with a real risk of rejection or violence.

There are controversies related to the process of coming out. Some LGBT+ movements emphasise the affirmative and positive role that coming out can play: they believe that coming out, especially when done publicly by well-known people, leads to greater acceptance of LGBT+ people in the society. However, many queer theorists believe that this equates to a self-labelling process, whereby someone places themselves within a system of oppression in which sexual orientations other than heterosexual are associated with negative characteristics and meanings.

This reinforces the point that the decision about whether to come out should be a personal one and should follow a process of consideration. The process of coming out is different for everyone, and it can take some time for people to feel comfortable and confident enough to talk about it with other people.

Youth work has an important role to play in supporting young people in their coming out process. If a young person decides to come out to a youth worker close to them, the youth worker should be prepared to listen, to demonstrate empathy and understanding, and to keep an open mind. The young person is sharing something very personal and very important. If a youth worker is uncertain of what to say, or thinks that the young person needs further advice, they should point them to services that provide specific support and counselling to LGBT+ people.

LGBT+ movements

The roots of organised LGBT+ movements can be traced back to the 1920s and 1930s, with the development of an urban gay and lesbian culture[8]. Homosexual organisations themselves only really began to develop after the Second World War. In the Netherlands, in 1946, gay men - and later lesbian women - got together under the nickname 'The Shakespeare Club', and then as an organisation called C.O.C. This stood for the 'Centre for Culture and Leisure', a cover name initially adopted after its foundation. C.O.C. is known as the oldest Lesbian, Gay, Bisexual and Transgender organisation in the world.

In the USA, the first attempts to set up a lesbian and gay organisation can be traced back to 1950 in Los Angeles, when a small group of men set up the Mattachine Society. Mostly male in membership, the Society was joined in 1955 by a lesbian organisation based in San Francisco, called the Daughters of Bilitis. In the 1950s, these organisations remained small, but they established chapters in several cities and published magazines that became a beacon of hope for readers.

The beginning of a gay political movement is today often traced back to 27 June 1969, and a raid by the New York City police on a Greenwich Village gay bar, The Stonewall Inn. Contrary to expectations, the patrons of the bar fought back, provoking three nights of rioting in the area, accompanied by the appearance of 'gay power' slogans on the buildings. Almost overnight, a massive grassroots gay liberation movement was born. Owing much to the radical protest of African-Americans, women, and anti-war protesters of the 1960s, gays challenged all forms of hostility and punishment which had been meted out by society. Choosing to 'come out of the closet' and publicly proclaim their identity, they gave substantial impetus to a wider movement for social change.

In general, the same developments can be seen in Western European countries, where the lesbian and gay world is no longer an underground subculture, but a well-organised community, particularly in larger cities. This often involves gay businesses, political clubs, social service agencies, community centres and religious congregations bringing people together. In a number of places, openly gay candidates run for elections.

In the course of these struggles, homosexual men and lesbian women came to realise that they did not and would not conform to dominant social gender roles. Homosexual people not only challenged the heterosexual norm, but also challenged the images of how men and women should behave, what they should look like and what roles they should fulfil in society. These confrontations with repressive social norms have been carried out in spectacular ways that have increased the visibility of the struggles, such as a 'kiss–in' of lesbian women on a German town square. They have also often used traditional political approaches, such as lobbying and advocacy. The presence of publicly 'out' lesbians and gays in politics, and organisations as the International Lesbian and Gay Association (ILGA) or the International Lesbian, Gay, Bisexual and Transgender Youth and Students Organisation (IGLYO) have contributed substantially to the inclusion of LGBT issues in discussions on equal opportunities, human rights and general social policy.

Because of the Stonewall riots in June, the month was chosen as LGBT Pride month, when a number of LGBT Pride marches and festivals are organised across the globe (although in some regions, they take place at other times as well). Such festivals and marches are organised not only to promote self-affirmation, dignity, and equality, but have also become an important way to increase the visibility of LGBT+ people and to mainstream the movement.

Gender-based violence towards LGBT+ people

Violence against LGBT+ people is often neglected when gender-based violence is discussed. It is not unusual, for example, for perpetrators of violence against LGBT+ people to 'justify' their actions by expressing disgust at gay sexuality or gay masculinities. Neglect of gender-based violence against LGBT+ people partly reflects a lack of awareness of such violence , but it is also a consequence of inadequate legal and institutional protections for LGBT+ people in many countries of Europe and in the rest of the world.

Homophobia, biphobia and transphobia are terms that describe a fear, dislike or hatred of lesbian, gay, bisexual and transgender people. Such hatred is usually deeply rooted in stereotypes and prejudices, and supported by a hostile social and political climate towards LGBT+ people. It can take many forms, for example:

- Telling offensive jokes, using banter or words that make fun of LGBT+ people. Sometimes these are told with no malicious intention, but they may still have a negative impact on LGBT+ people.
- Bullying at school, which can take many forms, such as exclusion, violent incidents targeting young LGBT+ people, or threats. Such behaviour often results in young people being frightened, hurt or left out. Furthermore, in some schools the climate may be very hostile towards people who do not conform to traditional gender norms, and may therefore intentionally or unintentionally promote homo-, bi- or transphobia.
- Hate speech and hate crimes: LGBT+ young people frequently experience hate speech, especially on the Internet. This may not necessarily be as a result of personal targeting: they may still be affected when LGBT+ people in general are targeted. Such behaviour can have a devastating impact on the lives of young LGBT+ people: it lowers their self-confidence and sense of self-worth, it hinders their coming out process, it makes them feel alone. There are examples of hate speech targeting LGBT+ people that lead to suicidal attempts. Hate crimes are crimes motivated by prejudice and intolerance, where an offender hurts another person, because of the victim's actual or perceived ethnicity, national origin, race, sexual orientation, gender identity, religious beliefs, or disability, etc. Hate crimes include assault, harassment, insults, rape, torture, damage to property, or murder.
- Discrimination, such as the exclusion of young LGBT+ people from education or the job market; the absence of gender-neutral toilets for people who do not identify with assigned sex or specific gender; a lack of, or limited access to, medical services; inadequate legislation to allow non-heterosexual couples to enter into legally recognised form of union or partnership, etc.
- Other types of violence, such as forcing gays and lesbians to undergo therapy altering their sexual orientation - procedures which are now banned in many countries
- In some countries, sexual orientation other than heterosexual is illegal and punished, even with death penalty.

Domestic violence in LGBT relationships

Domestic violence in LGBT+ relationships is harder to identify, both for the victims and for the services offering support, because 'mainstream' services for domestic violence do not always recognise domestic violence in same sex relationships, and there are few people who are experienced in dealing with its specific aspects. However, statistics show that violence in heterosexual, gay, and lesbian relationships occurs at approximately the same rate (one in four).

The main similarities and differences between same-gender and opposite-gender domestic violence are summarised below[9].

Similarities include the form of abuse, the control the perpetrator has over the victim, the isolation the abused may experience, and the dynamics of the 'cycle of violence'.

Differences include:

Isolation. The isolation that accompanies domestic violence can be compounded by being LGBT+ in a homophobic society. Silence about domestic violence within the LGBT+ community further isolates the victim, giving more power to the abuser. Added to this, is the problem of limited community space within LGBT+ networks: privacy may be difficult to maintain and leaving a relationship may be more difficult.

Heterosexist manipulation. An abuser may threaten to 'speak out about' a person's sexual orientation or gender identity to friends, family, co-workers, or a landlord. In addition to this, existing support services may require an individual to 'come out' against his or her will.

Fear of further oppression. As an oppressed and defamed group, the LGBT+ community is often hesitant to address issues that many fear will further 'stain' the community.

Gender myths. People assume that two men in a fight must be equals. Similarly, gay, bi- sexual and transgendered (GBT) men often reject the idea that they can be victims. Given social assumptions about 'deviance', it might also be assumed that the violence is part of a sadomasochistic relationship.

The context of historical oppression. LGBT+ people often approach shelters, social service agencies, domestic violence service-providers, the police, and the courts with great caution. LGBT+ victims may fear re-victimisation through homophobia, disbelief, rejection and degradation from institutions that have a history of exclusion, hostility and violence toward LGBT people.

The Human rights framework

It is often claimed that LGBT+ people want 'special' rights, such as the right for gay and lesbian people to marry and adopt children. LGBT+ rights are not special rights: they are the same universal human rights that apply to all human beings, regardless of sex, gender, sexual orientation or gender identity.

On 30 March 2010, the Council of Europe Committee of Ministers adopted Recommendation CM/Rec (2010)[10], on measures to combat discrimination on grounds of sexual orientation or gender identity. This Recommendation sets out the principles deriving from existing European and international instruments, with particular emphasis on the European Convention of Human Rights and case law from the European Court of Human Rights.

The Recommendation identifies specific measures to be adopted and effectively endorsed by member states to combat discrimination, ensure respect for LGBT persons, promote tolerance towards them, and ensure that victims have access to legal remedies. Such measures include, among others:

- Ensuring effective, prompt and impartial investigations into alleged crimes and other incidents, where the sexual orientation or gender identity of the victim is reasonably suspected to have constituted a motive for the perpetrator
- Taking action in cases of hate speech targeting LGBT+ people
- Guaranteeing freedom of association for LGBT+ people and providing support to LGBT+ organisations
- Repealing any discriminatory legislation criminalising same-sex sexual acts between consenting adults, including any differences with respect to the age of consent for same-sex sexual acts and heterosexual acts
- Implementing mechanisms protecting people from discrimination on grounds of sexual orientation or gender identity in employment and occupation in the public as well as in the private sector.
- Promoting mutual tolerance and respect in schools, regardless of sexual orientation or gender identity
- Encouraging dialogue with, and supporting sports associations and fan clubs, in developing awareness-raising activities regarding discrimination against lesbian, gay, bisexual and transgender persons in sport, and in condemning manifestations of intolerance towards them
- Protecting asylum seekers from discriminatory policies or practices on grounds of sexual orientation or gender identity.

The Parliamentary Assembly of the Council of Europe adopted in 2015 a Resolution on discrimination against transgender people in Europe (Resolution 2048/2015)[11], which calls on member States to adopt measures in the areas of anti-discrimination legislation and policies, legal gender recognition, gender reassignment treatment and health care, information, awareness raising and training. It is worth mentioning that in 2015, Malta became the first country in Europe to introduce legislation recognising the right to gender identity. This gave every individual the right to recognition of their gender identity and the right to be treated and identified according to this identity.

The Yogyakarta Principles

The Principles and State Obligations on the Application of International Human Rights Law in Relation to Sexual Orientation, Gender Identity, Gender Expression and Sex Characteristics, known as the Yogyakarta principles, were developed in Yogyakarta (Indonesia) in 2006 by a group of human rights experts from diverse regions and backgrounds. The document includes recommendations to all countries, as well as to UN bodies, national human rights institutions, the media, non-governmental organisations, and others, to implement human rights standards in relation to LGBT+ people. The Principles were revised in 2017 to include 10 new principlesand are now known as The Yogyakarta Principles+10. These new principles include the right to state protection, the right to legal recognition, or the right to freedom from criminalisation and sanction on the basis of sexual orientation, gender identity, gender expression or sex characteristics. Although it is not a legally binding document, the Principles have a very important role as they represent "an affirmation of existing international legal standards as they apply to all persons on grounds of their sexual orientation, gender identity, gender expression and sex characteristics. States must comply with these principles both as a legal obligation and as an aspect of their commitment to universal human rights."[12]

Masculinities

Gender is present in every aspect of our lives and affects everyone without exception. This includes men. Gender-based violence is rooted in, and reinforces, gender-based inequalities and cannot be understood outside social structures, gender norms and supporting or reinforcing roles.

A patriarchal perspective sees men as the centre of rationality and normality. It is no surprise that it has taken a long time for masculinity to be understood as part of gender construction, and to see men as gendered. The idea of masculinities refers to the position of men in the gender order. Whitehead and Barrett explain that:

> Masculinities are those behaviours, languages and practices, existing in specific cultural and organisational locations, which are commonly associated with men, thus culturally defined as not feminine[13].

There is no universal set of expectations around masculinity: within societies, there are dominant codes that exert pressure on, and create expectations around men - with consequences for women, children and society as a whole. The understanding of masculinity varies across time and socio-cultural contexts, and within groups and networks; and men also "perform" their masculinity differently and inconsistently. Just as masculinity is defined by its relationship with femininity, women too have an important role to play in the interpretation and understanding of masculinity, particularly in their interaction with men and boys.

Masculine identities

Masculine identities are constructed through difference and association: being a man involves both *not* being something other than a man, *and* being like certain other men. Masculinity involves displaying attitudes and behaviours that signify and validate maleness, and involves being recognised in particular ways by other men and women.

R.W Connell, in her book *Masculinities* (1995), argues that what is important to a meaningful analysis of gender and masculinity is the "…processes and relationships through which men and women conduct gendered lives. 'Masculinity', to the extent the term can be briefly defined at all, is simultaneously a place in gender relations, the practices through which men and women engage that place in gender, and the effects of these practices in bodily experience, personality and culture"[14].

Connell argues that it is important to consider the power relationships between different masculinities as well as their relationships with femininities in order to analyse how these relationships act to reproduce, support or challenge the distribution of power in society. She identifies five categories of masculinities, which have been criticised, and should be regarded as fluid rather than rigid:

- **Hegemonic masculinities** are masculinities that are highly visible, respected, and occupy a position of authority in relation to other masculinities, within a particular setting. Such masculinities may not be the most widespread form, but they are likely to be those most admired, and they represent standards for others. Examples might include decisive business leaders, popular boys in a peer group, and certain sportsmen. Hegemonic masculinities can be seen as dominant in the entire gender order. A successful claim to authority is the mark of hegemony, rather than acts of direct violence, although violence underpins and supports this authority. Hegemony is supported by the production of exemplars - symbols with recognised authority - even though most men cannot live up to the ideal.
- **Complicit masculinities**. To be complicit means to condone or support something, without being actively engaged in it. Complicit masculinities are those that benefit in general from the social dominance of men, while not actively seeking to oppress women. A complicit action would be to deny the existence of inequality or other problems, or merely not to question the way in which gender relations are generally ordered.
- **Subordinate masculinities**. Within the overall framework, there are gender relations of dominance and subordination between groups of men. The most common example is the dominance of heterosexual men and the subordination of homosexual men. From the point of view of hegemonic masculinities, homosexuality is easily assimilated to femininity, and is therefore seen to be inferior. Other examples include men who have made a conscious effort to contest and 'exit' from hegemonic and complicit positions, or those whose physical appearance does not conform to standards set by hegemonic exemplars.
- **Marginalised masculinities** are those that are categorised as different, on the basis of class, ethnicity or status. They may display and enjoy masculine power in certain contexts but are always ultimately compared to the hegemonic norms and images[15].
- **Protest masculinities** represent a pattern of masculinity constructed in local working-class settings, sometimes among ethnically marginalised men, which embody the same claims to power of typical hegemonic masculinities, but which lack the economic resources and institutional authority which underpin regional and global patterns.[16]

The crisis of masculinity and men's rights movements

Ever since the early 1990s, men and masculinities have been an issue of concern in relation to unemployment, changing family patterns, school failure, and violent crime. Some researchers argue that young men feel disoriented, and experience conflicting societal demands, which make it difficult to build their (gender) identities as young men. On the one hand, traditional expectations of masculinity demand toughness, strength and rationality, while on the other hand, 'modern men' are expected to possess soft skills, such as empathy and sensitivity. These seemingly conflicting requests can have a negative impact on the development and behaviour of boys and young men, leading to aggression, low self-esteem and drug abuse. In their study of young masculinities and femininities, Nayak and Kehily claim that "Identity only becomes an issue when it is in crisis, when something assumed to be fixed, coherent and stable is displaced by the experience of doubt and insecurity"[17].

'The work of Ken Harland with young men and boys in Northern Ireland has shown that young men experience ambivalence about their 'public' and 'private' personas. In public, there is great pressure to appear confident, and to display their masculinity in a forceful way; and there is a fear of being humiliated as a result of appearing weak or feminine. In 'private', young men face their anxieties, and try to address their fears and inner emotions, but they tend to have little support and few available mechanisms at their disposal to help them to become more skilled at expressing their emotions and reflecting on their identity and behaviour. For most young males, their daily experience tends to contradict societal perceptions of masculinity: they often feel powerless, fear the threat of daily violence, may be labelled 'stupid' at school, pay little attention to their health needs - particularly mental health - have not been in a sexual relationship or have little sexual experience, and feel that adults see them as 'immature.' Such conflicting experiences need appreciating in order to understand the internal pressures that many young males experience in constructing their masculine identity and in knowing what it means to be a man.

In the first half of the XX century, men's rights movements have increasingly begun to emerge as a way of opposing the claims of women's movements for emancipation and equal rights. From the men's liberation movement in the 1970s, two main branches evolved: pro-feminist men's movements and anti-feminist men's movements. The second of these are mostly branded as "men's rights movements". Some of the men's rights movements claim that men are in fact the oppressed and discriminated, arguing that men and society have been 'feminised' by the success of the women's movement. Most of the men's rights movements oppose feminism and argue for the maintenance or re-establishment of a patriarchal gender order. The emergence of the Internet has allowed such movements to reach wider audiences. Men's rights groups and father's rights groups are generally associated with a shift towards a more conservative approach to the family and gender relations, and such movements have become increasingly vocal in Europe. However, research also shows that in certain countries, policies encouraging men to take a more active fathering role have facilitated women's entry into the labour market. There are also indications of an increasing interest in feminist ideas even while men's rights movements have gained in popularity.[18]

Risk taking behaviours and young men

Young men often willingly jeopardise their health by engaging in high-risk activities, as a result of clinging to stereotypical images of men and masculinity. The notion of risk is a recurring theme in young men's health statistics. This can be seen by observing male risk-taking behaviours, such as driving without a seat belt, eating snack foods, fighting, street violence, not visiting doctors, alcohol abuse, car theft, and increased suicide rates. While the young men may have been aware of the dangers, they perceived risk-taking as a necessary aspect of male youth culture, and as an important way in which males demonstrate their masculinity to others.[19]

Research shows that violence plays an integral and complex role in male identity, and that it is an accepted and normal part of many boys' lives and experiences. Young men tend to refer to violence primarily in relation to men's violence towards other men. Violence has been seen as a way to assert one's masculinity in front of other men, or a way of dealing with things that might challenge aspects of masculinity and cause a feeling of shame.[20]

Violence fulfils a function in relation to stereotypical gender roles. Violence, as an integral and complex aspect of male identity also 'serves to maintain group solidarity, reinforce kinship ties, affirm allegiances and enhance status within the group'[21]. For other young men, the function is related to self-protection, where an attempt to use violence or aggression or threat is seen as a means of warding off a threat from another.

While it is certainly the case that gender-based violence affects women disproportionately, and while men are the main aggressors, they too experience violent consequences as a result of the assumptions and beliefs which underlie gender-based violence. Perhaps nothing shows this better than the history of conflict and genocide.

Gender and genocide studies have long focused on the under-reported stories of women, especially stories about rape and abuse within conflict, which have tended to be excluded from early accounts of the Holocaust and genocide up to the 1980s. A closer look shows that men too are gendered in genocidal processes. They are often the first group to be separated and massacred, allowing for the killing and exploitation of women and children. For example, on 12 July 1995, more than 8000 Bosnian Muslim men and boys were murdered in and around the town of Srebrenica by Bosnian Serb forces[22]. Adam Jones identified two types of genocides: gender selective slaughter of males, and "root-and-branch" genocides which target all sectors of the target population indiscriminately. Genocides targeting battle-age males are more frequent than the second type, portraying a brutal logic and understanding of masculinity: males are those who can serve in the military, and are therefore legitimate targets. However, this does not imply that women are saved from the worst types of genocidal violence. While the violence that they are exposed to is often less deadly, it is no less shocking: it may involve verbal humiliation, sexual slavery, individual and gang rape, or rape-murder on a large scale.[23]

Youth work and masculinities

Any youth work addressing gender-based violence needs to address the concepts and constructions of masculinity and femininity that young people are exposed to, and needs to support them to reflect critically on these concepts and on their own relationship to, and performance of gender. Traditionally, work against discrimination has focused on the empowerment of girls and women, and this needs to remain an important focus. However, working with boys and young men is also needed - partly in order to support them in exploring their identity and reflecting on their understanding of masculinity and on the social pressures surrounding this concept; but also in order to encourage them to engage actively against gender-based violence and for gender equality.

Sexuality

Sexuality is everywhere we look: in the books we read, the movies we watch, on television, in online videos, music video clips, online games, in advertisements, in the websites we visit, the way we dress or talk with other people, in our way of thinking about and imagining things. Sexuality is a part of us. It is probably difficult to find another domain of human life that is as loaded with controversial issues, stereotypes, prejudices, norms, and taboos.

Human sexuality is a complex issue. In different attempts to define this term, two aspects are usually taken into account: biological (essentialist approach) and socio-cultural (constructivist approach). Although sexuality has an important biological component - usually related to the imperative of reproduction - other components, such as personal needs and desires, emotions, practices and identities, are of equal, and sometimes greater, importance. The World Health Organisation defines sexuality as:

> (…) a central aspect of being human throughout life (that) encompasses sex, gender identities and roles, sexual orientation, eroticism, pleasure, intimacy and reproduction. Sexuality is experienced and expressed in thoughts, fantasies, desires, beliefs, attitudes, values, behaviours, practices, roles and relationships. While sexuality can include all of these dimensions, not all of them are always experienced or expressed. Sexuality is influenced by the interaction of biological, psychological, social, economic, political, cultural, legal, historical, religious and spiritual factors."[24]

One of the first pieces of sociological research to undermine the understanding of human sexuality as something invariable was done in the United States by Alfred Kinsey and his team, in the late forties and early fifties of the XX century. The results of this large-scale research were shocking, as they showed large discrepancies between social norms and expectations and actual human sexual behaviours and practices. Masturbation and sex between people of the same sex turned out to be common and treated as natural. The study contributed to a wider understanding of human sexuality beyond biology and physiology.

The idea of fixed categories of sexuality, as with the idea of unchanging, essential gender identities, is undermined by histories of sexuality that show changing practices and values attached to forms of sexual behaviour between people. One of the most famous of these is the work of the French philosopher Michel Foucault, in his three volume History of Sexuality. In volume 1, for instance, he shows that before 'homosexuality' became categorised as a form of sexual identity in the nineteenth century, sexual relations between men were regarded, in different contexts, as an act that may be celebrated or punished, but that did not define the identities of those involved. In his book, Foucault also showed how sexuality was determined throughout history and how it became a tool of power. His theories influenced both queer and feminist ideas and movements.

Views on human sexuality have changed throughout history, and sexuality is today increasingly seen as a dimension of life that everyone can define and shape according to their own particular needs. However, every society establishes certain norms in relation to sexual behaviours, and these are learnt in the process of socialisation. These norms are often built into laws that prohibit or restrict certain sexual behaviours. For example, in every society there is a legal 'age of consent': the age that people need to reach, in order to be considered capable of making a conscious decision to engage in sexual relationships. In most countries, this can be found in the criminal code, which makes it a crime to engage in any sexual act with a person below the age of consent. This age varies from country to country, but is usually between 14 to 18 years of age. Sexual violence is another example of a social norm built into legislation: sex is only legal if it is consensual. Practices which force a partner or partners to engage in sexual practices or behaviours, or which cause harm (psychological or physical) are punishable by law.

There are many issues related to human sexuality, such as sex work, pornography or abortion, that lead to heated debate. Such issues will always be subject to dispute, as they touch upon values and established social norms, which can never be neutral: for certain people, they will seem natural and important for preserving the social order, while for others, they will seem unfair, and a restriction of their autonomy and right to self-determination.

Diverse sexualities

There are many different types and forms of expression of sexuality and it can take a while for people to figure out what is "right" for them. Although there are many aspects of sexuality, such as gender identity, sexual identity or sexual orientation, issues of sexual diversity primarily centre about the later.

In terms of sexual orientation, people may identify themselves as straight (attracted to people of the opposite gender), gay or lesbian (attracted to people of the same gender), or bisexual (attracted to people of both genders). However, it is often not simply a choice between three alternatives that applies for the whole life. Sexual orientation should be rather seen on a spectrum from straight (heterosexual) to gay (homosexual) with many options in between. Yet, some people may not want to be identified with any sexual orientation. You can read more about sexual orientation in the section on LGBT+.

However, sexual diversity is much more than only sexual orientation, it also includes asexual, transsexual (transgender) or intersex people.

Asexuality

Not everyone needs sex to express themselves and to feel happy. An asexual person is someone who does not feel sexual attraction, and has no, or very little, sexual drive. This is not the same as celibacy, which people choose. Asexuality is an intrinsic part of a person, a part of their identity. Although the absence of sexual attraction or sexual drive may, in particular cases, be the result of health concerns, asexuality is not today considered to be a pathological condition. People who identify themselves as asexual have the same emotional needs as everyone else, and they may decide to live life on their own, and even to date and establish romantic relationships. However, they do not feel the need to be involved in sexual practices and behaviours. Asexual people may feel attracted to a particular gender, and may therefore self-identify as gay, lesbian, bisexual or straight.

Transsexuality

"Being born in a wrong body" is how many transsexual people would describe themselves. For example, their body may be female, but their gender identity male. Or the opposite may be the case: they have been born with a male body, but feel they are female. This phenomenon is called transsexuality (or gender dysphoria, in the medical literature). It is described as the case when someone has the typical physical anatomy belonging to one sex, but the gender identity of the opposite one. Some transsexual people prefer to be called transgender (transsexual is generally considered to be a subset of transgender), but some refuse this identification. Being born in the wrong body is a very painful experience. A transsexual person's life is a constant fight – against one's own body, against deteriorating mental health, against discrimination and violence. In general, the only way to relieve these symptoms is through sex reassignment surgery, during which a person obtains the body that corresponds with their gender identity. This normally demands a series of psychological tests, hormone therapy - usually until the end of their life – and a name and legal gender change, if the law permits this. There are still 22 countries in Europe (2017) that require mandatory sterilisation of transsexual people before sex reassignment surgery is allowed. This was ruled to be a human rights violation by the European Court of Human Rights (A. P., E. Garçon and S. Nicot against France)[25].

Intersex

A person's sex is assigned at birth: the doctors or others who assist women at labour usually decide if the new-born baby is male or female, on the basis of sex characteristics, such as the type of sex organs. Intersex people are born with sex characteristics (including genitals, gonads and chromosomes) that do not fit the typical binary classification of male or female bodies. In some cases, intersex traits may be visible at birth, but often they do not become clear until puberty. Some chromosomal intersex characteristics may never be visible at all.

Being intersex is related to biological sex characteristics and is distinct from a person's sexual orientation or gender identity. Unfortunately, in many places, the sex of someone who is intersex is decided by the medical staff, sometimes after consultation with the parents, and the child is forced to undergo a surgical procedure to make the genitals correspond to the assigned sex. Later on, in puberty, it may turn out that a person's sex was wrongly assigned. A 2013 statement by the United Nations Special Rapporteur on Torture condemns the non-consensual use of normalisation surgery on intersex people as they "(...) can cause scarring, loss of sexual sensation, pain, incontinence and lifelong depression and have also been criticized as being unscientific, potentially harmful and contributing to stigma."[26]

Sexuality education and youth work

Sexuality education covers a number of issues that are relevant for children and young people, relating to biological, emotional and social aspects of sexuality. The International Planned Parenthood Federation (IPPF) defines a rights-based approach to comprehensive sexuality education as something that "seeks to equip young people with the knowledge, skills, attitudes and values they need to determine and enjoy their sexuality – physically and emotionally, individually and in relationships. It views 'sexuality' holistically and within the context of emotional and social development. It recognizes that information alone is not enough. Young people need to be given the opportunity to acquire essential life skills and develop positive attitudes and values."[27] The IPFF defines seven essential components of sexuality education: gender, sexual and reproductive health and HIV, sexual rights and sexual citizenship, pleasure, violence, diversity and relationships.

Sexuality education is, most of all, about creating self-awareness about the human body, learning how to create and sustain healthy relationships, improving self-confidence, learning acceptance, and developing attitudes of tolerance and non-discrimination. However, there are many places where sexual education is either not provided to young people or it is purely informative, focusing on the biological aspects of human sexuality, while issues such as gender identity, sexual orientation, and even gender-based violence may be treated as taboo, and not talked about or labelled as "bad" or "immoral". Such an approach to sexuality education does not contribute to young people's well-being and may even lead to dramatic consequences for those who do not accept or identify with norms that have been imposed on them. In cases where the formal education system does not provide young people with sexuality education, they tend to look for information on the Internet or from their peers. However, this can lead to misleading information, as online sources often reduce the question of sexuality to sex practices only, and sexual partners are often objectified.

There are differing opinions as to whether sexual education should be done by youth workers, or whether it should rather be left to professionals in the field of human sexuality. However, youth workers are often in a position to provide important assistance to young people in talking through issues related to sexuality and answering their concerns. This can be done through informal discussions or in organised workshops that deal with such topics as negotiation and communication skills, antidiscrimination and human rights education.

The Council of Europe has produced educational resources related to sexuality education that can be used in working with children and young people. These can be found at *https://www.coe.int/en/web/pestalozzi/sexed*

Sexual and reproductive health and rights

The World Health Organisation defines sexual health as:

> "(…) a state of physical, emotional, mental and social well-being in relation to sexuality; it is not merely the absence of disease, dysfunction or infirmity. Sexual health requires a positive and respectful approach to sexuality and sexual relationships, as well as the possibility of having pleasurable and safe sexual experiences, free of coercion, discrimination and violence…"[28]

The definition of reproductive health developed by the United Nations Office of the High Commissioner for Human Rights, which is similar to the World Health Organisation's, includes an additional paragraph explaining that: "Reproductive health implies that people are able to have a satisfying and safe sex life and that they have the capacity to reproduce and the freedom to decide if, when and how often to do so".[29]

In order for the conditions for sexual and reproductive health to be met, the sexual and reproductive rights of a person must be respected and protected. Sexual and reproductive rights are human rights that are recognised in existing international and regional human rights documents – for example:

- the right to equality and non-discrimination;
- the right to be free from torture or cruel, inhumane or degrading treatment or punishment;
- the right to privacy;
- the right to the highest attainable standard of health ;
- the right to marry and to found a family and enter into marriage with free and full consent of the intending spouses, and to equality in and at the dissolution of marriage;

- the right to decide the number and spacing of one's children;
- the right to information and education;
- the right to freedom of opinion and expression; and
- the right to an effective remedy for violations of fundamental rights.

The Council of Europe's Commissioner for Human Rights in an Issue Paper on Women's Sexual and Reproductive Health and Rights in Europe (2017)[30] identified several obstacles to the fulfilment and protection of those rights, including:

- lack of or limited access to contraception and legal and safe abortion,
- existing harmful gender stereotypes, social norms and stigma regarding women's sexuality and reproductive capacities,
- violence, threats, hate speech and smear campaigns against people and organisations defending women's rights,
- sexuality education programmes throughout Europe that fall short of international human rights requirements and the World Health Organization's standards regarding comprehensive sexuality education
- inadequate access to effective remedies and reparation for victims of sexual and reproductive coercion, including past human rights abuse such as forced sterilisation of Roma women in some countries.

The European Court of Human Rights has dealt with many complaints against member states concerning issues of reproductive rights, for example: access to lawful abortion, embryo donation and scientific research, home birth, medically-assisted procreation, sterilisation operations and surrogacy.[31]

Endnotes

1 http://www.obn.org/cfundef/100antitheses.html

2 Based on: Todd. D. Nelson, Psychology of Prejudice, Pearsons Education, Inc. publishing as Allyn and Bacon, 2002

3 Read more about case law of the European Court of Human Rights related to gender equality at:
https://www.echr.coe.int/Documents/FS_Gender_Equality_ENG.pdf

4 Beijing Declaration, United Nations, 1995, http://www.un.org/womenwatch/daw/beijing/platform/declar.htm
(accessed 20 December 2017)

5 Sandra Fredman, Intersectional Discrimination in EU gender equality and non-discrimination role, Directorate Justice and Consumers, May 2016.

6 Sumi Cho, Kimberle Crenshaw, Leslie McCall, Towards a Field of Intersectionality Studies: Theory, Applications, and Praxis, in Signs, vol 38, no 4, 2013, pp. 785-810.

7 Fredman, op.cit., p. 37

8 Lentin, A. (2004). 'The problem of culture and human rights in the response to racism', in Titley, G. (Ed.) Resituating Culture. Strasbourg: Council of Europe Publishing. For a full discussion see Lentin, A. (2004). Racism and Anti-Racism in Europe. London: Pluto Press.

9 Excerpted from www.gmdvp.org and LAMBDA Gay and Lesbian Anti Violence Project (El Paso).

10 https://search.coe.int/cm/Pages/result_details.aspx?ObjectID=09000016805cf40a

11 http://assembly.coe.int/nw/xml/XRef/Xref-XML2HTML-EN.asp?fileid=21736&lang=en

12 Read more at: http://yogyakartaprinciples.org/wp-content/uploads/2017/11/A5_yogyakartaWEB-2.pdf

13 Whitehead, S.M., Barret, F.J., The Masculinities Reader, Polity Press, 2004

14 R.W. Connell, *Masculinities*, 2nd edition, University of California Press, Berkeley, 2005

15 Connell, ibid p. 76-81.

16 R.W. Connell, James Messerschmidt, Rethinking hegemonic masculinities, in GENDER & SOCIETY, Vol. 19 No. 6, December 2005, p. 829-859.

17 Nayak, Anoop; Kehily, Mary Jane, *Gender, Youth and Culture: Young Masculinities and Femininities*, 2nd edition, Palgrave Macmillan, Kindle Edition, 2013, p. 56

18 Sandy Ruxton, Nikki van der Gaag, *Men's involvement in gender equality – European perspectives*, Gender and Development, 21:1, 2013, p. 161-175.

19 Ken Harland, Young Men Talking – Voices from Belfast (1997) YouthAction Northern Ireland and Working with Men Publications, London

20 Ken Harland, Sam McCready, Boys, young men and violence : masculinities, education and practice, Palgrave Macmillan, 2015, p. 134

21 *Ibidem*, p.171.

22 The International Criminal Tribunal for the Crimes in the Former Yugoslavia ruled in 2004 that the crime constituted genocide. The ruling was upheld in 2007 by the International Court of Justice.

23 Adam Jones, Genocide. A Comprehensive Introduction, Routledge, 2006, p.328-329.

24 http://www.who.int/reproductivehealth/topics/sexual_health/sh_definitions/en/

25 https://hudoc.echr.coe.int/eng#{"itemid":["001-172556"]}

26 http://www.ohchr.org/Documents/HRBodies/HRCouncil/RegularSession/Session22/A.HRC.22.53_English.pdf

27 IPPF Framework for Comprehensive Sexuality Education (CSE), International Planned Parenthood Federation, London 2010, p. 6,

28 *http://www.who.int/reproductivehealth/topics/sexual_health/sh_definitions/en/*

29 Reproductive Rights are Human Rights. A Handbook for National Human Rights Institutions, United Nations 2014, *http://www.ohchr.org/Documents/Publications/NHRIHandbook.pdf*

30 Women's sexual and reproductive health and rights in Europe, Issue Paper published by the Council of Europe Commissioner for Human Rights, Council of Europe, December 2017 *https://rm.coe.int/women-s-sexual-and-reproductive-health-and-rights-in-europe-issue-pape/168076dead*

31 Reproductive rights, Factsheet, European Court of Human Rights, July 2017 *http://www.echr.coe.int/Documents/FS_Reproductive_ENG.pdf*

Poster created by the No Hate Ninjas (Portugal) for the No Hate Speech Movement youth campaign.

law /lɔː/

APPENDICES

Selected international legal human rights instruments related to gender-based violence

Glossary of terms related to gender and gender-based violence

Selected International Legal Human Rights Instruments Related to Gender-Based Violence

- The Universal Declaration of Human Rights (unofficial summary)
- The Universal Declaration of Human Rights
- Convention on the Elimination of All Forms of Discrimination against Women CEDAW (Summary)
- European Convention on Human Rights (simplified version of selected articles)
- Council of Europe Convention on Preventing and Combating Violence against Women and Domestic Violence (unofficial summary)

The Universal Declaration of Human Rights

(Unofficial summary)

Article 1	Right to Equality		**Article 15**	Right to a Nationality and the Freedom to Change It
Article 2	Freedom from Discrimination		**Article 16**	Right to Marriage and Family
Article 3	Right to Life, Liberty, Personal Security		**Article 17**	Right to Own Property
Article 4	Freedom from Slavery		**Article 18**	Freedom of Belief and Religion
Article 5	Freedom from Torture and Degrading Treatment		**Article 19**	Freedom of Opinion and Information
Article 6	Right to Recognition as a Person before the Law		**Article 20**	Right of Peaceful Assembly and Association
Article 7	Right to Equality before the Law		**Article 21**	Right to Participate in Government and in Free Elections
Article 8	Right to Remedy by Competent Tribunal		**Article 22**	Right to Social Security
Article 9	Freedom from Arbitrary Arrest and Exile		**Article 23**	Right to Desirable Work and to Join Trade Unions
Article 10	Right to Fair Public Hearing		**Article 24**	Right to Rest and Leisure
Article 11	Right to be Considered Innocent until Proven Guilty		**Article 25**	Right to Adequate Living Standard
Article 12	Freedom from Interference with Privacy, Family, Home and Correspondence		**Article 26**	Right to Education
			Article 27	Right to Participate in the Cultural Life of Community
Article 13	Right to Free Movement in and out of the Country		**Article 28**	Right to a Social Order that Articulates this Document
Article 14	Right to Asylum in other Countries from Persecution		**Article 29**	Community Duties Essential to Free and Full Development
			Article 30	Freedom from State or Personal Interference in the above Rights

The Universal Declaration of Human Rights

Adopted and proclaimed by General Assembly resolution 217 A (III) of 10 December 1948

On December 10, 1948 the General Assembly of the United Nations adopted and proclaimed the Universal Declaration of Human Rights the full text of which appears in the following pages. Following this historic act the Assembly called upon all Member countries to publicize the text of the Declaration and "to cause it to be disseminated, displayed, read and expound- ed principally in schools and other educational institutions, without distinction based on the political status of countries or territories."

PREAMBLE

Whereas recognition of the inherent dignity and of the equal and inalienable rights of all members of the human family is the foundation of freedom, justice and peace in the world,

Whereas disregard and contempt for human rights have re- sulted in barbarous acts which have outraged the conscience of mankind, and the advent of a world in which human be- ings shall enjoy freedom of speech and belief and freedom from fear and want has been proclaimed as the highest aspi- ration of the common people,

Whereas it is essential, if man is not to be compelled to have recourse, as a last resort, to rebellion against tyranny and oppression, that human rights should be protected by the rule of law,

Whereas it is essential to promote the development of friendly relations between nations,

Whereas the peoples of the United Nations have in the Charter reaffirmed their faith in fundamental human rights, in the dignity and worth of the human person and in the equal rights of men and women and have determined to promote social progress and better standards of life in larger freedom,

Whereas Member States have pledged themselves to achieve, in co-operation with the United Nations, the promotion of universal respect for and observance of human rights and fundamental freedoms,

Whereas a common understanding of these rights and free- doms is of the greatest importance for the full realization of this pledge,

Now, Therefore THE GENERAL ASSEMBLY proclaims THIS UNIVERSAL DECLARATION OF HUMAN RIGHTS as a common standard of achieve- ment for all peoples and all nations, to the end that every in- dividual and every organ of society, keeping this Declaration constantly in mind, shall strive by teaching and education to promote respect for these rights and freedoms and by pro- gressive measures, national and international, to secure their universal and effective recognition and observance, both among the peoples of Member States themselves and among the peoples of territories under their jurisdiction.

Article 1.

All human beings are born free and equal in dignity and rights. They are endowed with reason and conscience and should act towards one another in a spirit of brotherhood.

Article 2.

Everyone is entitled to all the rights and freedoms set forth in this Declaration, without distinction of any kind, such as race, colour, sex, language, religion, political or other opinion, national or social origin, property, birth or other status. Furthermore, no distinction shall be made on the basis of the political, jurisdictional or inter- national status of the country or territory to which a per- son belongs, whether it be independent, trust, non-self- governing or under any other limitation of sovereignty.

Article 3.

Everyone has the right to life, liberty and security of person.

Article 4.

No one shall be held in slavery or servitude; slavery and the slave trade shall be prohibited in all their forms.

Article 5.

No one shall be subjected to torture or to cruel, inhuman or degrading treatment or punishment.

Article 6.

Everyone has the right to recognition everywhere as a person before the law.

Article 7.

All are equal before the law and are entitled without any discrimination to equal protection of the law. All are enti- tled to equal protection against any discrimination in violation of this Declaration and against any incitement to such discrimination.

Article 8.

Everyone has the right to an effective remedy by the com- petent national tribunals for acts violating the fundamental rights granted him by the constitution or by law.

Article 9.

No one shall be subjected to arbitrary arrest, detention or exile.

Article 10.

Everyone is entitled in full equality to a fair and public hearing by an independent and impartial tribunal, in the determination of his rights and obligations and of any crim- inal charge against him.

Article 11.

1) Everyone charged with a penal offence has the right to be presumed innocent until proved guilty according to law in a public trial at which he has had all the guarantees necessary for his defense.
2) No one shall be held guilty of any penal offence on ac- count of any act or omission which did not constitute a penal offence, under national or international law, at the time when it was committed. Nor shall a heavier penalty be imposed than the one that was applicable at the time the penal offence was committed.

Article 12.

No one shall be subjected to arbitrary interference with his privacy, family, home or correspondence, nor to at- tacks upon his honour and reputation. Everyone has the right to the protection of the law against such interference or attacks.

Article 13.

1) Everyone has the right to freedom of movement and residence within the borders of each state.
2) Everyone has the right to leave any country, including his own, and to return to his country.

Article 14.

1) Everyone has the right to seek and to enjoy in other countries asylum from persecution.
2) This right may not be invoked in the case of prosecu- tions genuinely arising from non-political crimes or from acts contrary to the purposes and principles of the United Nations.

Article 15.

1) Everyone has the right to a nationality.
2) No one shall be arbitrarily deprived of his nationality nor denied the right to change his nationality.

Article 16.

Men and women of full age, without any limitation due to race, nationality or religion, have the right to marry and to found a family. They are entitled to equal rights as to marriage, during marriage and at its dissolution.

1) Marriage shall be entered into only with the free and full consent of the intending spouses.
2) The family is the natural and fundamental group unit of society and is entitled to protection by society and the State.

Article 17.

1) Everyone has the right to own property alone as well as in association with others.
2) No one shall be arbitrarily deprived of his property.

Article 18.

Everyone has the right to freedom of thought, conscience and religion; this right includes freedom to change his reli- gion or belief, and freedom, either alone or in community with others and in public or private, to manifest his religion or belief in teaching, practice, worship and observance.

Article 19.

Everyone has the right to freedom of opinion and expression; this right includes freedom to hold opinions without interference and to seek, receive and impart information and ideas through any media and regardless of frontiers.

Article 20.

1) Everyone has the right to freedom of peaceful assembly and association.
2) No one may be compelled to belong to an association.

Article 21.

1) Everyone has the right to take part in the government of his country, directly or through freely chosen representatives.
2) Everyone has the right of equal access to public service in his country.
3) The will of the people shall be the basis of the authority of government; this will shall be expressed in periodic and genuine elections which shall be by universal and equal suffrage and shall be held by secret vote or by equivalent free voting procedures.

Article 22.

Everyone, as a member of society, has the right to social security and is entitled to realization, through national effort and international co-operation and in accordance with the organization and resources of each State, of the economic, social and cultural rights indispensable for his dignity and the free development of his personality.

Article 23.

1) Everyone has the right to work, to free choice of em- ployment, to just and favourable conditions of work and to protection against unemployment.
2) Everyone, without any discrimination, has the right to equal pay for equal work.
3) Everyone who works has the right to just and favourable remuneration ensuring for himself and his family an existence worthy of human dignity, and supplemented, if necessary, by other means of social protection.
4) Everyone has the right to form and to join trade unions for the protection of his interests.

Article 24.

Everyone has the right to rest and leisure, including reasonable limitation of working hours and periodic holidays with pay.

Article 25.

1) Everyone has the right to a standard of living adequate for the health and well-being of himself and of his family, including food, clothing, housing and medical care and necessary social services, and the right to security in the event of unemployment, sickness, disability, widowhood, old age or other lack of livelihood in circumstances beyond his control.
2) Motherhood and childhood are entitled to special care and assistance. All children, whether born in or out of wedlock, shall enjoy the same social protection.

Article 26.

1) Everyone has the right to education. Education shall be free, at least in the elementary and fundamental stages. Elementary education shall be compulsory. Technical and professional education shall be made generally available and higher education shall be equally accessible to all on the basis of merit.

2) Education shall be directed to the full development of the human personality and to the strengthening of respect for human rights and fundamental freedoms. It shall pro- mote understanding, tolerance and friendship among all nations, racial or religious groups, and shall further the activities of the United Nations for the maintenance of peace.
3) Parents have a prior right to choose the kind of educa tion that shall be given to their children.

Article 27.

1) Everyone has the right freely to participate in the cultural life of the community, to enjoy the arts and to share in scientific advancement and its benefits.
2) Everyone has the right to the protection of the moral and material interests resulting from any scientific, literary or artistic production of which he is the author.

Article 28.

Everyone is entitled to a social and international order in which the rights and freedoms set forth in this Declaration can be fully realized.

Article 29.

1) Everyone has duties to the community in which alone the free and full development of his personality is possible.
2) In the exercise of his rights and freedoms, everyone shall be subject only to such limitations as are determined by law solely for the purpose of securing due recognition and respect for the rights and freedoms of others and of meeting the just requirements of morality, public order and the general welfare in a democratic society.
3) These rights and freedoms may in no case be exercised contrary to the purposes and principles of the United Nations.

Article 30.

Nothing in this Declaration may be interpreted as implying for any State, group or person any right to engage in any activity or to perform any act aimed at the destruction of any of the rights and freedoms set forth herein.

Convention on the Elimination of All Forms of Discrimination against Women – CEDAW (Summary)

Article 1

Definition of discrimination against women: any distinction, exclusion, or restriction, made on the basis of sex, with the purpose or effect of impairing the enjoyment by women of political, economic, social, cultural, or civil human rights on equal footing with men.

Article 2

States Parties condemn discrimination against women and undertake to pursue a policy of eliminating it in all its forms. States Parties undertake to: include the principles of equality of men and women in national constitutions; adopt legislation prohibiting all discrimination against women; ensure legal protection and effective remedy against discrimination; refrain from any act of discrimination against women and ensure that no public authorities or institutions engage in discrimination; take measures to eliminate discrimination against women by any person, organization or enterprise; take measures to modify or abolish existing laws, customs and practices which constitute discrimination against women.

Article 3

States Parties shall take all appropriate measures, especially in the political, social, economic and cultural fields, to ensure the full development and advancement of women, for the purpose of guaranteeing them enjoyment of human rights on equal footing with men.

Article 4

Affirmative action measures shall not be considered discrimination. Special measures protecting pregnancy shall not be considered discriminatory.

Article 5

States Parties shall take all appropriate measures: to modify social and cultural patterns of conduct of men and women which are based on ideas of inferiority or superiority or on stereotyped roles for men and women; to ensure that family education includes the recognition of the common responsibility of men and women in raising children.

Article 6

States Parties shall take all appropriate measures to suppress traffic in women and exploitation of prostitution.

Article 7

States Parties shall take all appropriate measures to eliminate discrimination against women in political and public life and shall ensure equal rights to vote and be eligible for election; to participate in forming government policy and to hold public office; to participate in NGOs.

Article 8

States Parties shall take all appropriate measures to ensure a woman's equal right to represent her government at the international level and participate in the work of international organizations.

Article 9

States Parties shall grant women equal rights to a nationality. Neither marriage nor change of nationality by the husband during marriage shall automatically change the nationality of the wife. Women shall have equal rights with men with respect to their children's nationality.

Article 10

States Parties shall ensure to women equal rights in the field of education. States Parties shall ensure the same conditions for career guidance, access to studies, the same teaching staff and equipment. Stereotyped roles of men and women are to be eliminated in all forms of education. States Parties shall ensure that women have the same opportunities to benefit from scholarships and the same access to continuing education. States Parties shall ensure the reduction of female drop-out rates and shall ensure that women have access to educational information to help ensure health and well-being of families, including information on family planning.

Article 11

States Parties shall take all appropriate measures to eliminate discrimination against women in employment and shall ensure, on the basis of equality of men and women, the same rights to work, to the same employment opportunities, to free choice of employment, to promotion, benefits, vocational training, equal remuneration, equal treatment in respect of work of equal value, the right to social security, unemployment, protection of health. States Parties shall prohibit dismissal on the grounds of pregnancy and discrimination in dismissals on the basis of marital status. States Parties shall take measures to introduce maternity leave with pay or social benefits.

Article 12

States Parties shall take all appropriate measures to eliminate discrimination against women in the field of health care and shall ensure women equal access to health care services and appropriate services in connection with pregnancy.

Article 13

States Parties shall take all appropriate measures to eliminate discrimination against women in other areas of economic and social life and shall ensure the same rights to family benefits, to bank loans, mortgages and other forms of credit.

Article 14

States Parties shall take into account the special problems of rural women and the significant roles they play in the economic survival of their families and shall ensure to them all rights in this convention. States Parties shall ensure equal rights of men and women to participate in and benefit from rural development, and shall ensure to rural women the rights to: participate in development planning; have access to adequate health care facilities and family planning; benefit from social security programs; receive training and education; have access to agricultural credit and loans, marketing, and appropriate technology; receive equal treatment in land reform; and have adequate living conditions, particularly in relation to housing, sanitation, electricity and water supply, transport and communications.

Article 15

Women shall have equality with men before the law. Women and men shall have the same rights regarding movement of persons and freedom to choose residence.

Article 16

States Parties shall take all appropriate measures to eliminate discrimination against women in all matters relating to marriage and family relations and shall ensure equal rights to enter marriage, to choose a spouse, to enter marriage only with full consent, the same rights and responsibilities within marriage and in divorce, the same rights and responsibilities as parents, the same rights to decide on the number and spacing of children, the same rights with regard to ownership of property. A minimum age shall be set for marriage.

Articles 17-22 detail how the CEDAW Committee works, including the role in the monitoring in the implementation of the Convention.

Articles 23 to 30 deal with the administration of CEDAW.

Optional Protocol introduces additional mechanisms for the implementation of CEDAW, including an inquiry procedure for the CEDAW committee to address systematic violations and a way for women and girls to submit complaints directly to the CEDAW committee if they consider their human rights protected by CEDAW are violated.

European Convention on Human Rights (simplified version of selected articles)

Summary of the preamble

The member governments of the Council of Europe work towards peace and greater unity based on human rights and fundamental freedoms. With this Convention they decide to take the first steps to enforce many of the rights contained in the Universal Declaration of Human Rights.

Article 1 - Obligation to respect human rights

States must ensure that everyone has the rights stated in this Convention.

Article 2 - Right to life

You have the right to life.

Article 3 - Prohibition of torture

No one ever has the right to hurt you or torture you. Even in detention your human dignity has to be respected.

Article 4 - Prohibition of slavery and forced labour

It is prohibited to treat you as a slave or to impose forced labour on you.

Article 5 - Right to liberty and security

You have the right to liberty. If you are arrested, you have the right to know why. If you are arrested you have the right to stand trial soon, or to be released until the trial takes place.

Article 6 - Right to a fair trial

You have the right to a fair trial before an unbiased and independent judge. If you are accused of having committed a crime, you are innocent until proved guilty. You have the right to be assisted by a lawyer who has to be paid by the state if you are poor.

Article 7 - No punishment without law

You cannot be held guilty of a crime if there was no law against it when you did it.

Article 8 - Right to respect for private and family life

You have the right to respect for your private and family life, your home and correspondence.

Article 9 - Freedom of thought, conscience and religion

You have the right to freedom of thought, conscience and religion. You have the right to practise your religion at home and in public and to change your religion if you want.

Article 10 - Freedom of expression

You have the right to responsibly say and write what you think and to give and receive information from others. This includes freedom of the press.

Article 11 - Freedom of assembly and association

You have the right to take part in peaceful meetings and to set up or join associations including trade unions.

Article 12 - Right to marry

You have the right to marry and to have a family.

Article 13 - Right to an effective remedy

If your rights are violated, you can complain about this officially to the courts or other public bodies.

Article 14 - Prohibition of discrimination

You have these rights regardless of your skin colour, sex, language, political or religious beliefs, or origins.

Article 15 - Derogation in time of emergency

In time of war or other public emergency, a government may do things which go against your rights, but only when strictly necessary. Even then, governments are not allowed, for example, to torture you or to kill you arbitrarily.

Article 16 - Restrictions on political activity of aliens

Governments may restrict the political activity of foreigners, even if this would be in conflict with Articles 10, 11 or 14.

Article 17 - Prohibition of abuse of rights

Nothing in this Convention can be used to damage the rights and freedoms in the Convention.

Article 18 - Limitation on use of restrictions of rights

Most of the rights in this Convention can be restricted by a general law which is applied to everyone. Such restrictions are only allowed if they are strictly necessary.

Articles 19 to 51

These articles explain how the European Court of Human Rights works.

Article 34 - Individual applications

If your rights contained in the Convention have been violated in one of the member states you should first appeal to all competent national authorities. If that does not work out for you, then you may appeal directly to the European Court of Human Rights in Strasbourg.

Article 52 - Inquiries by the Secretary General

If the Secretary General of the Council of Europe requests it, a government must explain how its national law protects the rights of this Convention.

Protocols to the Convention

Article 1 of Protocol No. 1 - Protection of property

You have the right to own property and use your possessions.

Article 2 of Protocol No. 1 - Right to education

You have the right to go to school.

Article 3 of Protocol No. 1 - Right to free elections

You have the right to elect the government of your country by secret vote.

Article 2 of Protocol No. 4 - Freedom of movement

If you are lawfully within a country, you have the right to go where you want and to live where you want within it.

Article 1 of Protocol No. 6 - Abolition of the death penalty

You cannot be condemned to death or executed by the state.

Article 2 of Protocol No. 7 - Right of appeal in criminal matters

You may appeal to a higher court if you have been convicted for committing a crime.

Article 3 of Protocol No. 7 - Compensation for wrongful conviction

You have the right to compensation if you have been convicted for committing a crime and it turns out that you were innocent.

Article 1 of Protocol No. 12 - General prohibition of discrimination

You cannot be discriminated against by public authorities for reasons of, for example, your skin colour, sex, language, political or religious beliefs, or origins.

This simplified version was prepared by the Directorate of Communication of the Council of Europe for educational purposes only. The only texts which have a legal basis are to be found in the official published versions of the Convention for the Protection of Human Rights and Fundamental Freedoms and its protocols.

Council of Europe Convention on Preventing and Combating Violence against Women and Domestic Violence (unofficial summary)

This Convention was adopted in Istanbul on 11 May 2011, and open for signature to states which are not members of the Council of Europe. As of June 2019, 34 countries have ratified the Convention. It is also known as the Istanbul Convention.

Chapter I – Purposes, definitions, equality and non-discrimination, general obligations

Article 1 - Purpose of the Convention

The Convention aims to protect women against all forms of violence; to prevent, prosecute and eliminate violence against women and domestic violence; to promote real equality between women and men; to provide assistance to organisations and law enforcement agencies to cooperate effectively, in order to adopt an integrated approach.

Article 2 - Scope of the Convention

The Convention is applicable in times of peace and conflict. It applies to all forms of violence against women, including domestic violence, but particular attention should be paid to women.

Article 3 - Definitions

Violence against women is a human rights violation and a form of discrimination against women. "Violence against women" refers to all acts of violence that result in, or are likely to result in physical, sexual, psychological or economic harm or suffering to women, including threats, coercion or arbitrary deprivation of liberty, whether occurring in public or private spaces. "

Domestic violence refers to all acts of physical, sexual, psychological or economic violence that occur within the family or domestic unit or between former or current spouses or partners, whether or not the perpetrator shares or has shared the same residence with the victim.

Gender is defined as the socially constructed roles, behaviours, activities and attributes that a given society considers appropriate for women and men.

Gender-based violence against women refers to all violence directed against a woman because she is a woman or that affects women disproportionately,

Victim is defined as any person subjected to behaviour which constitutes "violence against women" or "domestic violence"

The Convention states that the term "women" also includes girls under the age of 18.

Article 4 - Fundamental rights, equality and non-discrimination

Everyone is entitled to live free from violence in both the public and private sphere, and states must implement the necessary measures, including legislative to ensure this. States must condemn all forms of discrimination against women. This Convention should be applied without discrimination on any grounds. Special measures taken by states to prevent and protect women from gender-based violence do not constitute discrimination.

Article 5 - State obligations and due diligence

States and their authorities, officials, agents and other actors must refrain from engaging in gender-based violence against women and must take measures necessary to prevent, investigate, punish and provide reparation for acts of violence perpetrated by non-state actors.

Article 6 - Gender sensitive policies

States must include a gender perspective in monitoring the application of this Convention, promote and implement policies of equality between women and men and the empowerment of women.

Chapter II – Integrated policies and data collection

Article 7 - Comprehensive and co-ordinated policies

States must take measures at State-wide level to adopt and implement policies to prevent and combat all forms of violence against women. The rights of the victim must be placed at the centre of these measures. All relevant actors, including civil society, must be involved in design and implementation.

Article 8 - Financial resources

States must allocate appropriate financial and human resources to effectively implement policies and programmes to prevent and combat all forms of violence covered by the scope of the Convention. Resources should be available as well for NGOs and civil society.

Article 9 - Non-governmental organisations and civil society

The work of NGOs and civil society should be recognised, encouraged and supported by the State.

Article 10 - Co-ordinating body

States must establish one or more official bodies to ensure coordination, implementation, monitoring and evaluation of policies and measures.

Article 11 - Data collection and research

Disaggregated statistical data on all forms of violence, and should be collected at regular intervals. States should support research in the field of gender-based violence. Data collected should be made public.

Chapter III – Prevention

Article 12 - General obligations

States should aim to eradicate prejudice, customs, traditions and practices which are based on stereotypical roles for men and women; they should implement the necessary legislative measures to prevent violence against women, taking into account the specific needs of persons made vulnerable by certain circumstances; States should engage men and boys in prevention work, and adopt a human rights and victim centred approach.

Article 13 - Awareness raising

Awareness raising campaigns or programmes should be conducted on a regular basis with relevant partners and at all levels of society.

Article 14 - Education

States should include, where necessary, teaching material on: equality between men and women, non-stereotyped gender roles, respect, non-violent conflict resolution, gender-based violence against women, and the right to personal integrity - in all forms of education and at all levels.

Article 15 - Training of professionals

States should provide training for professionals on dealing with victims or perpetrators of gender-based violence.

Article 16 - Preventive intervention and treatment programmes

Support and treatment programmes should be established, aimed at preventing perpetrators from re-offending and supporting them to adopt non-violent behaviours. Such programmes should be developed with specialist support services for victims.

Article 17 - Participation of the private sector and the media

States should encourage the private sector and media to participate in the elaboration and implementation of policies to prevent violence against women, including in the development of programmes aimed at children, parents and educators on how to deal with the information and communication environment that provides access to degrading and harmful content.

Chapter IV – Protection and support

Article 18 - General obligations for protection and support

All measures taken by the State should be: based on a gendered understanding of violence against women and domestic violence; have a human rights and victim centred approach; have an integrated approach that takes into account the relationship between victims, perpetrators, children and their environment; avoids secondary victimisation; aims at empowerment and the economic independence of women; allows for a range of support services on the same premises; addresses the needs of vulnerable persons, including child victims. Support services shall not be dependent on pressing charges or testifying against a perpetrator.

Article 19 - Information

Victims should receive adequate and timely information on support services available.

Article 20 - General support services

The states should make sure that victims have access to services to facilitate their recovery from violence, including access to health care and social services.

Article 21 - Assistance in individual/collective complaints

Victims should have information and access to regional and international individual or collective complaints mechanisms. They should also be assisted in presenting any such complaints.

Article 22 - Specialist support services

These support services for victims should be provided, in an adequate geographical distribution, including immediate, short- and long-term services.

Article 23 - Shelters

States should take measures to make shelters for women and children available.

Article 24 - Telephone helplines

States must set up state-wide, round-the-clock, and free of charge telephone helplines.

Article 25 - Support for victims of sexual violence

States must set up rape crisis and sexual violence referral centres for victims to provide medical and counselling services.

Article 26 - Protection and support for child witnesses

The rights of child witnesses must be taken into account in designing support measures for victims, and due regard must be given to the best interests of the child.

Article 27 - Reporting

States should encourage any person to report acts of violence that they might witness or might believe is likely to occur to the relevant authorities.

Article 28 - Reporting by professionals

Confidentiality rules should not stop professionals from reporting acts of grave violence where they suspect that such acts might reoccur.

Chapter V – Substantive law

Article 29 - Civil lawsuits and remedies

Victims must have available adequate civil remedies against the perpetrator or against the State, if the State has failed to take preventive and protective measures.

Article 30 - Compensation

Victims have the right to claim compensation from both the perpetrator and from the State, in cases of sustained serious bodily injury or impairment of health, and if the damage is not covered by other sources. The compensation must be granted within the reasonable time.

Article 31 - Custody, visitation rights and safety

Incidents of violence should be taken into account in the determination of custody and visitation rights of children, and that the exercise of such rights does not endanger the victim or the children.

Article 32 - Civil consequences of forced marriages

Forced marriages concluded under force should be voided, annulled or dissolved without financial or administrative burden.

Article 33 – 40 Criminalisation of gender-based violence

The following types of violence should be criminalised: psychological violence, stalking; physical violence; sexual violence, including rape and causing another person to engage in non-consensual acts of a sexual nature with a third person, forced marriage of an adult or child, including luring an adult or child to enter the territory of another state with the aim of forcing them into marriage, female genital mutilation; forced abortion and forced sterilisation, when lacking the informed consent of the women and her understanding of the procedure; sexual harassment, whether it be verbal, non-verbal, or physical.

Article 41 - Aiding or abetting and attempt

Intentional aiding or abetting the commission of gender-based violence should be considered an offence. The same applies to attempts to commit it.

Article 42 - Unacceptable justifications for crimes, including crimes committed in the name of so-called "honour"

Culture, custom, tradition, religion, or so-called "honour" should not be regarded in criminal proceedings as justifications for acts of gender-based violence mentioned by the Convention.

Article 43 - Application of criminal offences

All offences established in accordance with the Convention should apply irrespective of the nature of the relationship between victim and perpetrator.

Article 44 - Jurisdiction

States must take measures to established jurisdiction over any offence mentioned in the Convention when the offence is committed on their territory, on board a ship flying their flag, on board of a plane registered under their laws, committed by one of their nationals or by a person who is a resident on their territory.

Article 45 - Sanctions and measures

The crimes established by this Convention should be punished by effective, proportionate and dissuasive sanctions. In addition, States may establish measures such as monitoring or supervision of convicted persons and withdrawal of parental rights, if this is in the best interests of the child.

Article 46 - Aggravating circumstances

Among many, the following circumstances should be considered aggravating in the determination of a sentence for the offence established in the Convention: offence against current or former spouse or partner as recognised by internal law, by a member of the family or a person cohabitating with the victim; when the offence was committed repeatedly; the offence was committed in a presence of a child; when extreme violence was involved; when the offence resulted in severe physical or psychological harm for the victim.

Article 47 - Sentences passed by another Party

Final sentences passed by another state should be taken into account when determining the sentence for perpetrators.

Article 48 - Prohibition of mandatory alternative dispute resolution processes and sentencing

States should prohibit mandatory alternative resolution processes, including mediation and conciliation, in relation to all forms of violence covered by the Convention.

Chapter VI – Investigation, prosecution, procedural law and protective measures

This chapter (Articles 49 – 58) contains a variety of provisions that cover a broad range of issues related to investigation, prosecution, procedural law and protection against all forms of violence covered by the scope of this Convention, in order to reinforce the rights and duties laid out in the previous chapters of the Convention. For example:

- Investigations and judicial proceeding in relation to all forms of violence covered by the Convention should proceed without delay, and should take into account the rights of the victim. (art. 49)
- In cases where there is an immediate danger, competent authorities can order a perpetrator to leave a residence and prohibit contact with the victim for a period of time. (art. 52)
- In criminal or civil trials, evidence relating to a victim's sexual history and conduct is permitted only when relevant and necessary. (art. 54)
- States can continue investigating and prosecuting a crime under the Convention, even if the victim withdraws her or his statement/complaint. (art. 55)
- Victims have the right to free legal aid. (art.57)

Chapter VII – Migration and asylum

Article 59 – Residence status

In cases of asylum and migration, victims of domestic or gender-based violence whose residence status is dependent on that of a spouse or partner can be granted an autonomous residence permit, irrespective of the duration of the marriage or partnership. States should take measures to support victims of forced marriages to regain residence status in the original state, where this has been lost as a result of the forced marriage.

Article 60 - Gender-based asylum claims

Gender-based violence against women should be recognised as a form of persecution and ground for granting asylum. Additionally, states must ensure a gender sensitive interpretation of the Convention relating to the Status of Refugees.

Article 61 - Non-refoulment

The principle of non-refoulment should respected in the case of victims of violence against women. Victims of gender-based violence shall not be returned to any country where their life might be at risk or where they may be subjected to torture or inhuman or degrading treatment.

Chapter VIII – International co-operation

This Chapter sets out the provisions on international co-operation between Parties to the Convention. The provisions are not confined to judicial co-operation in criminal and civil matters but are also concerned with co-operation in preventing all forms of violence covered by the scope of this Convention and assisting victims of that violence.

Chapter IX – Monitoring mechanism

Chapter IX of the Convention contains provisions which aim at ensuring the effective implementation of the Convention by the Parties. The monitoring mechanism is designed to cover the scope of this Convention. The Convention sets up a Group of experts on action against violence against women and domestic violence (hereafter "GREVIO") which is an expert body, composed of independent and highly qualified experts in the fields of human rights, gender equality, violence against women and domestic violence, criminal law and in assistance to and protection of victims of violence against women and domestic violence, with the task of "monitoring the implementation of this Convention by the Parties".

The Convention also establishes a Committee of the Parties, composed of the representatives of the Parties to the Convention.

Chapter X – relationship with other international instruments

This Chapter seeks to ensure that the Convention harmoniously coexists with other treaties – whether multilateral or bilateral – or instruments dealing with matters which the Convention also covers. It also states positively that Parties may conclude bilateral or multilateral agreements – or any other legal instrument – relating to the matters which the Convention governs.

Chapter XI – Amendments to the Convention

This Chapter states that the states may propose amendments to the provisions of the

Convention. They must be communicated to the Secretary General of the Council of Europe and to all Council of Europe member states, to any signatory, to any Party, to the European Union and to any state invited to sign or accede to the Convention. As a next step, the Committee of Ministers examines and adopts the amendment. Before deciding on the amendment, the Committee of Ministers shall consult and obtain the unanimous consent of all Parties to the Convention. Such a requirement recognises that all Parties to the Convention should be able to participate in the decision-making process concerning amendments and are on an equal footing.

Chapter XII – Final clauses

This Chapter includes final closing provisions such as related to effects of the Convention, dispute settlement, signature and entry into force, accession to the convention, territorial application, reservations, validity and review of reservations, denunciation and notification.

Chart of signatures and ratifications of the Istanbul Convention (CETS 210)

Status at 17 June 2019. Source: *https://www.coe.int/en/web/conventions*

	Signature	Ratification
Albania	19/12/2011	04/02/2013
Andorra	22/02/2013	22/04/2014
Armenia	18/01/2018	
Austria	11/05/2011	14/11/2013
Azerbaijan		
Belgium	11/09/2012	14/03/2016
Bosnia and Herzegovina	08/03/2013	07/11/2013
Bulgaria	21/04/2016	
Croatia	22/01/2013	12/06/2018
Cyprus	16/06/2015	10/11/2017
Czech Republic	02/05/2016	
Denmark	11/10/2013	23/04/2014
Estonia	02/12/2014	26/10/2017
Finland	11/05/2011	17/04/2015
France	11/05/2011	04/07/2014
Georgia	19/06/2014	19/05/2017
Germany	11/05/2011	12/10/2017

	Signature	Ratification
Greece	11/05/2011	18/06/2018
Hungary	14/03/2014	
Iceland	11/05/2011	26/04/2018
Ireland	05/11/2015	08/03/2019
Italy	27/09/2012	10/09/2013
Latvia	18/05/2016	
Liechtenstein	10/11/2016	
Lithuania	07/06/2013	
Luxembourg	11/05/2011	07/08/2018
Malta	21/05/2012	29/07/2014
Republic of Moldova	06/02/2017	
Monaco	20/09/2012	07/10/2014
Montenegro	11/05/2011	22/04/2013
The Netherlands	14/11/2012	18/11/2015
North Macedonia	08/07/2011	23/03/2018
Norway	07/07/2011	05/07/2017
Poland	18/12/2012	27/04/2015
Portugal	11/05/2011	05/02/2013
Romania	27/06/2014	23/05/2016
Russian Federation		
San Marino	30/04/2014	28/01/2016
Serbia	04/04/2012	21/11/2013
Slovak Republic	11/05/2011	
Slovenia	08/09/2011	05/02/2015
Spain	11/05/2011	10/04/2014
Sweden	11/05/2011	01/07/2014
Switzerland	11/09/2013	14/12/2017
Turkey	11/05/2011	14/03/2012
Ukraine	07/11/2011	
United Kingdom	08/06/2012	

Glossary
of terms related to gender and gender-based violence

Androgyny - used to describe the combination of masculine and feminine characteristics in one being. The term is used in biology, medicine, psychology, sociology, cultural studies, philosophy, literature or religious studies. In biology and medicine the term is applied when a person shows both male and female sex characteristics.

Asexual - an asexual person is someone who does not experience sexual attraction, has no or very little sexual drive. People who identify themselves as asexual have the same emotional needs as anybody else: they may decide to live their life on their own, they may decide to date and/or establish romantic relationships. They do not, however, feel the need get involved in sexual activity and behaviour.

Bisexuality - emotional, romantic and sexual attraction to both men and women.

Coming out - the process of making one's own sexual orientation or gender identity public. The term refers to LGBT people who decide to inform others about their sexual orientation / gender identity. Coming out can be limited to small groups of people, such as friends or family.

Date rape - sexual activity that is non-consensual and coerced by someone the victim knows and is involved in a romantic or potentially romantic relationship with. Date rape is sometimes forced by adding a sedative drug to a victim's drink to make them unconscious, so the person does not resist sexual activity.

Discrimination – any distinction, exclusion or restriction of preference, which is based on any ground such as race, culture, ethnic origin, nationality, gender, age, sexual orientation, religion, sking colour, disability, or other characteristics not relevant to the issue in question.

Domestic violence - acts of physical, sexual, psychological or economic violence that occur within the family or domestic unit or between former or current spouses or partners, whether or not the perpetrator shares or has shared the same residence as the victim.

Feminism - a social movement for women's rights. It is perhaps best known for the campaigns for universal suffrage, when women did not have the right to vote. Today, it focuses more on acting against sexism, gender-based violence and issues related to gender equality.

Gay - refers to a person who is homosexual, usually a man. However, it is sometimes used to describe homosexual people regardless of their gender ('gay people')

Gender - socially constructed notions of masculinity or femininity. The term 'gender' is different from the term 'sex', which focuses on biological differences. Gender is a psychological, cultural and social construct, developed in the process of socialisation, and is related with our own identity and how we feel about ourselves. For example, people may identify themselves as masculine, feminine, transgender, other or none (indeterminate/unspecified). Gender is not necessarily related to biological sex: a person's gender may or may not correspond to their biological sex.

Gender-based violence - any type of harm that is perpetrated against a person or group of people because of their actual or perceived sex, gender, sexual orientation and/or gender identity. Gender-based violence affects women disproportionately.

Gender binary – a term used to describe the belief that there are only two genders, male and female, and that someone's biological sex aligns with socially constructed notions of masculinity and femininity.

Gender-based discrimination – describes cases where someone is - or may be - treated less favourably than others simply because of their actual or perceived gender.

Gender expression - intentional or unintentional ways of communicating one's gender - including dressing style, movement, hair style, ways of interacting with others.

Gender roles - behaviours that are considered appropriate and are accepted in a given culture for people representing a specific gender. These are usually related to the concepts of masculinity and femininity.

Genderqueer - a term that describes a person who does not conform to a gender binary stereotype and whose gender identity goes beyond it.

Hate speech – advocacy, promotion or incitement, in any form, of the denigration, hatred or vilification of a person or group of persons, as well as any harassment, insult, negative stereotyping, stigmatisation or threat in respect of such a person or group of persons and the justification of all the preceding types of expression, on the ground of "race"[1], colour, descent, national or ethnic origin, age, disability, language, religion or belief, sex, gender, gender identity, sexual orientation and other personal characteristics or status. (ECRI)

Heterosexuality - emotional, romantic and sexual attraction to people of the opposite gender.

Homosexuality - emotional, romantic and sexual attraction to people of the same gender.

Intersectionality - a way of understanding and analysing the complexity of human behaviour, the world, and people, emphasising the fact that people hold different identities, which interact with one another and influence thought and action. In relation to gender discrimination and gender-based violence, the term is used to emphasise the fact that gender identity needs to be seen in relation to other identities, such as those related to ethnic origin, skin colour, age, ability/disability, religion, sexual orientation, etc. Gender discrimination or violence often includes, or is accompanied by, discrimination on other grounds as well - for example disability or ethnicity.

Intersex - Intersex people are born with sex characteristics - including genitals, gonads and chromosomes - which do not fit the typical binary notion of male or female bodies. Sometimes intersex traits are visible at birth, but often they will not become clear until puberty.

Lesbian - a word used to name a homosexual woman

LGBT - an acronym that stands for lesbian, gay, bisexual and transgender. Sometimes it is used in other forms, such as: LGBTIQ (including intersex and queer people) or LGBT+ to encompass a diversity of human sexual orientation and gender identity.

Misogyny - hatred or irrational fear of women, including prejudice, hostility, or feeling of disgust towards them.

Patriarchy - a social system based on male dominance. Patriarchy literally means "the rule of the father" and describes a system in which men are seen as the rightful holders of power in the family, in business, and in politics.

Physical violence - a type of violence where a person (or group of people) uses part of their body or an object to hurt someone else, or to take control of a victim.

Psychological violence (sometimes known as emotional violence) - a type of violence, where a person (or group of people) intentionally uses coercion and threats leading to fear, enabling them to gain control over another person or group of people. Psychological violence often precedes or accompanies physical and sexual violence in intimate relationships (domestic violence). However, it may also occur in any other type of setting, for example in the work place or school environment.

Rape - unconsensual sexual activity usually involving sexual intercourse or another form of penetration, committed using physical force, coercion or an abuse of authority. Causing another person to engage in non-consensual acts of a sexual nature with a third person can also constitute rape. A rape victim may be conscious or unconscious, and the perpetrator(s) may be a person or group of people known to the victim, or they may be strangers.

Queer - a general term referring to people not fitting into existing norms related to gender.

Sex - relates to different biological and physiological characteristics of males and females, such as the reproductive organs, chromosomes or hormones

Sexism - perceiving and judging people only on the basis of their belonging or perceived to belong to a particular sex or gender. Sexism leads to unfair treatment of people on the basis of sex or gender.

Sex reassignment surgery (or gender reassignment surgery) - a surgical procedure, which aims to make the body match a person's gender identity. It is usually performed on people who are transsexual. In the case of male-to-female, the person is castrated, and female genital organs are formed, together with other sex characteristics, such as female breasts. In female-to-male procedures, doctors a perform a mastectomy and male genital organs are formed. Other procedures may also be performed to make a person's body look more masculine or feminine.

Sexual harassment - any form of unwanted verbal, non-verbal or physical conduct of a sexual nature, which has the aim or effect of violating the dignity of a person, in particular when creating an intimidating, hostile, degrading, humiliating or offensive environment

Sexual orientation - patterns of emotional, romantic and sexual attraction to people. Traditionally, there are three sexual orientations: heterosexual (attraction to people of the opposite sex), bisexual (attraction to people of both sexes) and homosexual (attraction to people of the same sex). However, these three categories do not describe all possible forms of sexual identification: some people decide not to use any of these to identify their sexual orientation.

Sexual violence - any sexual act, attempt to obtain a sexual act, unwanted sexual comments or advances, or acts to traffic, or otherwise directed, against a person's sexuality using coercion, by any person regardless of their relationship to the victim, in any setting, including but not limited to home and work. (source: World Health Organisation)

Sexuality - a central aspect of being human throughout life (that) encompasses sex, gender identities and roles, sexual orientation, eroticism, pleasure, intimacy and reproduction. (source: World Health Organisation)

Socio-economic violence – a type of violence that aims at taking control of a person by making them economically dependent and diminishing their role in the society.

Stalking - repeatedly engaging in threatening conduct towards another person, causing her or him to fear for their safety. Stalkers may act individually or in a group, and their actions may include: pestering and annoying phone calls or text messages, life threats, following someone, repeated visits to their home, presenting gifts, or constant solicitation. Such behaviour may lead on to physical violence and even murder.

Verbal violence - a type of violence that occurs when someone uses language to humiliate and cause harm to a person, e.g. name calling, yelling, insulting, swearing, or threatening other forms of violence against the victim or against someone or something dear to them.

Trafficking in human beings - the recruitment, transportation, transfer, harbouring or receipt of persons, by means of the threat or use of force or other forms of coercion, of abduction, of fraud, of deception, of the abuse of power or of a position of vulnerability or of the giving or receiving of payments or benefits to achieve the consent of a person having control over another person, for the purpose of exploitation. (source: Council of Europe Convention Against Trafficking in Human Beings)

Transgender - an umbrella term used to describe certain people or different forms of behaviour and expression related to gender – for example, people whose biological sex is different from their gender identity and who are in need of gender reassignment surgery (transsexuality), people who do not fit into generally defined notions of masculinity or femininity or gender binary, people who define themselves as queer or genderqueer.

Transsexual - someone possessing the typical physical anatomy of one sex, but the gender identity of the opposite one. Transsexual is generally considered to be a subset of transgender, and some transsexual people refer to themselves as transgender.

Endnotes

1 Since all human beings belong to the same species, ECRI rejects theories based on the existence of different races. However, in this Recommendation ECRI uses this term "race" in order to ensure that those persons who are generally and erroneously perceived as belonging to another race are not excluded from the protection provided for by the Recommendation.

Sales agents for publications of the Council of Europe
Agents de vente des publications du Conseil de l'Europe

BELGIUM/BELGIQUE
La Librairie Européenne -
The European Bookshop
Rue de l'Orme, 1
BE-1040 BRUXELLES
Tel.: + 32 (0)2 231 04 35
Fax: + 32 (0)2 735 08 60
E-mail: info@libeurop.eu
http://www.libeurop.be

Jean De Lannoy/DL Services
c/o Michot Warehouses
Bergense steenweg 77
Chaussée de Mons
BE-1600 SINT PIETERS LEEUW
Fax: + 32 (0)2 706 52 27
E-mail: jean.de.lannoy@dl-servi.com
http://www.jean-de-lannoy.be

CANADA
Renouf Publishing Co. Ltd.
22-1010 Polytek Street
CDN-OTTAWA, ONT K1J 9J1
Tel.: + 1 613 745 2665
Fax: + 1 613 745 7660
Toll-Free Tel.: (866) 767-6766
E-mail: order.dept@renoufbooks.com
http://www.renoufbooks.com

CROATIA/CROATIE
Robert's Plus d.o.o.
Marasoviçeva 67
HR-21000 SPLIT
Tel.: + 385 21 315 800, 801, 802, 803
Fax: + 385 21 315 804
E-mail: robertsplus@robertsplus.hr

CZECH REPUBLIC/
RÉPUBLIQUE TCHÈQUE
Suweco CZ, s.r.o.
Klecakova 347
CZ-180 21 PRAHA 9
Tel.: + 420 2 424 59 204
Fax: + 420 2 848 21 646
E-mail: import@suweco.cz
http://www.suweco.cz

DENMARK/DANEMARK
GAD
Vimmelskaftet 32
DK-1161 KØBENHAVN K
Tel.: + 45 77 66 60 00
Fax: + 45 77 66 60 01
E-mail: reception@gad.dk
http://www.gad.dk

FINLAND/FINLANDE
Akateeminen Kirjakauppa
PO Box 128
Keskuskatu 1
FI-00100 HELSINKI
Tel.: + 358 (0)9 121 4430
Fax: + 358 (0)9 121 4242
E-mail: akatilaus@akateeminen.com
http://www.akateeminen.com

FRANCE
Please contact directly /
Merci de contacter directement
Council of Europe Publishing
Éditions du Conseil de l'Europe
F-67075 STRASBOURG Cedex
Tel.: + 33 (0)3 88 41 25 81
Fax: + 33 (0)3 88 41 39 10
E-mail: publishing@coe.int
http://book.coe.int

Librairie Kléber
1, rue des Francs-Bourgeois
F-67000 STRASBOURG
Tel.: + 33 (0)3 88 15 78 88
Fax: + 33 (0)3 88 15 78 80
E-mail: librairie-kleber@coe.int
http://www.librairie-kleber.com

NORWAY/NORVÈGE
Akademika
Postboks 84 Blindern
NO-0314 OSLO
Tel.: + 47 2 218 8100
Fax: + 47 2 218 8103
E-mail: support@akademika.no
http://www.akademika.no

POLAND/POLOGNE
Ars Polona JSC
25 Obroncow Street
PL-03-933 WARSZAWA
Tel.: + 48 (0)22 509 86 00
Fax: + 48 (0)22 509 86 10
E-mail: arspolona@arspolona.com.pl
http://www.arspolona.com.pl

PORTUGAL
Marka Lda
Rua dos Correeiros 61-3
PT-1100-162 LISBOA
Tel: 351 21 3224040
Fax: 351 21 3224044
E mail: apoio.clientes@marka.pt
www.marka.pt

RUSSIAN FEDERATION/
FÉDÉRATION DE RUSSIE
Ves Mir
17b, Butlerova ul. - Office 338
RU-117342 MOSCOW
Tel.: + 7 495 739 0971
Fax: + 7 495 739 0971
E-mail: orders@vesmirbooks.ru
http://www.vesmirbooks.ru

SWITZERLAND/SUISSE
Planetis Sàrl
16, chemin des Pins
CH-1273 ARZIER
Tel.: + 41 22 366 51 77
Fax: + 41 22 366 51 78
E-mail: info@planetis.ch

TAIWAN
Tycoon Information Inc.
5th Floor, No. 500, Chang-Chun Road
Taipei, Taiwan
Tel.: 886-2-8712 8886
Fax: 886-2-8712 4747, 8712 4777
E-mail: info@tycoon-info.com.tw
orders@tycoon-info.com.tw

UNITED KINGDOM/ROYAUME-UNI
The Stationery Office Ltd
PO Box 29
GB-NORWICH NR3 1GN
Tel.: + 44 (0)870 600 5522
Fax: + 44 (0)870 600 5533
E-mail: book.enquiries@tso.co.uk
http://www.tsoshop.co.uk

UNITED STATES and CANADA/
ÉTATS-UNIS et CANADA
Manhattan Publishing Co
670 White Plains Road
USA-10583 SCARSDALE, NY
Tel: + 1 914 472 4650
Fax: + 1 914 472 4316
E-mail: coe@manhattanpublishing.com
http://www.manhattanpublishing.com

Council of Europe Publishing/Éditions du Conseil de l'Europe
F-67075 STRASBOURG Cedex
Tel.: + 33 (0)3 88 41 25 81 – Fax: + 33 (0)3 88 41 39 10 – E-mail: publishing@coe.int – Website: http://book.coe.int